D1617117

JUST ONE VOTE

DATE DUE

JUST ONE VOTE

*From Jim Walding's Nomination
to Constitutional Defeat*

IAN STEWART

University of Manitoba Press

University of Manitoba Press
Winnipeg, Manitoba R3T 2M5 Canada
www.umanitoba.ca/uofmpress

Printed in Canada on acid-free paper.

Cover design: Doowah Design
Text design: Relish Design Studio

Library and Archives Canada Cataloguing in Publication

Stewart, Ian, 1953–
    Just one vote : from Jim Walding's nomination to constitutional defeat / Ian Stewart.

Includes bibliographical references and index.
ISBN 978-0-88755-711-8

    1. Walding, Jim. 2. New Democratic Party of Manitoba—Officials and employees—Selection and appointment—History. 3. Manitoba—Politics and government—1977-1988. 4. Manitoba—Politics and government—1988-1999. 5. Politicians—Manitoba—Biography. I. Title.

FC3378.2.S74 2009   971.27'03   C2008-907936-1

The University of Manitoba Press gratefully acknowledges the financial support for its publication program provided by the Federal Government of Canada through the Book Publishing Industry Development Program (BPIDP), the Canada Council for the Arts, the Manitoba Arts Council, and the Manitoba Department of Culture, Heritage, and Tourism.

Contents

For want of a nail
the shoe was lost.
For want of a shoe
the horse was lost.
For want of a horse
the rider was lost.
For want of a rider
the battle was lost.
For want of a battle
the kingdom was lost.
And all for the want
Of a horseshoe nail.

—*English Nursery Rhyme*

List of Tables

List of Illustrations

5.   Jim Walding Campaign Pamphlet, 1981.

6.   Jim Walding, Speaker's Portrait.

7.   Sig Laser Campaign Pamphlet, 1985.

8.   The three candidates: Gerri Unwin, Sig Laser, and Jim Walding. *Winnipeg Sun*, 12 January 1986.

9.   An anxious Jim Walding, together with wife Val (right) and supporter Elizabeth Dotremont, awaits results of second ballot at St. Vital NDP nominating meeting on 12 January 1986.

10. Jim Walding remains seated when members of the legislature are asked to stand to vote against a non-confidence motion on the Pawley government's budget, 8 March 1988.

11. Jim Walding, on 11 March 1988, meets reporters for the first time after the non-confidence vote.

Credits and Permissions

Plates 1, 4 courtesy University of Manitoba Archives and Special Collections, Tribune Collection (UMASC). Figure 7, Plates 2–3, 5 courtesy Archives of Manitoba (AM), Jim Walding Papers. Plate 6 courtesy Archives of Manitoba, Government Photograph, Jim Walding (82-3180) (Z-8-2-7-6). Plate 7 courtesy Sig Laser, personal papers. Figures 5, 8, Plate 8 courtesy Sun Media Corporation (SMC). Plates 9–11 courtesy *Winnipeg Free Press*.

Acknowledgements

I HAVE LONG BEEN FASCINATED by the fall of the Manitoba government on 8 March 1988. As will become apparent, the event had a highly theatrical quality. Jim Walding's decision that day to vote against his government's budget was the climax of a complex human drama guaranteed to grab the attention of even a casual political voyeur. This was, however, more than just an entrancing spectacle. It also highlighted the (not unrelated) significance of agency and of contingency, forces which, for entirely understandable reasons, political scientists have tended to downplay in their explanatory accounts.

In 1993, I undertook a brief exploration of the topic, but did not return to it full-time until 2005 when, thanks to a grant from the Acadia University Research Fund (Article 25.55) and the on-site encouragement of David Stewart, I spent a month ensconced in a Winnipeg motel. Thereafter, I found it impossible not to work steadily on the project. I am grateful to Acadia University, my academic home for the past quarter-century, for granting me the sabbatical leave in which to write this book, and to Bob Perrins, Dean of Arts, for funds to secure copyright releases. I am also grateful to Danielle Fraser, our departmental secretary, for efficiently dealing with any and all problems I indiscriminately passed her way. I must also thank Jude Carlson, Wayne Copeland, Brenda Deamel, Patrick Fortier, Bill Reid, Irene Rossman, Paul Williamson, and David Woodbury of the Manitoba NDP, Paul Black of the Nova Scotia NDP, Lorna Miner of the St. Vital Historical Society, Rob Derksen of the Manitoba Civil Service Superannuation Board, Maggie Buttrum and Mary Skanderburg of Elections Manitoba, and all the staff at the Archives of

Manitoba for going well out of their way to help an inquisitive academic. Thanks, as well, to Erica Sigurdson and Fraser Stewart for some last-minute research assistance, and to Paul Thomas and two anonymous referees for their insightful suggestions. I am grateful to David Carr, Glenn Bergen, and Cheryl Miki at the University of Manitoba Press, who made the production of this book such a pleasurable experience. Particular thanks are due to all the New Democrats of St. Vital (but especially Jim and Val Walding, Sig and Tannis Laser, and Gerri and Fred Unwin) who, with both grace and generosity, took me into their homes and patiently suffered my questions about long-ago events that many would just as soon have forgotten. I have tried in this account faithfully to represent their values, interests, and beliefs; if I have failed, the fault is mine alone.

This book was, for the most part, written during six months in Italy and four months in Malta. Many thanks are owed to Dr. Laura Ferri and Dr. Bianca Mancini of the Centro Siena-Toronto and to Dr. Isabelle Calleja of the University of Malta for providing a stimulating and supportive atmosphere in which to work. Thanks, as well, to Fred Eaglesmith who made pleasurable the daily transposition from longhand to typescript. Writing about Canada from across the pond is not without difficulties; my thanks to Ken Carty, Bill Cross, Don Desserud, Monroe Eagles, Lynda Erickson, Ned Franks, Andrew Heard, Stewart Hyson, Brenda O'Neill, Anthony Sayers, Paddy Smith, Kennedy Stewart, and Beert Verstraete, who responded promptly to my urgent appeals for nuggets of esoteric information. Finally, I must thank my beloved wife, Audrey, who cheerfully put up with my vacant stares while the minutiae of the Walding affair danced haphazardly across my mind and who carefully and intelligently critiqued the manuscript's first draft.

This book has a double dedication. First, to Dr. George Perlin, who initially tweaked my interest as an MA student in the internal workings of Canadian political parties. Besides, he's a hell of a nice guy. Second, to my parents, Ross and Greta, who for over five decades (gulp) have provided unstinting and unconditional love and support. Hope you like it.

1

Introduction

ON 12 JANUARY 1986, in a crowded Winnipeg high-school auditorium, Jim Walding was nominated as the New Democratic Party (NDP) candidate for the provincial constituency of St. Vital. Although Walding had been a member of the legislative assembly (MLA) for fifteen years, he had fallen out of favour with key elements in his party. Two challengers for the nomination came forward—Gerri Unwin, the president of the local constituency association, and Sig Laser, an aide to Premier Howard Pawley. Ultimately, Walding prevailed over Laser on a second ballot by a single vote.

On 3 June 1987, the Meech Lake Accord was signed with much fanfare by Prime Minister Brian Mulroney and the ten provincial premiers. The patriation of the Canadian Constitution and the additions of an amending formula and the Charter of Rights and Freedoms had, five years previously, occurred over the objections of the Quebec government. Such a circumstance seemed untenable in the long run, and after Mulroney gained office in 1984, he pledged to reintegrate Quebec into the Canadian "constitutional family." The Meech Lake Accord was designed principally to secure Quebec's consent to Canada's constitutional arrangements. With some alacrity, Premier Robert Bourassa pushed the Accord through Quebec's National Assembly on 23 June 1987 and set ticking Canada's three-year constitutional amendment clock. When that clock struck midnight on 23 June 1990, the Accord had successfully passed through the federal Parliament and the legislatures of eight of Canada's provinces (all but those of Newfoundland and Manitoba). Yet, because it required unanimous provincial consent, the Accord died.

It is a central contention of this book that a link can be drawn between these two seemingly unrelated events, between Jim Walding's nomination and the demise of the Meech Lake Accord. The association is not a straightforward instance of cause and effect; Walding's nomination did not directly cause the Accord to expire. Rather, Walding's nomination triggered a series of events that substantially lessened the likelihood that the Accord would succeed.

Such a contention inevitably provokes a series of counterfactual questions: What if Walding had lost the nomination contest? Would events have turned out differently? Would it have been more likely, in particular, that the Meech Lake Accord would have become part of our constitutional bedrock? The academy has traditionally dismissed these sorts of questions as either the sour grapes of sore losers or as the whimsical by-products of overheated and misdirected imaginations. Nevertheless, the study of counterfactual or virtual history has recently gained some academic traction. Geoffrey Hawthorn's *Plausible Worlds*[1] and Niall Ferguson's edited collection *Virtual History: Alternatives and Counterfactuals*[2] explore a range of counterfactual questions, including these: What if more effective steps had been taken to counteract the bubonic plague? What if Irish Home Rule had been enacted in 1912? What if Great Britain had stayed neutral during World War I? What if the United States had not occupied the southern half of the Korean Peninsula after World War II? In these and other cases, the authors contend that events could have turned out differently, that we ignore the power of contingency at our analytic peril.

Admittedly, there are countless possible counterfactual scenarios. How are we to distinguish those that are plausible from those that are not? In subsequent chapters, I will pay special heed to the potentially mutable behaviour of key political actors. According to Hawthorn, "actual agents have dispositions and abilities, kinds of knowledge and states of mind which, so we judge, preclude their considering some alternatives for themselves, and thereby preclude us from considering those alternatives as alternatives for them."[3]

Thus, a counterfactual analysis would be implausible, for example, if it required a fierce Walding loyalist to vote for one of his two challengers, but much less so if it hinged on an equally fierce Walding opponent missing the meeting because of car trouble.

Niall Ferguson raises the plausibility bar even higher. Not only must a human agent have considered an alternative course of action at the time, but there must also be evidence of same for a counterfactual scenario to be taken seriously.[4] Admittedly, the Ferguson volume deals principally with decisions of great public import for which exist an extensive archival base. Unfortunately, unheralded nomination tussles typically receive little media attention; thus, the only documentary evidence of what transpired on that long-ago January afternoon are brief newspaper stories from the following day and two pages of official minutes. Fortunately, all the Manitoba NDP files from that time are now lodged in the provincial archives, as are four boxes of Jim Walding's papers. In addition, Sig Laser generously provided access to his voluminous records (including detailed computer tracking of the voting inclinations of all St. Vital New Democrats). Moreover, I was able to undertake interviews to reconstruct the beliefs, motivations, and actions of the meeting's participants. Four hundred and five people voted in the contest's decisive second ballot; I have directly or indirectly contacted seventy-six of these individuals (or just under one-fifth of the total). Of particular importance were the interviews conducted with the three candidates, their respective spouses, key players on their campaign teams, and members of the riding executive at the time. As well, I interviewed thirteen individuals who were present at the meeting in a non-voting capacity and thirty-two others who were able to offer some perspective on the events (including former premiers Ed Schreyer and Howard Pawley).[5]

Relying on people's memories of an event that transpired over two decades ago is not without risks. "The palest ink," according to a Chinese proverb, "is clearer than the best memory."[6] And it cannot be denied that some recollections were manifestly in error; one respondent, for example, steadfastly maintained that the nomination meeting occurred in Glenlawn, rather than Norberry, school, and if the *Winnipeg Free Press* said otherwise, then the *Winnipeg Free Press* must have been in error (it was not). Nonetheless, I remain quite confident in the validity of the interview data. For reasons that will subsequently come clear, the nomination meeting was a formative event in the lives of many of the key players. As such, it has been seared into their memories in a way that was unlikely to fade over time. Moreover, speaking to so many of the participants permitted multiple confirmations of what transpired on that January afternoon in 1986; to a remarkable extent, their accounts dovetail nicely. Finally, my reconstruction of the nomination meeting has a structural integrity; there is nothing inexplicable in the motivations and actions of those present at the meeting, and their recollections of the event correspond almost completely to the documentary evidence to which I have had access. In short, I approach the interview data with no more than customary interpretive caution.[7]

We shall return to the matter of plausible counterfactuals in the concluding chapter. It is important to emphasize, however, that the bulk of this book is devoted to chronicling and explaining what did happen in St. Vital, rather than speculating on what might have happened. A growing academic literature exists on Canadian nomination contests, and it is important to situate this particular nomination meeting within that broader theoretical context.

True, this literature was slow to emerge. A half-century ago, John Meisel was able to provide only a "general impression" of Canadian nomination practices,[8] while his contemporary, Howard Scarrow, was likewise obliged to acknowledge that "little is known" about the phenomenon.[9] Even as recently as 1981, Robert Williams lamented that "no comprehensive survey of candidate recruitment practices has yet appeared" and that, as a result, this "filtering process ... is less well understood and much more shadowy in its operation" than the general elections that follow.[10] Such a disciplinary lacuna could not survive indefinitely. After all, the nomination choices of parties fundamentally constrain the voting choices of citizens. Studying the latter while ignoring the former was nonsensical (indeed, regulating the latter while entirely ignoring the former was equally nonsensical, as the Canadian state finally acknowledged when it amended the *Canada Elections Act* in 2003 to include oversight over federal nomination contests). Fortunately, the work, in particular, of Ken Carty, Bill Cross, Lynda Erickson, and Anthony Sayers has done much to fill out our understanding of Canadian nomination processes. What has emerged is a highly variegated picture. We now know that nomination practices have differed over time[11] and across space.[12] We know, as well, that much depends upon the relative health of the constituency association.[13] In fact, we even know that since national party constitutions tend to be "permissive,"[14] local organizations differ significantly on membership rules, on contest timing, on screening practices, and on many other matters.[15] As Robert Williams observes, "it is difficult to generalize about the process of candidate selection ... because no two cases are precisely the same and there may be considerable variation between the written rules and the actual practices followed."[16]

Even so, it is possible to perceive some patterns in this apparent disorder. It is clear, for example, that New Democratic Party nomination practices differ significantly from those of their major competitors. For one thing, NDP constituency organizations tend to have relatively stable membership numbers that, unlike their Liberal and Conservative counterparts, do not fluctuate wildly with the electoral cycle.[17] The enlistment of instant members for the sole purpose of packing a nomination contest is foreign to the NDP's organizational culture of demanding a serious and ongoing commitment to the party's goals. Thus, for most New Democratic riding associations, "nomination contests are the private internal affairs of a well-established membership."[18]

A second differentiating feature of NDP nomination contests is closely linked to the first; only those with long records of service in the party (or the trade union movement) will be regarded as credible candidates. Again, this can be distinguished from the more permissive culture of the Liberals and Conservatives where a recently converted notable might secure not just a constituency nomination, but even the party leadership. In contrast, the NDP rank and file need to be convinced of an individual's bona fides before entrusting them to carry the party banner. Any prospective candidate who is unable to satisfy this somewhat "exclusionary" criterion "can expect to gain little support from existing members."[19]

Finally, in contrast to the Liberals and Conservatives, the pool of candidates seeking, and winning, New Democratic nominations is typically more socially diverse. This is particularly obvious with respect to gender. The NDP has employed a variety of techniques to encourage more women to seek elected office (from providing financial assistance to females contesting nominations[20] to freezing an entire cluster of nomination meetings until a sufficient number of women in the area either enter a race or are actively solicited to do so[21]). In fact, one study discovered that while only about one-third of Conservative and Liberal constituency presidents reported that an attempt had been made to recruit female candidates, the corresponding figure for the NDP was 80 percent.[22] The results of these labours have long been apparent; the New Democratic Party consistently has a significantly higher proportion of women candidates than have their chief opponents.[23]

Anthony Sayers has undertaken the most systematic analysis of Canadian nominations. He discovered that the practices of mass parties such as the NDP differed sharply from those exhibited in cadre parties such as the Liberals and Conservatives. Where the party is at least competitive, the nomination struggle within an NDP association typically manifests what Sayers labels as "party democracy," a term which is "synonymous with the relatively impermeable, well-organized associations of mass parties that run closed, contested nominations."[24] To summarize: Canadian scholars have uncovered three key features that distinguish New Democratic nomination contests from those of other parties (a more stable membership, a greater need for candidates to have lengthy party resumés, and a higher proportion of female aspirants). This literature, however, is almost entirely derived from studies at the national level. Would we anticipate these findings would be equally applicable at the provincial level, that what is true for the federal NDP would be equally valid for the Manitoba NDP?[25] After all, federal constituencies, on average, contain more than twice as many people as provincial constituencies, and in a less-populated province like Manitoba, the difference would be even more pronounced. As well, the national NDP is consigned to minor-party status, while the Manitoba NDP is a major player in provincial politics. Nevertheless, the New Democratic Party has "by far the most integrated organization of the three main Canadian political parties," and "the widespread feeling of belonging to an undifferentiated movement"[26] would likely trump any differences of scale or of status. We would anticipate, therefore, that the nomination practices in the national NDP would closely resemble those in the Manitoba NDP. As the subsequent chapters will demonstrate, this expectation is well-grounded.

The scholarly literature on Canadian party nominations emphasizes one other theme directly relevant to this analysis: incumbents rarely face nomination challenges. True, there has been the occasional high-profile exception to this generalization. In 1887, for example, former Toronto mayor James Beatty was not only challenged, but actually lost a nomination contest in his hometown, and the same fate befell W.F. Maclean (the "Dean of Parliament") in 1926[27] and George Tustin, the Conservative whip, in 1957.[28] In the 1988 federal election, only 12 percent of incumbents were challenged for their nomination and only 2 percent were actually denied renomination.[29] These figures were essentially repeated in 1993; 10 percent of incumbents faced a contest and, again, only 2 percent lost their renomination bid.[30] The media attention provoked by an attempt to oust a sitting member might leave the mistaken impression that this is a common occurrence. In fact, as R.K. Carty and Lynda Erickson observe, these nomination challenges are "dramatic events precisely because they are infrequent."[31]

On the face of it, the "infrequent" challenges to incumbents might seem surprising. The politically ambitious, after all, have little interest in running as sacrificial lambs in hopeless constituencies and much prefer ridings that have a history of supporting the candidatures of their fellow partisans. Where such a disposition seems deeply entrenched—such as the thirty-eight-year (and counting) proclivity of most rural Albertan constituencies to elect Conservative MLAS—securing the nomination is tantamount to a ticket to the provincial legislature.[32]

Why, then, is it "widely conceded that an incumbent who wishes to be renominated usually can be?"[33] Three factors are at play. First, there are comparative advantages associated with incumbency. Sitting legislators generally start any renomination battle with a clear advantage in name recognition. For at least the previous term of office, they have been the public face of the party in the riding. If they are even remotely adept at self-promotion, they should have imprinted their name and face in their constituents' collective consciousness through countless public appearances. Incumbents should also have used their time as elected officials to provide both personal and impersonal benefits to supporters, and, as proven winners, they should also be able to count on healthy financial backing. Finally, they should have peopled the constituency executive with loyalists who will ensure that such matters as the timing, location, and rules of the nomination meeting are to the incumbent's advantage.

Second, party headquarters is rarely enthusiastic about challenges to sitting legislators. Such tussles tend, whatever the outcome, to produce an embittered and divided constituency association, one which is unlikely to be an effective fighting force in the coming election. Thus, the Quebec Liberal Party, prior to 1960, "simply assumed" the renomination of sitting members (although an irate rank and file occasionally nominated an "Independent Liberal" and, in one instance, the insurgent was successful).[34] Similarly, party leader Jean Chrétien decreed that all Liberal incumbents were to be renominated for the 1993 election and, despite some grumblings at the grassroots, this objective was achieved.[35] In general, the party brass will regard challenges to a sitting member as an explicit threat to party solidarity and an implicit attack on party authority.

Third, rank-and-file members of the riding association are likely to feel some loyalty to the incumbent. This was the individual, after all, who triumphed over their (oft-disliked) partisan foes in at least one preceding election. Most constituency activists would have worked many hours to secure the incumbent's election; to resist his or her renomination would essentially undercut the validity of their previous efforts. Some members of the riding association develop a strong affective bond with their "champion" and regard a nomination challenge as a personal slight. Thus, when Bill Fair had the temerity to challenge the iconic John Diefenbaker for the 1972 nomination in Prince Albert, Fair's entourage could safely enter the auditorium only through a door from the back alley (and that egress was achieved only after the aborting of a plan by four aggrieved Diefenbakerites to kidnap Fair and take him to Lac La Ronge for the day).[36] In short, the resources of the incumbent, the hostility of the party brass, and the loyalty of the rank-and-file members make nominating challenges to sitting members rare occurrences (and successful challenges rarer still).

Thus, Jim Walding, as a fifteen-year MLA, should have been relatively safe from challenge, and this assessment is not perceptibly altered when matters of region, of party, and of governmental status are considered. True, the constituency of St. Vital lies in western Canada, a part of the country where populist challenges to authority are an integral part of the political culture. It is likely no coincidence that Roger-Joseph Teillet, member of Parliament for the Winnipeg riding of St. Boniface, became, in 1968, the first cabinet minister in Canadian history to lose a nomination tussle.[37] One study of the 1988 federal election discovered that while 24 percent of western Canadian incumbents confronted challenges, the comparable figure for the remainder of the country was only 9 percent.[38] And in 2000, as many as one-fifth of the MPS from the western-based Canadian Alliance faced contested nominations (although, in this instance, it is not straightforward to disentangle the impact of region from that of party).[39]

Yet if Walding's hold on his nomination was made more tenuous simply owing to the location of his riding, both his party and his party's status in government should have had the opposite effect. Although this question has not been systematically studied, the data from 2004 are suggestive. In an election where a number of Liberal incumbents (including Sheila Copps) faced challenges, not one of the NDP's forty-nine contested nominations involved a sitting member, indicative of "the stronger internal norms of solidarity in the NDP stemming from their historical experience as a minority movement."[40] As well, it is important to recall that the Manitoba New Democratic Party was in office when Walding's renomination was contested in 1986. Carty and Erickson suggest that governments place a "greater premium" on internal solidarity "which is reflected in the reluctance of active party members to challenge their local MP."[41] In summary, therefore, it was unlikely that Jim Walding would be challenged for the St. Vital NDP nomination in 1986, and matters of region, of party, and of governmental status do not significantly alter this conclusion.

In actuality, Jim Walding's renomination was contested. Thus, although subsequent chapters will demonstrate that much of this nomination battle was certainly consistent with the NDP's normal nomination practices, this book is ultimately the analysis of a deviant case. It is unusual for an incumbent to be challenged. It is even more unusual for the contest to be decided by a single ballot. It is most unusual of all for such significant socio-political consequences to flow from this result. Highlighting the exceptionalism of the Walding case should throw into sharper relief the typicality of most Canadian nominating conventions.

The plan for this book is straightforward. The next chapter will outline the geographic, social, and political backdrop for what follows by considering the nature of both St. Vital (as a community and as a constituency) and the Manitoba New Democratic Party. Chapter 3 will introduce Jim Walding as our protagonist and detail his growing estrangement from his party during his first fourteen years as an MLA. Chapter 4 focuses on the nomination challenges from Gerri Unwin and Sig Laser and on the ensuing campaign, while Chapter 5 reconstructs the 12 January 1986 nomination meeting for St. Vital. The focus of Chapter 6 is the chain of events triggered by this meeting, up to and including the fall of the Pawley government. The penultimate chapter considers the fallout from these events, not just on the key players and local New Democrats, but also on all Manitobans and, indeed, on all Canadians. The concluding chapter returns to the central questions raised in this introduction: Was this an atypical nomination meeting? Why did Walding win? What were the implications of that victory? Can a plausible counterfactual scenario be constructed? And, most importantly, could 12 January 1986 have been the day Canada's peaceable kingdom was "lost?"

2

The Setting

IN THE WAKE OF THE RED RIVER REBELLION, Manitoba became, in 1870, Canada's fifth province. Manitoba entered Confederation with little territory (the "postage stamp" province), with a population that was predominantly Métis, and with constitutional guarantees for the French language. Over the next half-century, however, all three of these foundational facts would be uprooted. New lands were added to Manitoba until it grew to eighteen times its original size. Three waves of immigrants flooded into the province. First to arrive were a group of transplanted Ontarians who quickly occupied the most fertile farmland in Manitoba's southwest corner. Determined to remake the province in Ontario's image, and with the original Métis inhabitants both outnumbered and displaced, the provincial administration of Thomas Greenway in 1890 precipitously (and, as we shall subsequently see, unconstitutionally) annulled the *Manitoba Act*'s recognition of French as an official language. The influx of a (principally working-class) wave of British immigrants was followed in relatively short order by a final group of settlers from northern, central, and eastern Europe. These later arrivals tended to congregate in the poorer neighbourhoods in the northern and eastern parts of Winnipeg and on the less fertile land to the north and east of the city. Thus, by the outbreak of World War I, two quite different societies were separated by a line that bisected Winnipeg and ran from the Lake of the Woods in the province's southeast corner to just south of Swan Lake in the northwest.[1] Largely overlapping cleavages of region, of ethnicity, and of class made Manitoba a highly polarized place.

Figure 1: Manitoba's Political Diagonal

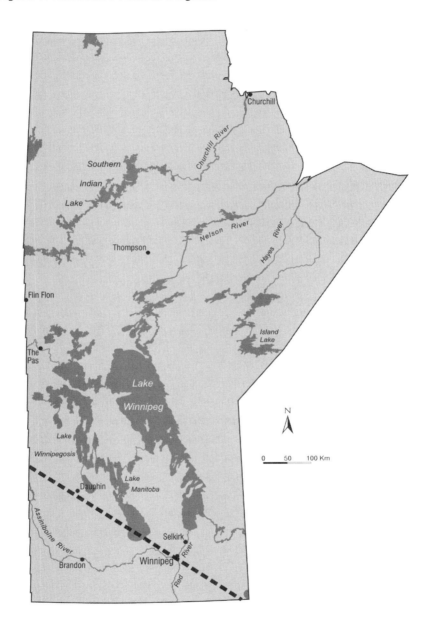

Inevitably, later immigrants transplanted to Manitoba many of the disparate ideas then current in Europe for profound social change. As a result, left-wing factionalism was endemic in Manitoba prior to and during the First World War; in the 1910 provincial election, for example, Manitoba Labor Party stalwart Fred Dixon was narrowly defeated when, four days prior to the balloting, the Socialist Party gratuitously nominated a candidate to split the vote.[2] In fact, it was only the decisive defeat of the Winnipeg General Strike of 1919 (and the consequent discrediting of both syndicalism and Bolshevism) that brought some order to Manitoba's political left. Under the moderate leadership of British trade unionists, Fabians, and Christian socialists, the Independent Labor Party (ILP) was established in 1920. In the intensely polarized, post-strike milieu, the ILP enjoyed a level of success matched elsewhere in Canada only in Cape Breton and Ontario. With 21 percent of the vote, the fledgling party managed in 1920 to elect eleven members to the legislative assembly, including three who were serving strike-related jail terms at the time. In the next two years, both J.S. Woodsworth and S.J. Farmer won election as ILP candidates (the former as an MP, the latter as the mayor of Winnipeg).[3] In provincial politics, this was to be the high-water mark of ILP support. With ethnic Manitobans practising the "politics of deference"[4] (voting for government candidates in order to evade the inaccurate ethnic scapegoating that occurred during and after the General Strike[5]), with class consciousness receding during the prosperous decade of the 1920s, and with the imposition of an electoral map dramatically skewed against urban voters, the ILP fell back to six, three, and five seats in the next three provincial elections (with between 10 and 17 percent of the popular vote).

The formation of the Co-operative Commonwealth Federation (CCF) in 1933 offered some hope, if a marriage between urban labour and rural progressives could be effected, that the Manitoba left could grow beyond its North Winnipeg bastion. In actuality, urban-rural animosities remained palpable, and, with the United Farmers of Manitoba (UFM) declining to affiliate with the new party, the CCF's seven seats from 12 percent of the popular vote in 1936 hardly represented an improvement on the ILP's record. At the outset of the Second World War, Manitoba Premier John Bracken proposed the creation of an all-party government, ostensibly to help the province secure better financial terms from Ottawa and to avoid unseemly and debilitating partisanship in a time of national crisis. Bracken, who tended to regard governing as an exercise more akin to administration than to politics, had previously made similar overtures to the Opposition parties, but these had been consistently spurned by a CCF anxious to avoid the sort of cooptation that had befallen the federal wing of the Progressives in the 1920s. Yet despite the vigorous protests of national party secretary David Lewis, Bracken's offer was accepted and CCF leader S.J. Farmer became minister of labour in an all-party government.

As it turned out, participation in this grand coalition (independent socialist Lewis St. George Stubbs was the only "opposition" member in the assembly), was a mistake for the CCF. The party had agreed to limit the electoral challenges to its coalition partners;[6] thus, in the 1941 provincial election it ran only ten candidates, winning 17 percent of the provincial vote and electing a paltry total of three MLAS. Worse yet, it soon became clear that participation in the government would bring few policy benefits. Farmer's bill to reform the provincial labour code was designated as a "free" vote, and when many of his cabinet colleagues (including the premier) voted against the changes, the bill was easily defeated. Bracken moved to the leadership of the national Progressive Conservatives in 1942, and the CCF took the opportunity to return to the Opposition benches.

Because it seemed to demonstrate not only the efficacy of the party's economic prescriptions, but also the appropriateness of its social recommendations, World War II was generally a boon for the CCF. Admittedly, their electoral results proved to be a significant disappointment in Ontario. Yet in Manitoba's other neighbour, Saskatchewan, the CCF actually came to power, and poll results for the national wing were, at least for a brief while, surprisingly strong. In Manitoba, CCF membership grew from 800 in 1942 to 3300 in 1943 and over 4000 in 1944.[7] As the only party now sitting in Opposition, moreover, the CCF was well-situated to take advantage of any popular discontent with the coalition administration (now under the premiership of Stuart

Garson). In the 1945 provincial campaign, the CCF, at 35 percent, polled more votes than any other party. Yet with Winnipeg allocated only ten of fifty-five seats (despite having almost half of the provincial population), only ten CCF candidates were elected. Worse yet, any momentum generated was soon dissipated in a debilitating struggle with the communist Labour Progressive Party, a struggle that led to the suspension and/or expulsion from the CCF of three of the party's MLAS.

The party thus entered a period of decline. Membership fell off; even their feeble counterparts in Alberta had more members than the Manitoba CCF in the post-war period.[8] The party's financial circumstances were also dire; their newspaper was shut down in 1952 and the provincial secretary was the sole (and, at times, unpaid) employee in the provincial office.[9] In both the 1949 and 1953 elections, the party had no hope of forming the government since it ran candidates in fewer than half the ridings. As the ardently anti-CCF *Winnipeg Free Press* gloated, "No more irrefutable certification of impotence could be given."[10] Under the circumstances, electing seven and five MLAS in these two elections was all that could be expected.

Two factors served to reverse this decline. First, the long-standing coalition government disintegrated in 1950 when the Conservatives moved into Opposition. It has frequently been observed that greater than minimal winning coalitions are inherently unstable;[11] with the CCF no longer a credible contender for office, the need for the Conservatives and the Liberal-Progressives to continue their coalescence abated sharply. Once in Opposition, Conservative attacks on regressive and antiquated government practices helped to legitimize long-standing CCF complaints. Second, Liberal-Progressive Premier Douglas Campbell (who personally sat in the Manitoba legislative assembly for forty-seven uninterrupted years!) undertook electoral reform, ostensibly on "his own initiative."[12] Using a formula that equated seven urban voters to four in the rural areas, Winnipeg's seat allocation grew from ten before World War II to twelve immediately thereafter to twenty prior to the 1958 vote. Using language that seems archaic to modern ears, CCF leader Lloyd Stinson railed in the legislature against the inequities inherent in the new scheme: "Why should four housewives in Portage la Prairie be equal to seven in Brandon?"[13] Even so, the reform was a godsend to a party based principally in Winnipeg; in the 1958 election, the party reached an historic high with eleven MLAS, even though at 20 percent their vote share was fourteen points lower than it had been in 1945.

The 1958 election ushered in what has been dubbed as "Manitoba's Quiet Revolution."[14] Replacing the Bracken-Garson-Campbell *ancien régime* was a modernizing, statist, and Keynesian government headed by Conservative Duff Roblin. Holding the balance of power, the CCF bartered their support in the legislature for the passage of some progressive economic and social policies. With the Liberal-Progressives in freefall, however, Roblin was able to gain much of the political credit for these initiatives and swept to a majority government in the following year's election (with the CCF essentially holding its position with ten seats and 22 percent of the vote).

In 1958, the national wing of the Co-operative Commonwealth Federation suffered a crushing reversal at the polls. With the defeat of both M.J. Coldwell and Stanley Knowles, only eight CCF MPs would sit in the new Parliament. For many supporters, this setback indicated that the CCF experiment had run its course; three years later, after extensive negotiations with the fledgling Canadian Labour Congress, the CCF was folded into the New Democratic Party. In Manitoba, however, this transition from CCF to NDP was anything but seamless. Led by Al Mackling and Howard Pawley (both of whom, as we shall see, would be key players in the party's evolution a quarter-century hence), dissidents raised a number of objections to the new party. In particular, it was feared that the sins linked to "big labour" in the public's mind would be visited upon the NDP, that the party's commitment to socialist goals would be significantly attenuated, and that the provision for trade union affiliation would ensure organized labour's hegemony in the new party.[15] As Howard Pawley subsequently acknowledged, "I didn't think it would work. Philosophically, I thought it was wrong."[16] Ultimately, the Pawley-Mackling forces were defeated, but not before introducing a series of resolutions, which, according to Knowles, manifested "a shocking display of ignorant and incredibly narrow-minded self-interest."[17] At the 1960 conference of the Manitoba CCF, by a two-to-one margin, delegates voted their party out of existence.

In the short run, the metamorphosis into the NDP appeared to be a mistake. In the 1962 election, the party fielded candidates in only thirty-nine of fifty-seven ridings, saw their legislative caucus reduced to seven from ten, and lost votes in every riding but one.[18] The following year, NDP membership rolls hemorrhaged by more than 50 percent, and while the 1966 election saw a return to the CCF's 1959 high-water marks of support, few presaged their "meteoric" rise to power only three years later.[19]

In actuality, the NDP was exceedingly fortunate. The once mighty Roblin government grew, as do most administrations after a decade in office, increasingly tired and out of touch. The public outcry over an unpopular sales-tax measure encouraged Roblin to jump into national politics, and the deeply conservative predilections of his successor, Walter Weir, had little appeal outside of the southwestern corner of the province. Weir resisted the introduction of medicare in Manitoba and at one federal-provincial conference made the remarkable observation that "Manitobans didn't want or need public housing but would build their own houses as their fore-fathers had done."[20] Better yet for the NDP, the Opposition Liberals were now led by Bobby Bend, whose inclinations were no more progressive than those of the premier. Into this political vacuum came Ed Schreyer who returned from a stint as a member of Parliament to secure the NDP leadership (and benefit from extensive media coverage) a scant seventeen days before the provincial vote. Unlike all previous leaders of the Manitoba CCF and NDP, Schreyer had a youthful persona, a rural background, and a non-Anglo-Saxon heritage. With another round of redistribution having given Winnipeg an additional seven seats in the legislature, with the other two party leaders having little appeal outside the British southwest, and with an unprecedented $45,000 election budget, Schreyer's New Democrats were able to parlay a fifteen-point hike in their share of the popular vote (to 38 percent) into twenty-eight seats in the legislature (just one short of a majority).[21] All of the NDP seats were in Winnipeg or in rural areas to the northeast of the city; the province's "Deep South"[22] remained an electoral wasteland. Even so, fifty years to the day after the Winnipeg General Strike leaders had formally capitulated, the political left finally gained power in Manitoba.

In many respects, the preceding chronology was reproduced, in miniature, in the socio-political evolution of St. Vital. Established in 1822 by French-speaking settlers (and subsequently named to commemorate the selfless labours of Bishop Vital-Grandin), St. Vital is, after Kildonan, the second-oldest community in Manitoba. For over four decades, St. Vital's prosperity was based on an entirely unsustainable harvest of buffalo; one such hunt in 1840 brought back over 1,000,000 pounds of buffalo meat to the Red River district (despite having left many times that amount to rot on the plains).[23] The failure of the buffalo hunt in the late 1860s, combined with a downturn in the community's other economic engine (the cart and boat brigades), left residents ill-disposed to accept the arrival of a party of Canadians intent on imposing the square survey system in place of the traditional river-lot system.[24] On 11 October 1869, Louis Riel (grandson of the first white woman to settle in the Canadian West and son of the man whose acts of defiance had successfully ended the Hudson Bay Company's monopoly on the fur trade in western Canada) left his mother's home in St. Vital to confront the interlopers. Backed by seventeen unarmed Métis, Riel declared, "The Canadian Government has no right to make surveys in the Territory without the express permission of the people of the Settlement."[25] Although initially disinclined to stop their work, the surveyors decided otherwise when Riel's confederates started to remove their "hampering" overcoats.[26] Thus began the chain of events that culminated in the Red River Rebellion, the establishment of the province of Manitoba, and the exile and execution of Riel.

The tumultuous occurrences of 1869 and 1870 did not initially alter the fundamental character of St. Vital as a French-speaking community with an economy based on subsistence agriculture. Over the next four decades, however, large numbers of anglophones came to reside in St. Vital, a demographic transformation that was masked by the fact that, until 1910, all councillors and all reeves (including Louis Riel's brother, Joseph, who served three terms as reeve in the 1890s) were French-speaking. In short order, English residents completely overhauled the community's political elite. St. Vital's first anglophone councillor secured office in 1910, and the initial anglophone reeve was elected in 1912; after that date, a francophone never again held the position of reeve. In fact, while council minutes were kept only in French prior to 1910, they would be maintained only in English after 1913 (with a brief interregnum in which both languages were recorded). The English councils were far more concerned with economic development than had been their French predecessors. The rural municipality of St. Vital was officially incorporated, water, sewer, and electrical services became readily available, and subdividing of pastureland proceeded apace. Over the next decade, council mandated a street-car line, concrete sidewalks, and the paving of St. Mary's Road (even though at the time only one resident of St. Vital owned a car).[27] In a paean to this economic progress, the first English-speaking reeve, Richard Wilson, celebrated the fact that many of Winnipeg's "largest business and professional men have already secured holdings varying in area from one to ten acres, ample grounds on which to erect palatial homes.... Truly a new era has dawned for St. Vital."[28]

Thus, as in Manitoba more generally, the place and power of francophones was abruptly constrained in St. Vital. The community may have been the home of Louis Riel, but after 1913 this reality was increasingly perceived through the lens of commercial ambition. Plans to purchase and restore one of Riel's dwellings, for example, were enthusiastically supported by a local editorialist: "There can be no denying that as a tourist attraction, the Riel property would provide a splendid promotional opportunity. Rebels are almost always loved by Americans, and we may as well face the economic reality that tourist attractions in Manitoba are specifically designed to snare a share of that particular market.... In the parlance of our times, [Louis Riel] is a merchandisable commodity."[29]

With large numbers of British and eastern European immigrants settling in the greater Winnipeg area, the proportion of francophones in St. Vital dwindled steadily (symbolized by the car-crash death of Louis Riel's highly visible nephew in the late 1940s).[30] By 1951, just fewer than 13 percent of the community's 19,000 inhabitants were of French ethnic origin (with 63 percent British, 10 percent German, Polish, or Ukrainian, and 14 percent other ethnicities).[31]

Only rarely did tensions flare up between St. Vital's francophones and anglophones. One such occasion occurred in the winter of 1963–64 when six (mostly French-speaking) families pulled their children out of school to protest the imposition of bus fees for parochial school students. After a three-month standoff, the matter was settled, but not until after St. Vital MLA Fred Groves had complained of receiving "vicious, ignorant and crude, anonymous letters," had condemned the presumed complicity of "the ecclesiastical authorities of St. Boniface," and had declared both his opposition to "any aid directly or indirectly to parochial schools" and his commitment "to defend the rights of the majority."[32] At most times, however, there were only faint echoes of the historic pre-eminence of the French language in St. Vital.

In electoral politics as well, the community's evolution closely coincided with that of the province. Recall the diagonal that separated the prosperous, conservative, Anglo-Saxon southwest of Manitoba from the poorer, more radical, and more ethnically diverse northeast. Located on Winnipeg's southeastern periphery, St. Vital effectively straddled this line and thus reproduced, in miniature, the province's political tensions. Table 1, which summarizes the community's electoral history from the First World War to the Schreyer breakthrough of 1969, reveals a number of patterns.

Table 1: Electoral Support in St. Boniface/St. Vital, 1920 to 1969[33]

	Lib/Progressive	Conservative	Labour/CCF/NDP	Social Credit	Liberal	Independent/Farmer
1920		1434*			730	942/675/404
1922			1124		1176	2024*
1927		1990*	1469		1790	1188
1932	3283	3483	3477*		1116	
1936	3630	2747	3157*	1730		
1941	3684*		2759	1404		
1945	3939		6349*			483/874/1710
1949	3936*/2647	2730	3905*/1483			
1953	4530*/3580*	2101/737	2707/1293	1420		3189
1958	2331	3616*	1334			242
1959	1946	4599*	1858			
1962		3626*	1023		2605	
1966		4432*	2310		2927	
1969		2587*	2564		2034	

*elected

First, it must be emphasized that between 1920 and 1953 the community of St. Vital was subsumed in the larger constituency of St. Boniface. The representational justification for this grouping is difficult to detect. While St. Vital had a relatively modest population of 1800 at the end of the First World War, it had grown to just under 11,000 inhabitants by 1933, more than sufficient to justify a stand-alone riding. With the rural southwest intent on freezing its post-General Strike advantage, however, any changes to the electoral map were strongly resisted. As a result, St. Boniface grew to be by far the largest constituency in the province. In 1945, for example, St. Boniface contained 24,052 registered electors; the next largest constituency (St. Clements) had only 15,074, while tiny Rupertsland had but 1100 voters. In fact, while much has been made of how the electoral map minimized Winnipeg's political impact, that city's 155,824 voters were entitled to ten MLAS, a level of malapportionment significantly less severe than that experienced by the electorate of St. Boniface. For 1949 and 1953, this injustice was partially alleviated by the ad hoc change of St. Boniface into a dual-member riding, before St. Vital became a riding unto itself prior to the 1958 election.

Second, for the provincial elections between 1927 and 1953 inclusive, St. Boniface, like all constituencies outside Winnipeg, employed the preferential ballot system. Voters ranked candidates in order of preference, and if no one received a majority on the initial tally then those candidates with the lowest totals were successively eliminated and their ballots redistributed until a winner emerged. Under the right circumstances, the preferential ballot can effectively blunt the electoral impact of socialist parties (and, in fact, it was explicitly adopted for that purpose in 1952 in British Columbia). Nevertheless, as can be seen from Table 1, this system actually worked to the advantage of the political left in St. Boniface. Both in 1932 (for the ILP) and in 1936 (for the ILP/CCF), Harold Lawrence was elected to the provincial legislature despite receiving fewer first-place selections than an opponent (markedly so on the latter occasion). These were, in fact, the only instances in either election when someone was able to use the second-choice selections of eliminated candidates to leap-frog to victory.

Third, it is clear from Table 1 that, at least for the first three decades after the Winnipeg General Strike, the political left performed well in St. Boniface. The St. Vital portion of the constituency was certainly buffeted by the Great Depression; in 1934, 21 percent of the community's 11,000 inhabitants were on relief.[34] Thus, Harold Lawrence's two triumphs in the 1930s were not especially surprising. In addition, Edwin Hansford was twice elected for the ccf in the 1940s (on one occasion, with an impressive 47 percent of the vote). In fact, as Table 2 makes apparent, from 1922 to 1949 the left was consistently ten to eighteen percentage points more popular in the constituency of St. Boniface than overall in the province of Manitoba. Yet Table 2 also reveals that this gap essentially disappeared over the next two decades. These were prosperous times for St. Vital. As an essentially residential community, St. Vital experienced the full impact of the post-war baby boom. Construction of the floodway eased the annual damage heretofore caused by the Seine and Red River overflows, new houses, roads, and schools were built (although some long-standing residents insisted on retaining their backyard privies),[35] St. Vital's population doubled from just over 15,000 in 1946 to just over 30,000 two decades on,[36] and, on 9 June 1962, St. Vital was officially incorporated as a city. During this expansionary period, no ccf or ndp candidate came close to being elected in St. Vital. In fact, one long-standing partisan was surprised to discover upon his arrival in 1961 that the St. Vital ndp had no local organization, no annual meeting, just a loose association of enthusiasts.

Yet the data from Tables 1 and 2 obscure one important reality about elections in St. Vital. If St. Vital can be said to straddle Manitoba's political diagonal, then it is not too fanciful to suggest that this line runs straight down St. Mary's Road, a route which bisects the constituency, before continuing on to the southeast corner of the province. Consider, for example, the results from the 1966 provincial election (Figure 2 shows the constituency boundaries at that time). Overall, Conservative Donald Craik easily retained the constituency for his party, winning 46 percent of the vote (to 30 percent for the Liberal and 24 percent for Bill Hutton, the New Democratic candidate). Dividing the constituency along St. Mary's Road,[38] however, reveals quite a different picture.

Table 2: ILP/CCF/NDP Support in St. Boniface/St. Vital and Manitoba, 1920 to 1969[37] (%)

Year	St. Boniface/ St. Vital	Manitoba	Difference
1920	0	21	-21
1922	26	16	10
1927	23	10	13
1932	31	17	14
1936	28	12	16
1941	35	17	18
1945	47	34	13
1949	37	26	11
1953	20	17	3
1958	18	20	-2
1959	22	22	0
1962	13	15	-2
1966	24	23	1
1969	36	38	-2

Table 3 illustrates that in the eighteen polls east of St. Mary's Road, Hutton was competitive with Craik; in the seventeen polls west of St. Mary's Road, however, Craik effectively tripled Hutton's total. In fact, in one particular poll in the wealthy Kingston Row neighbourhood, Hutton secured only thirteen of the 310 ballots cast. Small wonder that a prominent doctor, and one of the few New Democrats in the area, requested the "biggest NDP sign he could get in order to put some colour into a neighbourhood in which there were 50 blue PC signs." To be successful in St. Vital, the NDP would need to establish a stronger presence on the "other" side of the diagonal.

Table 3: NDP Support in St. Vital, East and West of St. Mary's Road, 1966[40]

	Craik (PC)	Honeyman (Lib)	Hutton (NDP)
Polls East of St. Mary's Road	1862	1254	1444
Polls West of St. Mary's Road	2490	1622	840

Thus, by the end of the 1960s, it had become apparent that if the NDP were to become serious contenders for power in Manitoba, they would have to make substantial progress in ridings that were located neither in their

Figure 2: Greater Winnipeg and St. Vital, 1966[39]

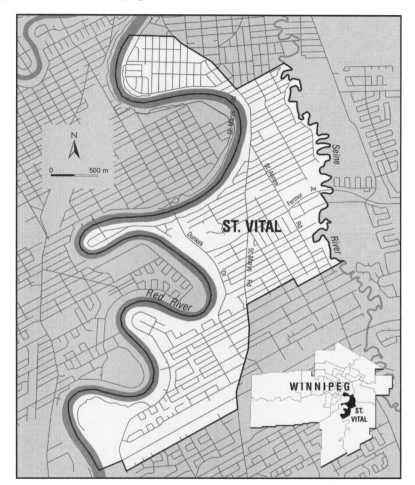

North Winnipeg redoubt, nor in the electoral wasteland of the southwest. St. Vital was just such a constituency. In the previous four provincial elections, the voters of St. Vital had supported the CCF/NDP in numbers commensurate with the party's province-wide backing. In the breakthrough election of 1969, the same pattern obtained. With provincial support for the NDP vaulting from 23 to 38 percent, the electors of St. Vital likewise provided unprecedented backing to the party. The local candidate won 36 percent of the vote (an increase of 12 percent over 1966) and came within twenty-three votes of securing St. Vital for the NDP. The name of this candidate was Jim Walding.

3

The Incumbent

JIM WALDING WAS BORN on 9 May 1937 in Rushden, Northamptonshire, England.[1] After marrying his wife, Valerie, at the age of twenty, Walding served three years in the Royal Inniskilling Fusiliers (including a stint in West Berlin) before immigrating to Canada in 1961.[2] The couple soon adopted three children, and Walding continued his career in Winnipeg as a dispensing optician and contact lens fitter.

It would have been impossible to predict that Walding would become the NDP candidate for St. Vital in the 1969 provincial election. In Britain, he had been a supporter of Labour, but had not been active in the party. Once in Canada, he had joined the NDP in 1963 and, prior to his nomination, had already served on the provincial executive; in fact, as chair of the special events committee, he had organized a fundraising social for Joe Borowski's February 1969 by-election victory in Churchill. Even so, he had been in Canada for only eight years and in that time, aside from the usual labours for home and school committees, had done little to raise his profile in the community. Moreover, as one might expect from someone who listed his hobbies as "reading, bridge, and chess," Walding did not possess the outgoing personality of the stereotypical politician. On the contrary, he was frequently described by contemporaries as shy, aloof, and reserved. At public meetings, it was not uncommon for Walding to stand quietly to one side while Val, his energetic, extroverted, and ambitious wife, chatted animatedly with party members and constituents. Finally, Walding did not even live in the St. Vital constituency at the time. He had, in fact, earlier in 1969, unsuccessfully sought the NDP nomination in the riding of Radisson. That defeat might have marked both the beginning and the end of Jim Walding's political career had not George Schamber, a prominent St. Vital New Democrat, decided to disregard the dictum that Canadian parties "select candidates with knowledge of and attachment to the riding."[3] Schamber drove to the Walding home and announced that he would be "tickled pink" if Jim would seek the party's nomination in St. Vital. Although initially reluctant to entertain the idea, the combined persuasive powers of his wife and his guest overcame all objections: Jim Walding would stand for the NDP in St. Vital.

On the strength of their four successive victories in St. Vital, the Progressive Conservatives were the obvious favourites to take the riding again in 1969. Redistribution, however, had induced the incumbent to run in a neighbouring constituency, so the Tories nominated Jack Hardy, the sitting mayor of St. Vital as their standard-bearer. Hardy had served eight years on St. Vital council (the last four as mayor), and he justified his candidacy on the grounds that "men with municipal experience were urgently needed at the provincial level of government."[4] Yet with widespread enthusiasm for new NDP leader Ed Schreyer and with the boundary change having taken seven polls west of St. Mary's Road out of the constituency, the result in St. Vital was going to be closer in 1969 than it had been three years previously. In the end, it was a very tight three-way race. Hardy's final twenty-three-vote margin was built on the traditional Conservative strength west of St. Mary's Road; in eastern polls, Walding had actually secured 414 more votes than his chief rival.

With twenty-eight seats in the provincial legislature, Schreyer's New Democrats were one short of majority status, although the defection of St. Boniface Liberal MLA Larry Desjardins to the government side stabilized the situation somewhat. With the election of Manitoba's first social democratic administration, the composition of the province's political elite was dramatically altered. Like the new premier, the NDP caucus and cabinet were demonstrably younger, better educated, and less Anglo-Saxon than their predecessors in office. The party's rural MLAS were concentrated disproportionately in the northeast, rather than the southwest, while their urban members tended to be professionals, rather than businessmen.[5] "For the first time anyone could recall," it was observed, "the exclusive Manitoba

Club (would) list no ministers among its members."[6] During its initial mandate, the Schreyer government introduced a range of social welfare reforms—it lowered the age of majority, instituted a rentalsman, heightened social assistance, introduced pharmacare, and raised the minimum wage. Its two signature programs from the early years, however, were Autopac (a compulsory public auto insurance scheme, which was enacted in 1970 in what former premier Howard Pawley claimed "was the fiercest battle in Manitoba history since the 1919 strike") and Unicity (a plan to amalgamate Greater Winnipeg's ten municipalities into a single unit, which was scheduled to come into effect on 1 January 1972).

But for Jack Hardy's increasingly erratic behaviour, Jim Walding would have been merely an interested spectator to these events. Contrary to the expectations of most observers, the St. Vital MLA chose in the fall of 1969 to re-offer for the city's mayoralty. With the provincial legislature only sitting for about one hundred days annually, Hardy claimed he could devote the remainder of the year "to seeing to the affairs of the city."[7] Despite punctuating his mayoralty campaign with a Nixonesque claim ("Never in all my years of public office have I made personal gain"),[8] Hardy was handily re-elected. Yet after labouring so hard to secure two positions of prominence in the community, Hardy soon made it clear that he wanted neither of them. He made frequent trips out of the province and, by the fall of 1970, his house was up for sale.[9] Shortly thereafter, Hardy confirmed that he would become the assistant city manager in Terrace, British Columbia. "I have to earn a living," claimed Hardy, "and in Manitoba it is totally impossible for a politician to do it solely in politics."[10] Yet despite leaving the province in early December 1970, Hardy did not formally resign from the legislature until mid-February 1971,[11] and even then the Conservative leader refused for over a week to pass on the resignation letter, while rumours circulated that Hardy might commute from Terrace for the upcoming legislative session.[12] With the Ste. Rose riding also vacant (the Liberal incumbent had been appointed to the Senate), it must have been tempting for the premier to take at least brief advantage of his newfound working majority. Instead, he called for by-elections in both constituencies to be held on 5 April 1971.

In the interval since his narrow defeat in 1969, Walding had buffed his credentials by serving as a board member on the Manitoba Centennial Corporation. When Schreyer announced the date of the St. Vital by-election, Walding did not give the matter much thought: "I looked around and it seemed obvious to run again," he recalled. But other New Democrats harboured doubts about Jim Walding. The stakes were much higher than they had been in 1969; a victory this time in St. Vital would go some way to stabilizing the government's situation in the legislature. Many local New Democrats importuned long-time executive member Hugh McMeel to let his name stand, but McMeel declined because he "had a lot of faith in Jim Walding at that time"; in fact, McMeel, Schamber, and at least five others on the local executive publicly endorsed Walding's candidacy.[13] Nevertheless, several members of caucus led by Radisson MLA Harry Shafransky (who had vanquished Walding in a nomination tussle two years previously) recruited local educator Keith Huss to contest the nomination, and Bill Hutton, the 1966 candidate, also joined the fray. Yet despite an onlooker's report that he appeared "scared" at the nomination meeting, "Silent" Jim Walding (as he was dubbed at the time by the local newspaper)[14] was able to win easily on the first ballot.[15] It would be fifteen years until he would again face a challenge to his nomination.

Inevitably, the subsequent campaign was dominated by the government's Unicity proposals. Amalgamation was opposed both by the Conservative candidate, who complained that the plan had been presented "with arrogance and without cost estimates"[16] and by his Liberal counterpart who railed that it was "typical of twisted and unpractical NDP ideology" to submerge St. Vital's identity into a bureaucratic "mishmash,"[17] and who pointedly promised that, if elected, he would "not be a 'Silent Jim.'"[18] These attacks were echoed, at every opportunity, by St. Vital's mayor and the entire city council. Indeed, in the final week of the campaign, Mayor Winslow took the unusual (and potentially dangerous) step of publicly questioning Walding's integrity. "I for one cannot sit idly by," claimed His Worship, "and let the people be deceived into believing claims such as those of Mr. Walding which to put it bluntly are just not true."[19] With a local newspaper poll indicating that public opinion in St.

Vital was running more than two-to-one against the Unicity proposal,[20] Walding's election to the legislature was anything but assured.

Despite these voices ranged against him, Walding was not without significant electoral assets. Unicity aside, Schreyer and his government were still enjoying high approval ratings; thus the premier was as prominently featured as the candidate in most of Walding's campaign literature. The cover of one such pamphlet simply contained the words: "Two Young Men," while the inside pages emphasized the links between Schreyer and Walding. Another leaflet announced, "This is the big issue in this by-election: The people of our community want to give Ed Schreyer the majority he needs to continue his program of moderation and progress for all Manitobans." In addition to the premier's popularity, Walding could also count on a formidable army of volunteer workers (including nomination foes Harry Shafransky and Keith Huss). Even in upscale neighbourhoods like Kingston Row, three complete canvasses were undertaken on Walding's behalf, and the candidate himself managed to visit almost every household in the riding at least once.[21]

Of course, the Unicity issue could not be entirely ducked, although at a televised all-candidates debate, the NDP nominee was noticeably disinclined to discuss the matter; according to Walding, "the central city proposal was not an issue as far as the average voter was concerned."[22] When he did touch upon the Unicity plan, Walding emphasized the potential for significant property tax reductions in St. Vital; one campaign pamphlet suggested it made "more sense to leave our residential area undisturbed by industry, while allowing us to take advantage of industrial assessment anywhere in the urban area."

On 5 April 1971, Jim Walding was elected to the provincial legislature. As Brian Mulroney was to demonstrate in the free trade election of 1988, being on the "wrong" side of an engaged public opinion is not always fatal, as long as the "right" side is disunited. Although the turnout in St. Vital jumped from 68 percent in 1969 to 83 percent in 1971, Walding's share of the vote remained steady at 36 percent, while Liberal Dan Kennedy rose to 33 percent and Conservative Ken Pratt (undoubtedly crippled by Jack Hardy's shenanigans) fell to 31 percent. Pratt made the accurate, albeit ungracious, assessment, "I think it shows the majority of the people are against the government and the one-city plan."[23] To the surprise of most, the government also won the Ste. Rose by-election despite what the premier labelled as a "vindictive, dirty, and underhanded" Liberal campaign.[24] The NDP candidate vaulted from 18 to 42 percent of the vote to end a forty-four-year Liberal stranglehold on the constituency. Winning both by-elections gave the NDP thirty of the fifty-seven seats in the provincial assembly and touched off a "wild" election-night celebration at Walding's headquarters in which "jubilant party workers, ecstatic cabinet ministers and a premier who couldn't stop smiling, partied for hours."[25] Only Walding himself seemed "relatively calm and unaffected by his win"; he acknowledged that he had no specific legislative initiatives to advance, adding "as a novice, it will be my job to learn the procedure and to support the government to the best of my ability."[26]

During the by-election campaign, Walding's two major promises had been to "make regular written reports to every home" and to "hold meetings throughout St. Vital where I will report and answer questions and pay careful attention to your problems." Now an MLA, Walding's regular columns in the *St. Vital Lance* and annual reports from the legislature (not sent at public expense) satisfied the first pledge, and to fulfill the second Walding approached St. Vital council about using city hall to meet constituents every second Saturday morning. The irony of this proposal, given Walding's support for Unicity,[27] was not lost on the councillors. "Some nerve," summarized one alderman, while another responded, "I have fought and worked hard for this city. I have a lot against that man."[28] Even so, council eventually acceded to the request and Walding began to develop a reputation for exceptional constituency service.

As a neophyte backbencher, Walding's legislative responsibilities were relatively light. He sat on several standing committees (and chaired the private bills committee) during his initial term, while also joining the Manitoba delegation to the 1972 meeting of the Commonwealth Parliamentary Association. Despite this modest workload, Walding gave up his career as an optician shortly after being elected to become a full-time politician, and, as a result, the Waldings were subsisting ("quite frugally" in the assessment of one confidante) on the annual MLA stipend of $7200. Ironically, this basic indemnity was supplemented for Greater Winnipeg members in 1971 by a tax-free allowance of $2400; had the raise come any earlier, it is likely that Jack Hardy would not have resigned his seat.

The Waldings had another important decision to make. They had continued to reside outside St. Vital during the by-election, but now they felt it was important to buy a house inside the constituency boundaries. The precise location of their new domicile, however, was to be driven by strategic considerations. In the 1971 by-election, the greatest gain had been made by the Liberals who, despite no longer being credible contenders for power, had vaulted to 33 percent from 28 percent two years previously. Most of the credit for this resurgence in St. Vital had been bestowed upon Dan Kennedy, the Liberal candidate. An ambitious, articulate, and photogenic young lawyer, Kennedy promised to be a formidable obstacle to Walding's re-election plans. Accordingly, with the aid of a statistically inclined son, the Waldings undertook a poll-by-poll analysis of the by-election results and discovered that the core of Kennedy's support was located in four contiguous polls in the Norwood Flats west of St. Mary's Road. So it was to a home in that neighbourhood that the Waldings relocated. Dan Kennedy, as Val Walding recalled, "was actually a very strong Liberal. That is why we moved into the area where we moved in because we knew where the Liberal vote was. And we had to switch the Liberal vote."

The 1973 provincial election would put Val Walding's theory to the test. In the interval, there had been much grumbling among Liberal and Conservative partisans about the inherent unfairness of having a socialist government when a clear majority of the electorate supported free-enterprise parties. In fact, one Conservative MLA indicated that the result of the St. Vital by-election had given "real impetus" to the movement to found a new right-wing vehicle (perhaps to be called the Manitoba Party or the United Party).[29] While this plan foundered, there was still the very real prospect that the Liberals and Conservatives would, on a seat-by-seat basis, agree to run only a candidate from that party most likely to defeat the NDP standard-bearer. Thus, one proposal for southeast Winnipeg envisaged the Liberals staying out of Riel and Radisson, while the Conservatives would likewise in St. Boniface and St. Vital. Yet when the *Winnipeg Tribune* ran a front-page story on the potential deal, the president of the St. Vital PC constituency association was quick to issue a denial: "At no time has the Conservative association of St. Vital held informal or formal discussions with any member of the Liberal Executive nor has any individual member, to my knowledge, held any discussions privately. It is inconceivable that a constituency which has been a traditionally strong Conservative Seat and is presently well organized and fortunate to have a well-experienced, successful, local candidate with an excellent track record, should espouse the idea of supporting an accommodation candidate."[30] Shortly thereafter, the president of the Riel Liberal association attempted to reinvigorate the trade-off initiative by announcing that he was resigning his post and supporting the local Conservative candidate. He claimed that there had been "much discussion" about the proposal in both Riel and St. Vital but that "the coalition plan was defeated because of the interference from the respective headquarters of the two parties. Conservative headquarters applied pressure to the previous executive in St. Vital, and Liberal headquarters did the same in Riel."[31]

Fortunately for Jim Walding (and other New Democratic candidates in the area), nothing came of these machinations. Walding's nomination for the 28 June 1973 provincial vote was unopposed, and he ran both on the Schreyer government's legislative record (with which, according to one of his campaign pamphlets, he was "generally satisfied") and on his own record of service to his constituents ("the most satisfying aspect of being an MLA is the ability to help people"). Walding made few specific policy promises, although he expressed an interest in promoting hydroelectric development and in improving services for the disabled (and one pamphlet made the enigmatic observation that Walding "feels that Manitobans are fortunate in having a low growth rate and believes we can use this growth rate to good advantage").

The results of the 1973 election were an affirmation of the status quo. With St. Boniface MLA Larry Desjardins now officially a member of the NDP, the governing party won thirty-one ridings (with a four-point rise in popular support over 1969 to 42 percent), the Opposition Progressive Conservatives dropped one seat to twenty-one, while the Liberals (although losing five points in the popular vote) retained their allotment of five seats. Once again, Ed Schreyer's party would govern with a bare majority.[32]

In St. Vital, NDP support continued to track the province-wide figure, as Jim Walding secured 39 percent of the vote (up three points from the by-election victory). As Val Walding had surmised, the greatest threat to her husband's re-election came from Dan Kennedy, who had been unopposed for the Liberal nomination and who had, in carefully coded language, declared his confidence that St. Vital "would return a candidate reflecting the general views of the majority of the constituency."[33] Kennedy enjoyed the private backing of a number of local Tories and the very public backing of the mercurial Jack Hardy. "I may reside in British Columbia but the riding, and the former City of St. Vital still retain a soft spot in my head," declared Hardy. "Of the three candidates, my personal feeling is that regardless of political alliance, Dan Kennedy is the best man for the job, he is far superior to the other two."[34] In the end, Walding squeaked back into office with a margin of 105 over Kennedy, with the Conservative candidate more than 1500 votes further back.

Had Val Walding's home-relocation strategy paid any dividends? In the four polls that had been at the core of Kennedy's 1971 surge, turnout dropped marginally in 1973. Even so, it is noteworthy that while Kennedy received thirty-seven fewer votes in these polls than two years previously (and the Conservative candidate lost even more), Walding's total actually rose by nine votes among his newfound neighbours, a significant contribution to his final margin of victory. Having been twice edged by Dan Kennedy, nobody in the NDP camp was anxious for a third engagement. Before the next election, St. Vital New Democrats tried to take Kennedy out of play by putting his name forward for a judgeship (although it was the federal Liberals who finalized an appointment to the bench in 1978).[35]

With only four novice NDP MLAs having been elected in 1973, Walding was still, even after his second successive electoral triumph, one of the least experienced members of caucus. There was, therefore, no expectation that he would be appointed to cabinet; Walding himself acknowledged that, under Schreyer, being an MLA "was as high as I expected to go and I was content to be a backbencher." Walding did continue to chair the private bills committee and was also appointed as a commissioner on the board of the Manitoba Telephone System. Most significantly, he was made chair of the NDP caucus, where his performance received mixed reviews. Walding was a relatively passive chair; rather than impose a personal agenda, Walding was always inquiring of his caucus mates, "What is your will and pleasure?" Some found this open-mindedness refreshing, but others chafed under the apparent lack of direction. Noted one critic, one cannot "just assume that some general will is going to emerge by osmosis."

There was no such carping about Walding's service to his constituents. "In the early years," according to one informant, "Jim Walding was the best MLA in Manitoba, no question." Not a single interviewee disputed the gist of this statement. At a time when MLAS did not generally have constituency offices, Walding worked tirelessly to meet the needs of his electors. He went door-to-door between elections, he continued his fortnightly town-hall meetings, and he frequently sent out questionnaires, all to find out what was on the minds of the good citizens of St. Vital. A cynical observer might well question the sincerity of any politician who would pledge, "I will always be available to help with any problem that needs solving." Yet Walding seemed genuinely committed to living up to this 1973 election promise. One Christmas morning, Walding was telephoned by a woman agitated that her son would be spending the day behind bars; after a series of calls, Walding was able to secure a day pass for the miscreant. Another constituent who was working for the advancement of deaf children recalled his delight when Walding arranged a personal interview with the minister of education. Walding was particularly solicitous towards the needs of his elderly constituents and he would spend long hours completing their income-tax returns.

But Jim was not the only Walding devoted to constituency service. One informant recalled that "Jim was very hard-working and Val was even harder working; Val was the mover and shaker in the family." It was Val who organized fall dinners and Christmas teas. It was Val who helped many of the older women with their hair. It was Val who most mornings had the neighbourhood old-timers over for coffee. It was Val who glad-handed at social events and spoke ten words to every one uttered by her husband. Some constituents may have resented Val's high profile, but few could deny her political skills. One long-standing member summarized them thus: "Jim Walding was a decent and conscientious guy, but his wife had the brains and ambition." Together, they worked with uncommon vigour to keep the constituents of St. Vital happy.

By 1976, it was clear that the second Schreyer administration was running out of steam, and an internal poll in seven swing ridings (including St. Vital) confirmed that the governing party was in trouble. Admittedly, Ed Schreyer remained the most popular party leader with the backing of 50 percent of the respondents. By contrast, Tory Sterling Lyon and Liberal Charles Huband stood at 15 and 6 percent respectively, levels of support that indicated, in one pithy summary, they were "dogmeat as popular leaders."[36] On the other hand, the survey also indicated that voters were concerned about high taxes, high unemployment, and high inflation, and that, as a result, the PCs were ahead of the NDP in five of the seven key ridings. In St. Vital, in particular, support for the Liberals had apparently collapsed, leaving the Tories almost eight points ahead of the New Democrats. Putting the best face on this dismal circumstance, the report noted that with one-third of St. Vital respondents still undecided, "the PC margin could be overcome with a strong campaign."[37]

The Waldings set out to provide that campaign. Even before the nomination meeting, Jim and Val had spent two months undertaking almost two complete canvasses of the constituency. Instead of the customary fifty signatures, Walding's nomination papers contained 443 names; according to official agent Hugh McMeel, this "was to give as many voters as possible the opportunity to nominate Jim."[38] Again unopposed for the nomination, Walding's campaign speeches and literature emphasized three, by now familiar, themes. First, in order to capitalize on the premier's popularity, there were frequent references to "the Schreyer government," and his picture was everywhere. Second, Walding stressed the government's popular accomplishments (Autopac, rent control, pharmacare) and promised more of the same (expanded dental-care protection, comprehensive accident insurance, and the like). "The issue is quite clear," noted Walding in typically understated rhetoric. "Do the people of Manitoba want a continuation of the progressive and common sense policies of the last eight years or is it time for a change?"[39] Finally, Walding trumpeted his service to his constituents. He was, after all, the only candidate to reside in the constituency and he would justify his "reputation for providing a level of service previously unknown" by remaining available "twenty-four hours a day" at his home phone number. Testimonials from happy constituents were prominently displayed in his campaign literature. One constituent had phoned Walding for background information to support a job application. "Imagine my surprise," he recounted, "when the very next day, Jim knocked on my door with all the information I wanted. No politician had ever given me that kind of service before."

Opposing Walding were two political neophytes, both of whom claimed they were best situated to defeat the NDP. Public-opinion soundings indicated that only the Tories could do so province-wide, but the St. Vital Liberal candidate muddied the waters with his approximately accurate contention that in 1973 "the Liberal Party lost by a mere 80 votes and the Conservatives were a full 1600 votes behind the Liberals, which ought to encourage those people who want to defeat the NDP" to vote Liberal.[40] Media reports emphasized Walding's apparent vulnerability. The incumbent, according to one columnist in the *Winnipeg Tribune*, "won the last race by a slim majority but what has he done since? He doesn't state the issues but his leader could carry him through."[41] Aided by a vigorous campaign team,[42] Walding increased his share of the vote by three points to 42 percent, and he had a comfortable cushion of 500 votes over his Tory opponent, while the Liberals, without Dan Kennedy as their candidate, were an additional 1200 votes in arrears.

Provincially, however, the 1977 election was a disappointment for the NDP, who dropped only three points in the popular vote to 39 percent, but lost eight seats in the provincial assembly. With a whopping 49 percent of the popular vote, Sterling Lyon's PCS easily secured a majority government.[43] The big losers of the election were the Liberals who, after campaigning to the right for two elections under former leaders Bobby Bend and Izzy Asper (and who thus lost some of their progressive voters to the NDP), now tacked sharply leftward under new leader Charles Huband. Among other things, the Liberals now promised to retain rent controls, subsidize low-income tenants, and inject funds into job creation, public housing, and solar energy. While this new Liberal emphasis may have won a few voters back from the NDP, the right wing of the party defected en masse to the Progressive Conservatives, and the Liberals were reduced to a single seat in the legislature.

It is important not to minimize Jim Walding's achievement in 1977. At a time when electoral support for the NDP was marginally receding, Walding incrementally increased his own share of the vote. Leaving aside Saul Cherniak, who had left the cabinet in 1975 after a lengthy tenure as minister of finance, Walding was one of only five New Democratic backbenchers who secured re-election in 1977; both Harry Shafransky and Wally Johannson, fellow back-benchers in the nearby constituencies of Radisson and St. Matthews went down to defeat. Of the seven swing ridings that had been assiduously surveyed by the party prior to the campaign, only St. Vital returned a New Democrat.

His third successive electoral victory fortified Jim Walding's standing in the party. He resumed his position as caucus chair and also was named chair of the public accounts committee (traditionally the only legislative commit-tee chaired by an Opposition member). In addition, Walding was frequently employed by his party to deliver free-time political broadcasts on both radio and television. By the late 1970s, New Democrats were confident that Premier Lyon's neo-liberal prescriptions were not working; Manitoba was experien-cing the lowest economic growth in the country, provincial unemployment was higher than at any time since the Great Depression, and the cost of living was rising faster in Winnipeg than in any other major city. Walding's soft-spoken style and reserved demeanour lent credibility to the charges that Sterling Lyon was heading "a sleepy, arrogant, and doctrinaire govern-ment,"[44] that the government restraint program had "turned out to be short-term pain for long-term agony,"[45] and that Manitoba was in danger of "becoming known as the Newfoundland of the Prairies."[46]

Because much of the Lyon government's economic development strategy was based on natural resource megaprojects, Walding's most important role during these years was to serve as Manitoba Hydro critic. By all accounts, he performed well in this capacity. Another MLA from that period, Harvey Bostrum, recalled that Walding was "an effective critic in the legislature, and a surprisingly good heckler, although his subtle, pointed barbs were not said loudly enough. Walding may have been soft-spoken, but he was respected by the other side of the house for being thorough." Walding closely reviewed the loans and contracts undertaken by Manitoba Hydro and he effectively probed whether the public utility was subsidizing out-of-province consumers by exporting power at rates below cost. In these endeavours, Walding was aided by a well-placed contact inside Manitoba Hydro. According to Val, her husband received "a lot of brown envelopes," and, thus, "never had to ask a question if he didn't already know the answer." On one occasion, Walding enraged the government by reading in the legislature from a confidential submission to the Manitoba Hydro board.[47] When Howard Pawley became party leader in 1979, Walding provided a comprehensive briefing on the hydro file, and Pawley's retrospective summary of Walding's performance as hydro critic was unreservedly positive: "He did very well on that, extremely well, and he did it in a very scholarly, rational, balanced manner, and it added to his credibility."

Pawley's ascension to the party leadership had been occasioned by Ed Schreyer's unexpected appointment as Governor General. In 1969, Walding had backed the eventual winner with his active participation in the Committee to Elect Ed Schreyer. A decade later, Walding was similarly astute, although he initially supported Sid Green in a caucus vote for interim leader.[48] Most MLAs remained neutral in the subsequent leadership race, but one of the contest's losers noted that Pawley was "greatly aided" by Jim Walding and two other caucus mates.[49] In St. Vital, the Waldings organized a function at their home for Howard and Adele Pawley, and it seems certain that most of the constituency's delegates supported Pawley at the convention.

Yet at the same time, there were a few early signs of a rift between Walding and the provincial office. It was customary at the time for party headquarters to levy an annual assessment on each constituency. Walding balked at this arrangement, preferring each level to be financially autonomous. When he got no support from the riding executive, however, he momentarily backed away from this position. Even more disquieting was Walding's response to a provincial council motion that, as caucus chairman, he would serve on a committee to administer the sharing of federal rebates (along with MP Bill Blaikie and Nels Thibault, first vice-president of the Manitoba NDP). In a brusque letter to provincial secretary Jan D'Arcy, Walding declared, "Unfortunately, I was not present when the motion was proposed, I regret I will not be able to serve on the committee and trust you will be able to find a replacement."[50] Even so, a party meeting on the eve of the 1981 campaign had, in marked contrast to its assessment of other constituencies, no doubt about the NDP's health in St. Vital. Its terse summary: "good executive and candidate."[51]

When Premier Lyon announced that Manitobans would go to the polls in November 1981, he defended his government's record as "prudent" and "workmanlike," rather than "flashy."[52] Yet with almost all major economic indicators having worsened during his term in office, the premier was understandably anxious for voters to look forward, rather than backward. Accordingly, he based his re-election campaign on a trio of megaprojects: a $600 million potash mine, a $500 million aluminum smelter, and a $3.3 billion western provinces power grid (the last two of which would permit construction to resume on the moth-balled Limestone power plant). None of these plans had been finalized, and Opposition spokespersons could legitimately query whether, having staked its political credibility on these megaprojects, the government would now be negotiating with the private sector and with other governments from a position of weakness. Lyon had no time for such concerns. "We can all agree," he maintained, "that these major projects represent a first and most important step into the kind of prosperity that other parts of western Canada now enjoy."[53] And while public-relations professionals questioned the wisdom of a slogan that commenced with two negatives,[54] "Don't Stop Us Now" became Lyon's campaign mantra.

Despite its impressive 49 percent vote share in 1977, this was manifestly a government ripe for defeat. Yet the NDP were also not without difficulties. Three government MLAS (including Sid Green) had bolted to form a new political party, the Progressives, and there were obvious dangers that the anti-government vote would be fragmented. As well, while Manitoban voters perceived

Pawley to be honest and fair, they also saw him as a weak and indecisive leader.[55] In the end, neither the Progressives nor the Liberals pulled many ballots, and in a straight two-way race, the NDP elected thirty-four MLAS on an eight-point jump (to 47 percent) in the popular vote.

At the campaign's outset, there was no guarantee that Jim Walding would be numbered among the government's members. As can be seen from contrasting Figures 2 and 3, redistribution had sharply pulled St. Vital to the southwest. The constituency had lost to St. Boniface a number of polls to the east of St. Mary's Road, while gaining polls to the west of that divide from the Tory stronghold of Riel. As Table 4 makes clear, had these boundaries been in effect four years previously (and making the admittedly erroneous assumption that local candidates have no impact on voting choice), then Jim Walding's plurality would have been reduced from 534 to 220 votes.

Figure 3: St. Vital after Redistribution, 1981[56]

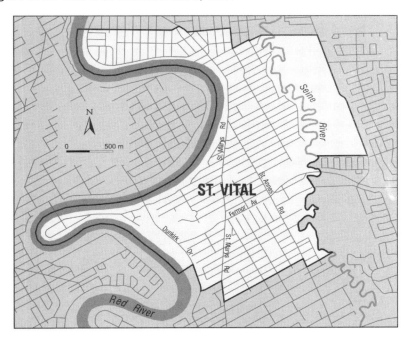

Table 4: Impact of Redistribution on St. Vital, 1981[57]

	Votes Lost to St. Boniface	Votes Retained	Votes Gained from Riel	Net Change
NDP	549	2966	1585	+1036
PC	537	2610	1887	+1350
Liberal	421	1492	490	+69

Walding also had to be concerned that the Conservatives had recruited a star candidate, John Robertson, to contest St. Vital. Robertson was a high-profile journalist with an enviable record of public service (long-standing chair of the Manitoba Marathon, active in the Canadian Association for the Mentally Retarded, and so on). According to Robertson, he was willing to abandon his $75,000 per year job as host of CBC's *24 Hours* because he wanted "to give something back" to Manitobans (although he also flippantly attributed his decision to male menopause).[58] In contrast to the reserved and self-effacing Walding, Robertson was boisterous, entertaining, and self-confident; "humility is not one of my stronger points,"[59] he acknowledged, and the frequent third-person references to himself certainly did not contradict this assessment.

In addition to a high public profile, Robertson was blessed with two further advantages. First, the Liberal vote in St. Vital was continuing to melt away. In fact, Eddie Coutu, the Liberal candidate in 1977 appeared at Robertson's unopposed nomination to announce his support. While Coutu still hoped the Liberals could eventually rebound in St. Vital, "that's in the future," he said; the immediate imperative was to defeat the NDP.[60] Second, the Conservatives were obviously intent on pouring resources into the St. Vital contest. Table 5 reveals that, in both 1973 and 1977, each of the other parties spent comparable amounts in the constituency. In 1981, however, Robertson's campaign expenditures dwarfed those of his two rivals. Walding's mild reply to the blizzard of PC promotional material descending on St. Vital was typical: "Being known is not necessarily a good thing."[61]

Table 5: St. Vital Campaign Expenditures, 1973 to 1981[62] ($)

	PC	NDP	Liberal
1973	4614	4591	4270
1977	4901	5395	5240
1981	24,232	8556	4732

In fact, Robertson's fondness for publicity may not always have been an electoral blessing. In his previous incarnation as a journalist, Robertson had been accustomed to skewering political figures from all parties, including PCs. Thus, when his newfound colleague, natural resources minister Harry Enns, outrageously called reporter Ingeborg Boyens "Ingewhore," Robertson's personal apology was equally over the top. The journalist was a victim, claimed Robertson, of "a baseless and senseless chauvinist tantrum which should outrage the sensitivities of every decent human being in this province.... And for a minister of this government to publicly refer to you as 'Ingewhore' makes me weep with shame that he and I wear the same colors in this election."[63] Ironically, given what was soon to transpire, the voters of St. Vital may have concluded that John Robertson was too much of a maverick to be an effective advocate inside any PC administration.

In the 1981 election, Jim Walding was convincingly returned to office with an impressive 53 percent of the popular vote (to Robertson's 41 percent and a paltry 6 percent for the Liberal candidate). Door-to-door canvassers had become aware of the incumbent's popularity with constituents;[64] as Robertson subsequently acknowledged, "the reason I lost was Jim Walding, Jim Walding, and Jim Walding." Victory, however, had not been won cheaply. Whereas previous campaigns had either broken even or registered a small profit, such was not the case in 1981. Some days later, a committee of three (including veteran stalwarts Hugh McMeel and George Schamber) went to see Walding, who inquired about the size of the campaign debt. "When told it was four figures," one recalled, "Walding pulled out his cheque book and wrote a cheque for the entire amount. 'Let's just clear that up,' he said."

Jim Walding had now been elected on four successive occasions; excluding the premier, only four of his caucus colleagues had more seniority. He was generally regarded as studious and intelligent,[65] he had played a key role in discrediting the Lyon government's energy practices, he occupied a potential swing riding, and he had helped Howard Pawley secure the party leadership. During the 1981 campaign, Walding mentioned to George Schamber that Pawley had promised him a cabinet post in the event of a NDP win, a pledge that Val Walding claimed had been overheard by several people at a constituency gathering. And yet, when Pawley announced his cabinet, Jim Walding's name was not included.[66]

What was Pawley's rationale? Obviously, not everyone could be included; indeed, with only twelve cabinet chairs to be divvied up among the remaining thirty-three members of caucus, Pawley was bound to disappoint almost twice as many as he pleased.[67] Had Walding represented a riding in the rural southwest, his place at the cabinet table would likely have been assured, but there was no shortage of ministerial prospects from the Greater Winnipeg area. As well, the 1981 election represented a generational change in the Manitoba NDP. Many of the older group of Schreyerites had not re-offered; they had been replaced by a talented and ambitious batch of newcomers (such as Vic Schroeder, Maureen Hemphill, and Eugene Kostyra). Aside from the premier, only six members of caucus had prior ministerial experience from the Schreyer years and even these individuals were not safe. Both Russell Doern and Al Mackling (Pawley's best man at his wedding and comrade-in-arms from two decades previously in the fight against folding the CCF into the NDP) found themselves left out,[68] while Sam Uskiw was only included at the eleventh hour. Still only forty-four, it seemed that Jim Walding's time had mysteriously come and gone.

Yet Walding's exclusion was by no means a foregone conclusion. "I will say to you openly," recalled Pawley, "that [prior to the 1981 campaign] I would have assumed that he [Walding] would have been in any Pawley cabinet." What apparently changed Pawley's thinking on the subject was a specific incident. Recall that Sterling Lyon had based his re-election bid on a trio of proposed megaprojects. In a bid to silence critics that these plans were, at best, half-baked, Lyon announced during the campaign that the three Prairie provinces had struck an interim agreement on a western power grid. The deal would be formally signed, according to the premier, "within a matter of weeks and certainly no later than the end of the year."[69] Even with the Saskatchewan government raising doubts about such a time-table, the NDP was deeply concerned that this announcement would signifi-cantly enhance Lyon's credibility. Pawley, who had been campaigning by bus in the provincial hinterland, raced back to Winnipeg and convened an emergency meeting to discuss the party's response: "We put through an urgent call for a number of key individuals, including the hydro critic Walding, to come to the Fort Garry Hotel and meet with us. Jim Walding did not come. I remember at the time us being very upset, because there was no possible excuse for why he could not drop what he was doing and come in. It was short notice, but when you are the hydro critic, you should come. Then the following day, I had to appear and campaign at a mall ... and he again failed to appear." Pawley's account, which is essentially confirmed by campaign co-chair Wilson Parasiuk, was disputed by Walding who claimed: "I was not aware of nor was I invited to a meeting at the Fort Garry Hotel. I was similarly not invited to attend Pawley's campaigning at a mall."[70] As to the latter, Walding's campaign manager Pat Portsmouth confirmed that the provincial office had requested that Walding appear at both Howard Paw-ley's nomination meeting and at a shopping mall in a neighbouring consti-uency. Walding was disinclined to campaign outside St. Vital, but under Portsmouth's strong urging, agreed to attend at least one of these events and opted for the Pawley nomination. Whether or not the missed Fort Garry meeting was also simply a matter of miscommunication, the impression had been lodged in Pawley's mind that Walding "was not a team player, that he was very much an individualist" and that he should therefore be left out of cabinet.

Walding registered his unhappiness, along with two others who had been similarly spurned, by being conspicuously absent from the new cabinet's swearing-in ceremony. Yet if Jim Walding was deeply disappointed by Paw-ley's rejection, his wife's response, by all accounts, was significantly stron-ger. Val was intensely ambitious for Jim; "he was not as interested," claimed one veteran New Democrat, "in climbing the ladder as she was." In fact, it was suggested that Jim "wanted a cabinet position because Val really felt he should have a cabinet position." Pawley's thwarting of that ambition left her "livid" and "bitter."

Howard Pawley did offer Jim Walding the post of Speaker. Even leaving aside the need to assuage hurt feelings, the proposal made sense. First, Walding had extensive experience as a committee chair and was obviously comfortable in that role. Second, he had no apparent policy agenda, so the requirements of neutrality would not constitute an unbearable constraint. Third, the Opposition did not perceive Walding to be blindly partisan; some years later, in fact, it was revealed that the PC caucus had been presented with two possible nominees for Speaker, and had indicated a preference for Walding.[71] Finally, despite immigrating to Canada, the Waldings were unabashed anglophiles. They enjoyed hosting teas, publications about the Queen and the monarchy were prominently displayed in their home, and their two sons had the princely names of Phillip and Andrew. These may have been unusual enthusiasms for a socialist MLA, but they dovetailed neatly with acting as the guardian of British parliamentary traditions.

Even so, Walding was unsure about accepting Pawley's offer. He informed members of his constituency association executive that, without their backing, he would not serve as Speaker. Virtually to a person, however, they enthusiastically supported an appointment that promised to combine extra salary and perks with a lighter workload. One executive member called on Walding's pride ("You know, Jim, you've got the power of the House; you're going to be running it"), while another appealed to his humility ("You know you will have much more free time to be with your constituents if you are Speaker than if you were a cabinet minister. That's what you like to do; when they need you, you are available for them"). Thus, on 17 December 1981, Jim Walding wrote the premier that he would "be pleased to accept the nomination for Speaker";[72] to others, he asserted that the post would at least be an improvement over the "dull" job of being a backbencher.[73]

From the outset, Walding was intent on increasing the prestige and perquisites of the speakership. Somewhat unusually, Walding's acceptance letter to Pawley had included data that emphasized that, at $6000, the Manitoba Speaker's remuneration was substantially less generous than that enjoyed by his or her counterparts in the remainder of the country. In fact, only in Prince Edward Island was the Speaker paid less handsomely, and the average figure for the remaining eight provinces was over $20,000. Upon assuming his new position in February 1982, Walding instructed the legislative counsel to draw up a bill whereby the Speaker would receive "a salary equal to the highest remuneration fixed under the *Executive Government Organization Act* for members of the Executive Council other than the President of the Council."[74] Such a change would have effectively increased the Speaker's indemnity to $20,600. Walding sent the draft legislation to Pawley, but the premier's own review of Speakers' salaries led him to conclude that the Manitoba figure only needed to be elevated to a level commensurate to ministers without portfolio (or $15,600). In any case, Pawley announced that he was forwarding the matter to the bipartisan Legislative Assembly Management Committee (LAMC) for consideration.[75] Walding was unimpressed. He wrote to Pawley that he had not meant to be "presumptuous" in preparing a bill; he had only done so "to assist you in honouring your commitment. You will recall," continued Walding, "that when we discussed this matter prior to the Session you gave me your undertaking to amend the Legislative Assembly Act to accord the Speaker the same status as your Ministers, and further, that it would be done before the end of the Session."[76] Walding lost this particular battle. Both parties' representatives on LAMC agreed that the Speaker should be paid less than even the humblest member of executive council, and the government enacted the recommendation to set the stipend at $12,000 (with an additional $1000 research allowance). One year later, Walding was financially rebuffed a second time. Although his predecessor had received an annual average of $2000 (at $50 per day) to fulfill his intersession administrative duties, Walding submitted a claim for $7000 (which would have had the de facto effect of raising his salary to that of a cabinet minister). Health minister Larry Desjardins adjudged this to be "excessive," and the government instituted a flat fee of $3500 for Walding's intersession responsibilities.[77]

Skirmishing over salary aside, it was apparent from the outset that Walding enjoyed his increased stature. He promptly cancelled his ordinary passport in order to receive a special green passport, he spent two weeks in the Bahamas representing Manitoba at the Commonwealth Parliamentary Association, and he regularly entertained dignitaries at his suite of rooms in the legislative assembly. Unfortunately, while attending a Speaker's conference in Ottawa in May 1982, Walding suffered a mild stroke on his forty-fifth birthday. After receiving treatment, Walding attempted to check himself out of a Gatineau hospital on the grounds that he was the Speaker of the Manitoba legislature. "I don't care if you're the Queen of England," replied the attending doctor, "you're not going until your blood pressure is down." The stroke left Walding with something of a balance difficulty and an even more embittered spouse. Disregarding the high stress levels experienced by most ministers, Val was heard to complain, "We will sue the damn government. Jim wouldn't have these damn problems if he had been left alone and put in the cabinet."

For most of 1982, there was little criticism of Walding's performance as the assembly's presiding officer. Even Sterling Lyon, who as premier had repeatedly hectored his own party's representative in the chair, had praise for Walding. "I can state categorically," wrote Lyon in the spring of 1982, "that we in Opposition have found Mr. Walding to be an eminently fair Speaker, whose 'evenhandedness' is apparent to all."[78] This assessment was to change drastically by year's end. On the afternoon of 9 December 1982, Walding had merely cautioned Tory Bud Sherman for revisiting charges of ministerial impropriety. After a supper break, however, Walding returned to the chair with a ruling that Sherman had to withdraw his comments immediately. Sherman declined to do so, and was promptly expelled for the rest of the evening's sitting. When it subsequently leaked out that Howard Pawley and Attorney General Roland Penner had gone to the Speaker's rooms over the supper recess (on the seemingly lame pretext that they were seeking out a transcript of the day's proceedings),[79] the Tories claimed that Walding had been pressured into making his ruling and that his independence had been fatally compromised. Their motion of non-confidence in the Speaker (the first ever in Manitoba) was defeated on a straight party vote, but not before there was "some pushing and shoving in the corridors."[80] Feelings of ill will intensified two months on when Walding cut off a "quasi-speech" by Lyon during question period despite having earlier permitted an equally long-winded reply by the premier.[81] Walding further angered the Opposition later in the session when he allowed two government backbenchers to make successive inquiries during question period, in apparent contradiction of an established protocol. "We are going to have even-handedness here or a new Speaker," was Lyon's inflammatory response. Speaking directly to Walding, he said: "You do not carry the confidence of this side of the house ... and I suggest sir, you reflect on your position over the weekend." When Lyon declined to withdraw his remarks ("Never. You're through."), Walding had little choice but to name the Opposition leader who was then expelled from the chamber for an unusually harsh four days.[82]

For the next fortnight, the Tories maintained their attacks on the Speaker. They alleged he was stonewalling a motion from the House rules committee calling for an analysis of the past twenty-five years of Speakers' rulings.[83] They rose on spurious points of order to repeat the precise words that had led to Lyon's expulsion.[84] They called on the government to end the crisis by replacing the Speaker. "The House's confidence in the Speaker is shattered,"[85] claimed Bud Sherman, and the *Winnipeg Free Press* concurred that "Mr. Walding may now be so damaged by the events that his usefulness as a speaker is at an end."[86] A visibly rattled Walding soon began to have memory lapses in the chair,[87] but irrespective of any private misgivings about his performance, the government made clear from the outset that to jettison the Speaker would be tantamount to capitulation. Accordingly, Attorney General Penner gave Walding a resounding vote of confidence. "You have acted in exemplary fashion. You have defended the office of the Speaker, which must always be defended," declared Penner. "The Speaker has the right to make wrong decisions from time to time, but the office of the Speaker must be defended."[88] Within a year, however, with Walding squarely at the centre of a controversy over French-language rights, Penner would come to rue his words.

The key period in Walding's speakership occurred between May 1983 and February 1984. During that time, the Manitoba legislature (already a "highly adversarial" chamber)[89] was riven by the Pawley government's constitutional proposals over French-language services. Much has already been written about this episode,[90] so we will concentrate here on Walding's distinctive contribution. Recall from Chapter 2 the Greenway government's unilateral abrogation in 1890 of the constitutional safeguards for the French language contained in the *Manitoba Act* of 1870. Eighty-nine years later, the Supreme Court of Canada finally had occasion to comment on this circumstance; in the Forest case, they ruled that French and English still had equal status in Manitoba's courts, legislature, and statute books. In 1981, Roger Bilodeau challenged the legality of a traffic ticket written only in English and, despite losing at the Manitoba Court of Appeal, took the case to the Supreme Court. Suddenly, the entire Manitoba statute book (including the legislation under which the existing provincial assembly had been elected) was under threat of being declared invalid. Two lawyers retained by the province assessed this eventuality as being "unlikely,"[91] but one acknowledged that there was "a significant risk of a ruling to the contrary."[92]

To forestall the chaos that could be precipitated by an adverse decision, the Pawley administration negotiated a constitutional deal with the federal government and the Société Franco-Manitobaine.[93] In return for the withdrawal of the Bilodeau case, the Manitoba government agreed, first, to recognize the constitutional equality of French and English by enacting all laws and regulations in both official languages after 1985, second, to translate around 10 percent of the existing statute book into French, and third, to provide services in French from a specified list of government agencies and tribunals. These seemingly modest proposals elicited a firestorm of controversy. Critics of the deal claimed that the government was too fearful of a worst-case judicial outcome[94] (although people routinely buy house and car insurance under essentially analogous circumstances). They argued it was too expensive[95] (although the federal government was chipping in over $2 million and the potential costs to the province of translating the entire statute book were massive). They suggested that the deal was the thin edge of the wedge, that municipalities and school boards would soon be forced into bilingualism[96] (although they were explicitly excluded), and that anglophones would soon confront constricted employment opportunities in the provincial bureaucracy[97] (although only 3 percent of government jobs would require a working knowledge of French, and most of these individuals were already in place). Finally, they complained that the deal gave unfair advantage, both real and symbolic, to a group that comprised less than 7 percent of the provincial population[98] (although that advantage had been constitutionally entrenched at Manitoba's creation).

Leading the charge against the government proposals was Opposition leader Sterling Lyon. Ironically, while still in office, Lyon had responded to the Forest decision by translating some laws into French and expanding French-language services; in a memo to all ministers and deputy ministers, Lyon praised these initiatives as part of "a pragmatic, imaginative and common sense approach."[99] Yet, inside the legislature, Lyon now raised public fears of an "intransigent assertion of rights by language zealots in the bureaucracy."[100] As well, Tory spokespersons baited francophone MLAS; Gerard Lecuyer was dubbed "Kermit [the frog]," while Lyon himself responded to a Lecuyer interjection with: "Do we hear something from the lily pad over on the far bench there?"[101] Assisting the Conservatives was embittered NDP MLA Russell Doern who, after being excluded from Pawley's cabinet despite fifteen years of experience as an MLA, found a new political purpose in leading an anti-bilingualism crusade. Doern spent $3500 of his own money for a half-page advertisement in the *Winnipeg Free Press* urging readers to signal their opposition to the government plan.[102] Over 12,000 responded, and many included money to help Doern defray his costs, including one individual who had been unemployed for the previous fifteen months, but who still had "$1 for this cause."[103] Although the Pawley government sent out information leaflets that emphasized that the proposal was "quite different from federal bilingualism," that "the federal model of bilingualism will not be applied in this province," and that "Manitoba has rejected the federal government's approach,"[104] opponents were unconvinced. According to Doern, "It is clear that the person who was really calling the shots behind the scenes was none other than the Prime Minister of Canada: the Rt. Hon. Pierre Elliott Trudeau."[105]

The public response to this paranoia and fear-mongering was sadly predictable. Hastily organized municipal plebiscites in the fall of 1983 revealed that 77 percent of Winnipeg voters and 79 percent of their rural counterparts opposed the government's plan, while NDP candidates for Winnipeg city council were blindsided by the issue.[106] A group of elderly women (dubbed "Hell's Grannies" by the NDP) seemed to be particularly agitated; among other activities, they systematically went through supermarkets turning the French-language labels on products away from the view of consumers.[107] Committee hearings in the fall provided a public platform for the expression of incendiary views. Should the deal proceed, English-speaking Manitobans "will settle it on their own on the streets," warned the reeve of Moosehorn. "The police can't always be watching."[108]

Under sustained assault both inside and outside the legislature, the Pawley government retreated. They had initially hoped to have the package approved no later than August 1983, but Tory filibustering and a concession to hold public hearings throughout the province dashed that aspiration. By the time Gary Filmon succeeded Sterling Lyon as PC leader in December 1983, the government was not appreciably closer to securing legislative approval than it had been eight months previously. Even so, Pawley's New Democrats were not yet disenchanted with Jim Walding's speakership. While Walding had tolerated a good deal of obstructionism by the Opposition (the Tories had on some occasions ignored the ringing of division bells for "unprecedented 10-hour and 20-hour periods"),[109] he had also expelled Lyon from the chamber for repeatedly questioning Pawley's honesty.[110] As well, Walding had ruled against the Conservatives when they had tried to introduce a lengthy series of only minutely different amendments; while the NDP were both "surprised" and "pleased" with the Speaker's decision,[111] the Tories took umbrage and walked out of the chamber. The Opposition House leader claimed that Walding's ruling "defie[d] description," while Lyon branded it "ridiculous, incredible and an outrage."[112]

When the Manitoba legislature resumed sitting on 5 January 1984 after a five-month recess, it was already the longest session in provincial history; only the French-language initiative was on the agenda. In an attempt to break the log-jam, the government had replaced Roland Penner as House leader with Andy Anstett[113] and had conceded to a key Opposition demand. The extension of French-language services was no longer part of the constitutional resolution; instead, it was to be effected by simple legislation. Hopes that Filmon would prove more tractable than Lyon, however, were soon quashed. The Conservatives still objected to that portion of the constitutional resolution that described French and English as "official" languages of Manitoba. Although legal counsel had indicated that there was only "a remote possibility" that such wording could in the future lead to an expansion of bilingualism,[114] the Tories' demand for absolute certainty on the matter, given judicial inscrutability, could never be met. For their part, the government could hardly concede on this final point without completely betraying the original deal signed with the Société Franco-Manitobaine. Inside the legislature, the Opposition refused to deal with the French-language services bill until they had their way with the already truncated constitutional resolution, so walkouts and extended ringing of the division bells became an almost daily occurrence.

Outside the legislature, the government's partial retreat did little to dampen the public protests, and despite expanded police protection, the premier was swarmed with shouts of "Heil Howard" at one constituency meeting.[115] A group styling itself "Grassroots Manitoba" organized numerous rallies against bilingualism. At one, the cry went up: "Bring Anstett, we want to hang him."[116] At another, eighty-nine-year-old Douglas Campbell (premier for one decade, MLA for almost five) told two thousand protesters, "This is the finest demonstration of democracy in action that I have ever seen in my many years of public life."[117] Support for the NDP continued to free fall; one poll showed them with the backing of only 12 percent of the electorate.[118]

An increasingly desperate administration turned for help to Jim Walding. Even closure, the ultimate weapon in any government's parliamentary arsenal, was proving to be of no avail. The Opposition had tolerated its use (for the first time in fifty-four years in Manitoba) on second reading of the French-language services bill, but repeated attempts to introduce closure on the constitutional resolution merely provoked further Opposition walkouts. A motion to limit the ringing of division bells to two hours met the same predictable response. A move to replace the Speaker with someone more pliable would presumably have confronted the identical difficulty (although influential voices in caucus were urging Pawley in that direction).[119] Only a willingness on Walding's part to call a vote despite the absence of Opposition members from the chamber offered a way out of the impasse. At least initially, the government House leader was reluctant to approach Walding: "I have never been one," asserted Anstett, "who felt that the government or Opposition had the right to try and influence the Speaker."[120] As the furor dragged on into February 1984, however, Anstett's position changed. "In terms of approaching the Speaker, certainly it's possible," he said. "The filibuster can't go on forever."[121] According to Anstett, Walding had "the obligation and duty to ensure the legislature functions in the spirit and intent of parliamentary law."[122] Echoed acting premier Larry Desjardins: "After a certain time the Speaker has a duty and a responsibility to step in."[123] Anstett did, in fact, have a private meeting with the Speaker soon thereafter, but received little encouragement; Walding apparently "made it very clear that the house must make its own decision."[124]

On 16 February 1984, the Tories ratcheted up the pressure by announcing that they would be staying out of the chamber indefinitely. After five further days of continuous bell-ringing, the premier's patience snapped. He fired off a letter to Walding on 21 February, virtually ordering the Speaker to call a vote (see Appendix B).[125] When Walding declined in a letter written the same day (see Appendix B),[126] he was publicly rebuked by Pawley. "There is no reason he can't intervene. I can find no rule (that keeps him) from calling in the members," the premier declared. "I feel the Speaker has a responsibility to uphold the British Parliamentary System."[127] Two days later, Walding did write to Anstett requesting a meeting with the two House leaders so that the Speaker could be "brought up to date on the status of ongoing negotiations" and offer "assistance with a view to satisfactorily resolving this situation."[128] A disgusted Anstett did not bother to reply.[129] By 27 February 1984, the division bells had already rung continuously for eleven days,[130] and there was no indication of an imminent cessation. Running out of money (and unable to employ special warrants while the House was still technically in session), the government was left with only one option. The House was prorogued and both the French-language services bill and the constitutional resolution died on the order paper. Ironically, Roger Bilodeau eventually recommenced his appeal to the Supreme Court and, one year later, won precisely the victory that the Pawley government's initiative had been designed to forestall.

How are we to understand the Speaker's role during this controversy? Both then and subsequently, Walding insisted that he was merely following established practice. "There had been a precedent in Ottawa a year or two before that," Walding recalled. "Madame Sauvé was in a similar position, but she said no, so we took that as a precedent." It is true that, as Speaker, Jeanne Sauvé refused to call a vote in Parliament when the Opposition Tories let the bells ring to protest an omnibus energy bill. It is also true that Walding was not alone in following Sauvé's lead; Speakers in both Saskatchewan and Ontario likewise refused to intervene when bell-ringing was employed in their bailiwicks (albeit for nowhere near as long as the 382 hours endured by Manitobans).[131] It is further true, noted legislative clerk Binx Remnant, that Manitoba's rules committee had twice previously had an opportunity to put limits on the practice of bell-ringing (in 1971 and again in 1983, when Walding had placed the matter on the agenda) and had, on both occasions, refused to act.[132] Raymond Hébert, who provides the most complete and balanced account of the episode can find no fault with Walding's decisions. "The record indicates," claims Hébert, "that Walding was scrupulously even-handed in his conduct of House affairs through one of the most turbulent periods in Manitoba history."[133]

This judgement, however, is far from universal. Tom McMahon has undertaken a wide-ranging analysis of bell-ringing as a form of parliamentary obstruction. McMahon concludes that a Speaker "should not be seen pleading lack of jurisdiction in his own court."[134] Yet throughout the furor, Walding claimed that his hands were effectively tied, that, as he wrote to the premier on 21 February, "any unilateral action ... could only be a betrayal of the impartiality of the Chair and would seriously undermine the integrity of the Speakership."[135] After all, no Speaker in British parliamentary history had ever permitted a vote in the absence of the Opposition.[136] Yet McMahon is still unconvinced. Whether or not Walding intervened to silence the bells, he was creating a precedent in the Manitoba legislature. "To do nothing during a bell-ringing is to make a decision," McMahon notes. "The views of those refusing to vote are implicitly sanctioned."[137] Admittedly, Walding had throughout his political career been an extremely passive chair. As well, Lyon's charge that Walding had been suborned by a suppertime visit from the premier likely constituted the formative event of his speakership. Thus, it was always likely that Walding would take the path of least resistance. McMahon might aptly decry this inactivity as "a lack of leadership," but Walding was clearly within his rights not to stop the bells and call a vote.

From another perspective, however, it was obviously troubling that Walding chose to exercise his discretion in a fashion guaranteed to frustrate the government's agenda. While the Speaker properly made no public comments on the French-language initiatives, his private observations were clearly unsympathetic. One attendee at a constituency executive meeting was surprised by Walding's comment on the matter: "He was adamantly opposed to the bill. His personal opinion basically agreed with Sterling Lyon and the Conservative position that some previous legislation dealt with the issue by giving services to the francophone community and that the Supreme Court wasn't going to come down and order this stuff to be done in a way that was impractical and very expensive." Similarly, a veteran New Democrat recalled that Walding "was a bit of an opponent of entrenched French-language services. At an executive meeting of the constituency association, Walding had quite a different slant. He wondered why the courts should be setting policy; shouldn't the political process take care of it?" As ardent anglophiles, neither Jim nor Val Walding could have been expected to have much sympathy with elevating French to a limited coequal status with English. "Certainly, the French-language issue was not one they would have been happy with," recalled Howard Pawley. "Everyone knew that." Walding deposited numerous letters from constituents on this issue in the public archives; without exception, these are hostile to the government's initiative. Perhaps Walding only received communications from foes of bilingualism. Perhaps he selected for posterity only those missives that decried the government's proposal. Either possibility hints at Walding's own views. It is also suggestive that one of the few voices of dissent at the Manitoba NDP's annual policy convention (held on the third weekend of February 1984 at the height of the crisis) came from a member of Walding's inner circle. According to St. Vital school trustee Jim Buchanan, the government needed to withdraw their language proposals. "It's not a matter of whether it's right or wrong," claimed Buchanan. "People are opposed to it. How do you legislate something when 80 percent of the people are against it?"[138] It is further suggestive that Russell Doern was a guest at the summer 1983 wedding of the Waldings' son, and that in his fight against bilingualism he claimed to have "received encouragement from those in attendance."[139] In fact, Val Walding, both then and since, was singled out as "very active in the Grassroots Manitoba crusade."[140] Small wonder, therefore, that some New Democrats came to believe that "Walding was using procedure to stop the substance of French-language reform. He and Val hated that bill.… It was pathetic. The bill died because the Speaker and his wife didn't want the bill."

The final ingredient in Walding's motivational mélange may well have been feelings of revenge. Walding clearly had expected to enter the cabinet in 1981 and felt some measure of betrayal at being excluded. Sabotaging Pawley's French-language initiative would be his way of getting even. Certainly, the Speaker took no time to consider the points raised in the premier's letter of 21 February 1984; on the contrary, his "sharply worded rebuff"[141] came back within two hours. Walding claimed in the letter to have been "surprised" at Pawley's request since the House was "close to effecting a change in its Rules." As Walding well knew, the paralyzed assembly was nowhere near to "effecting" such a change, and the Speaker's willful disingenuousness on this point can only be understood as a barb at Pawley. The government knew that Walding had felt "slighted" by his 1981 exclusion; it was only in the language controversy, however, that they discovered "just how much malice he bore."[142]

Whatever his motivation, Walding's handling of the French-language constitutional initiative marked a deep rupture between himself and his party. Later in the spring, Andy Anstett successfully challenged Walding's ruling on a complex procedural matter (ironically, on a bill designed to limit future bell-ringing episodes). Since it is highly unconventional (albeit not improper) for government MLAS to support en masse a challenge to the Speaker, the Conservatives took the episode as evidence that the NDP were trying to "embarrass" or "burn" Walding into resigning.[143] When asked point-blank if he would be disappointed if the Speaker stepped down, Anstett "took a long pause" before evasively stating: "We won't engage in speculation on resignations."[144] For his part, Walding fired back with a statement that while they were technically correct, Anstett's actions were "somewhat unorthodox" and "could amount to a discourtesy to the house."[145]

Two days later, Val Walding waded into the fray by claiming that some NDP MLAS had launched "a smear campaign" against her husband. "They're NDPers who have turned over," she claimed. "It makes me so mad when they spread lies." Claims that she had appeared at anti-government rallies were "absolute garbage," and those making the allegations could not be genuine New Democrats. Rather, "they're probably Liberals. They're vicious."[146]

Friction with the government characterized the remaining eighteen months of Jim Walding's speakership. In July 1984, he prolonged an embarrassing battle over relocating Russell Doern's office by permitting the renegade MLA to plead his case before LAMC.[147] Shortly thereafter, there was a challenge to Walding's presumed right to represent Manitoba at the upcoming Isle of Man conference of the Commonwealth Parliamentary Association. After a meeting with Walding and the NDP caucus chair, Pawley agreed that the Speaker could attend on this occasion, but that, in future, Walding would "consult with me, as Premier, prior to the selection of a Manitoba delegate to such Conferences."[148] Walding waited six weeks before replying. "Common courtesy indicates that I reply directly to you, although on reflection the matter is more appropriate to the administration of the Manitoba New Democratic Party," he wrote. "Accordingly, I am taking the liberty of writing to the party president, with a copy to you, with a resolution of this situation."[149] In November, Walding wrote to the premier asking that the office of the legislative counsel not be moved until the matter had been considered by LAMC. Without replying to the request (although a letter had purportedly been drafted), Pawley unilaterally proceeded with the relocation four weeks later.[150]

Meanwhile, Jim Walding, the MLA for St. Vital, was being just as difficult as Jim Walding, the Speaker. To sustain its activities, the Manitoba NDP annually placed an individualized levy on the fifty-seven constituency associations; included in the St. Vital assessment was a $2000 indemnity charged against the sitting MLA (as was the case in all other ridings held by the party). Walding had faithfully paid his indemnity up to and including 1982, the first year of his speakership. In fact, a mid-year accounting in 1981 had identified Walding as one of only five members of caucus who had fully paid that year's indemnity.[151] But Walding became increasingly convinced that any partisan involvement was inconsistent with the impartiality required of the Speaker. He failed to make his 1983 payment, and by mid-summer 1984 Pawley was sufficiently concerned that, after discussing the matter at length with Walding, he instructed his executive assistant to undertake a follow-up meeting.[152] Once again, Walding was unmoved by Pawley's entreaties and instead instructed his solicitor to draw up a trust agreement. Under the terms of the arrangement, dated 18 October 1984, Walding deposited $4000 in an interest-bearing account ($2000 for each of 1983 and 1984), and pledged to continue annual deposits of $2000 for the life of the agreement. The provisions for terminating this fund were quite ingenious. If Walding left the speakership and rejoined the NDP caucus, the accumulated monies would be immediately conveyed to the provincial secretary of the Manitoba NDP. If, on the other hand, Walding did not rejoin the NDP caucus by the first sitting of the *next* legislature, then the funds would be returned to him. In effect, Walding had given the party a financial incentive to work for both his renomination and his re-election.

The following day, Walding sent a copy of the trust agreement to party president Shirley Lord. "While this solution may not seem to be ideal from all points of view," Walding observed, "it is necessary to maintain the integrity of the Chair and recognizes the reality of the Speakership in Manitoba."[153] Lord was unimpressed. "It is our position that the trust agreement is not satisfactory," she replied, although as "a compromise to immediate payment, we will consider payment of the funds into a trust which unequivocally provides for payment to the Party."[154] Neither this suggestion nor a subsequent missive made any impression on Walding; he had executed the trust in good faith, the distribution of the funds was now out of his control, and if Lord had any further questions, "I should be pleased to have my solicitor provide the answers."[155]

The contretemps over Walding's indemnity was symptomatic of a wider malaise at the riding level. During Walding's first decade as an MLA, the combined labours of himself, his wife, and an enthusiastic and dedicated band of volunteers had created a vibrant organization. In 1981, the St. Vital NDP raised more money for the provincial party than all but six other constituency associations,[156] and as late as April 1982 Walding could truthfully write, "I can say personally that my constituents continue to contact me with their problems, and I am still active in my constituency."[157] By the end of the year, this was no longer valid. Soon after becoming Speaker, recalled one long-standing activist, "the constituency was left adrift. Before 1981, Walding was always involved at every executive meeting; afterwards, he came to meetings but was disengaged. He felt that he was neutral and shouldn't even be at the meeting." Other Speakers, in Manitoba and elsewhere, have managed to combine non-partisanship in the legislature with a modest, restrained partisanship in the constituency, but Walding seemed disinclined to try, and the team of volunteers who had repeatedly worked so hard on his campaigns felt betrayed. Fundraising initiatives seized up. Val was no longer organizing constituency dinners; despite some obstruction, these were eventually taken over by members of the executive.

With Walding not contributing his portion of the assessment, this organizational lassitude left the association hopelessly unable to meet its financial obligations. As of June 1984, it owed the provincial office over $10,000 of an annual assessment of $11,900; only two other NDP constituency associations were further in arrears.[158] In the fall of 1984, the provincial executive gave St. Vital and sixteen other malingering riding associations a "2 for 1" credit (writing down two dollars of debt for every one dollar of new monies), but the same problems re-emerged the next year. At the end of August 1985, St. Vital was again the third most indebted constituency, with over $9500 due to the provincial office.[159]

Walding's standoffishness from constituency affairs seemed not only to be a matter of principle; he was also perceived by his long-time supporters to be both unhappy and unhealthy. One observed that Walding "wasn't a happy man even before the shit hit the fan [over the bell-ringing]. He just seemed to withdraw. Val was very upset; she was very ambitious for Jim. Val pushed and pulled and this upset the constituency members." Another concurred: "After 1981, Jim Walding was not a happy person. Jim's family did not like him taking the Speaker's job." There were also questions about whether Walding ever entirely recovered from his stroke in the spring of 1982; neither his nerves nor his balance were as steady as before. Walding's health, concluded one executive member, was "failing him at the end; he had no energy or drive."

Little wonder, then, that Walding began to drop hints that he might not run again. "When the next election is called," he mused in 1982, "I'll have spent 14 years in the Legislature. That's a long time and maybe as much as anyone should stay."[160] Reaction to his handling of the French-language services bill (where he alienated most of the members of his riding executive and seemingly everyone of consequence at the provincial level) might have been expected to confirm a decision to step aside. "Those were very tense days," confirmed Walding. "My wife was my only source of strength."[161] Yet despite this profound isolation from his party, Walding announced in April 1985 that he was not yet ready to retire. "I had some reservation because of my health," Walding claimed. "But now my health has improved and I intend to seek re-election."[162]

But would this re-election take place in St. Vital? For some time, Walding had been enamoured of Stanley Knowles's idea to create a separate constituency for the Speaker. In the fall of 1984, Walding requested and received copies of Knowles's draft legislation and of the subsequent parliamentary debates.[163] Some months later, he instructed Manitoba's legislative counsel to write a bill based on the Knowles's model. *An Act to Amend the Electoral Divisions Act and the Legislative Assembly Act to Make Provision for the Independence of the Speaker* proposed to create a fifty-eighth constituency (to be known as Broadway); MLAs elected by the House to be Speaker would resign their constituency (and thus precipitate a by-election) to become the MLA for Broadway, a position they would retain, without the need to contest general elections, until such time as the House decided otherwise.[164]

To build support for this proposal, as yet unreleased, Walding sent the results of a constituency survey to all MLAS[165] and followed this up with a press conference a week later. The poll's key finding was that 55 percent of respondents felt it was a "liability" to be represented in the legislature by the Speaker, while only 22 percent considered it to be an "asset." "I haven't felt it was a liability; but when this information comes forward," Walding told reporters, "I have to wonder … whether it will reflect adversely on a speaker seeking re-election."[166] Admittedly, the accuracy of the data could legitimately be questioned; Walding had sent surveys to 8000 St. Vital households and received only 310 replies. Nevertheless, he hoped the results would "initiate a general discussion among the public on a speaker's role."[167]

There is no evidence that this wider debate took place. Nevertheless, Walding took the unusual step on 30 April 1985 of reading a three-page document at the outset of the House's business. The key section of this statement outlined the problems associated with the existing status of the Speaker:

> The more a Speaker strives for a position of impartiality, the more he becomes separated from the constituency and the Party which endorsed him in the previous election. There is an inherent unfairness in the Legislature which places one of its Members, and one only, in the position of being expected to support the initiatives of the Government of the Day while at the same time being required to act with fairness and impartiality. Suggestions have been made to me both implicitly and explicitly that a Speaker's political allegiance should supersede the requirement for impartiality and this has been the cause of considerable tension. The expectation of partiality and impartiality is clearly impossible, and has caused me considerable personal distress.

Walding closed his statement by drawing attention to Knowles's proposal for a special Speaker's constituency and by pledging to meet with Manitoba's party leaders "to discuss solutions to this long-standing problem and to propose specific remedies."[168]

Walding's plan soon foundered. Hoping to elicit external support, he sent copies of his statement to potentially interested dignitaries and experts across the country (including John Bosley, Jeanne Sauvé, James McGrath, and, of course, Stanley Knowles). Most of the replies, however, were either pro forma or unhelpful; former premier (now senator) Duff Roblin, for example, noted that, at least during his time in the Manitoba legislature, "occupants of the [Speaker's] office were able to discharge their duties effectively."[169] When Walding sent a copy of his statement for publication in the *Canadian Parliamentary Review*, the Alberta Speaker, Gerard Ameron-gen, weighed in with a contrary perspective. According to Amerongen, Speakers were actually statistically more likely than other parliamentarians to be re-elected, were more effective than even ministers at representing their constituencies, and could easily be partial outside the House, while remaining impartial in the chair. Worse yet, Amerongen concluded that Speakers "should continue to be elected first by constituents and then by the House" and that they "should not become civil servants nor be without an ordinary constituency."[170]

The response from influential voices in the province was no more enthusiastic. Two former Manitoba Speakers categorically rejected Walding's analysis, and one suggested that in making his proposals, Walding "was abusing the privilege of the chair."[171] Both Gary Filmon and Howard Pawley also expressed doubts. "I'm prepared to listen to the Speaker," acknowledged the premier, but "I don't feel basically that there is need for change."[172] Finally, both major newspapers condemned the Speaker's proposal. "There's a simple solution to Mr. Walding's dilemma that doesn't involve strange ideas about creating yet another mandarin in the provincial bureaucracy," opined the *Winnipeg Sun*. "If you don't like the job, Mr. Walding, quit."[173] Likewise, the *Winnipeg Free Press* suggested that Walding's proposal came across as "a personal plea," as something "designed primarily to get him out of his difficulties." A permanent Speaker might yet be instituted in Manitoba, but by his speech, Walding had "effectively removed himself from contention for the job."[174]

With the escape hatch of an ongoing Speaker's appointment effectively closed down, Jim Walding's long run in the legislature seemed to be under some threat. One pundit suggested Walding was "on the NDP hit list," that he was lodged "in a political never-never land, with an indication that even if he seeks re-election, his nomination may be contested."[175] Of course, such talk is notoriously cheap; in most instances, however, it is only, in the words of Tom Brook, the "backroom bluster that most campaign insiders are quite good at and when it comes time to fish or cut bait, most incumbents face little or no challenge, no matter how embarrassing they may have been to their parties or constituents."[176] In St. Vital, however, the fishing season was just beginning.

4

The Campaign

INCUMBENTS ARE RARELY CHALLENGED, but Jim Walding seemed certain to be an exception. For many years, George Schamber and Hugh McMeel had been two of Walding's most stalwart supporters.[1] It had been Schamber who had originally invited Walding to seek the NDP nomination in St. Vital and had served as the constituency association president for twelve consecutive years thereafter. McMeel had on multiple occasions served as Walding's official agent and had officially nominated him in 1977. In fact, when a radio station erroneously reported that Walding had triumphed in the 1969 election, McMeel had gotten out of his car in a rainstorm to plaster more Walding campaign signs on his rear and side windows. Yet both men were now deeply disenchanted. Schamber's pithy summary was that Walding had gone "off the deep end," while McMeel claimed, "If no one else had challenged him, I would have."

As it turned out, McMeel was able to stay on the sidelines. With the possibility of a fall 1985 election, rumours of a nomination tussle began to circulate openly in late August. Anxious to stir the pot, Gary Filmon claimed that "there's a move to dump Mr. Walding."[2] The Speaker declined comment, but a source euphemistically labelled as "very close to Walding" could not resist, and claimed the move had the blessing not only of the election planning committee (EPC), but also, intriguingly, of "some of Premier Howard Pawley's top aides." Two potential challengers were identified by the Walding source: Nancy Buchan, a St. Boniface health consultant, and Sig Laser, a St. Vital resident who also happened to be the premier's executive assistant. Both Buchan and Laser confirmed their interest in the nomination and both indicated their intentions would soon be made public. For the moment, however, influential voices on the St. Vital executive provided lukewarm endorsements of the incumbent. Putting on a brave public face, George Schamber claimed, "Jim took his job seriously and there's some minor grumblings about the way he did his job. But he has a lot of supporters." Echoed association president Gerri Unwin, "Some people think he did the right thing, some think he was wrong."

Yet when a challenge to Walding was formally announced on 23 September, it came not from Buchan or Laser, but from Unwin. As association president, Unwin had grown progressively more frustrated by Walding's detachment from constituency affairs. "Jim just wasn't Jim anymore," she recalled. "He was a different person." Other members of the executive echoed her doubts about Walding and urged her to stand for the nomination. While her attendance at a day-long staff development workshop on 11 September signalled ambivalence (a prospective candidate would have other concerns than the "'What' and 'Why' of Records"), she obviously came to a decision shortly thereafter. At the 21 and 22 September meeting of the NDP's provincial council, Unwin's candidacy was an open secret. The report of the Status of Women Committee named Unwin as one of five women who "have announced [their] intention to seek the nomination in their ridings,"[3] while the St. Vital association's communication to council was slightly more opaque. After acknowledging the ongoing concern that the constituency "assessment [was] not being met," the report observed that there were "2 other potential candidates" and that "membership should increase."[4] The following day, Unwin publicly confirmed her status as one of Walding's challengers. "I believe St. Vital needs a government MLA willing to work hard on behalf of the people," she declared, before ambiguously remarking, "I believe Jim's past record speaks for itself."[5] Basing a challenge on Walding's unsatisfactory service to the constituency would clearly have been inconceivable in any prior election. Walding was not entirely surprised by Unwin's announcement. "I've heard the same rumours (of a challenge). I have no way of validating them," Walding observed. "I thought we were above that sort of thing."[6]

If it is unusual for a sitting legislator to be challenged for the nomination, it is even more unusual for there to be more than a single aspiring usurper. A study of the 1988 federal election discovered that five out of every six incumbent challenges involved only one other candidate.[7] Gerri Unwin's announcement, it was subsequently acknowledged, did dissuade Norma Buchan from entering the fray; instead, Buchan opted to take on (unsuccessfully) another sitting New Democrat (Doreen Dodick in the neighbouring riding of Riel).[8] Sig Laser, however, was not so easily discouraged. On 17 October, he entered the contest claiming that the St. Vital constituency association had "slipped into disarray" owing to Walding's "neglect."[9] Laser insisted that most of the riding's members welcomed a genuine fight for the nomination. "It's how we decide as New Democrats what sort of a party we are going to be. It's how we judge our past performance and voice our hopes for the future," Laser asserted. "We've already brought new people into the party and renewed links with previous members who for one reason or another had drifted away."[10] Once again, Walding was not amused. He insisted that he would vanquish all challengers and again was forced to respond to charges that Val had been active in the Grassroots Manitoba fight against bilingualism. Insisted Walding, "It's absolutely not true."[11]

At the 17 October launch, Laser revealed that he had already signed up two hundred new members; he had, in fact, been campaigning vigorously in the five-week interval since reading his horoscope in the 10 September 1985 edition of the *Winnipeg Free Press*. As a Libra, Laser was advised: "You have every reason to feel confident about your career.... Do not be surprised if you become a candidate for a major leadership post."[12] Two days later, Laser hired a full-time organizer, David Street. Perhaps Laser should have announced his candidacy straightaway. But with a young family to support, he needed to retain his job in Pawley's office for as long as possible. Of course, NDP ministerial aides were expected to perform extracurricular political work; Bruce Buckley, likewise engaged as an assistant to the premier, had taken leaves both in 1984 to manage the re-election bid of a New Democratic member of Parliament[13] and in 1985 to assist in the campaign of the party's Ontario branch.[14] Yet even if it was undertaken after hours, challenging a sitting New Democrat was incompatible with continued employment in executive council. During the summer, Laser had taken pains to disguise his intentions. On 9 June, he had gone to an NDP candidate workshop (Unwin would not attend a similar event until 17 November); rather deviously, Laser had signified his constituency to be the rural Tory stronghold of Turtle Mountain. Over the next two months, Laser cleared the decks for a nomination bid by resigning as membership chair from the St. Vital executive and growing less circumspect about his intentions. On 13 September, he began formally to track potential allies by phoning other members of the constituency executive. Most were noncommittal, but the notation beside Gerri Unwin's name from that date is intriguing: "Possible supporter. Sig must work." On 24 September (one day after Unwin's campaign launch), quite a different set of comments appear: "We know better now," "She is trying to beat up on the poor Speaker," and, enigmatically, "We must not alienate."

The circumstances under which both Unwin and Laser ended up in the race left a residue of ill will between the two camps. Although Laser could not make an official announcement until he had left the premier's office (which happened on 4 October), he nevertheless felt that he had effectively staked his claim by mid-September. In conversation between the two, Unwin had indicated that Laser should do whatever he felt was right, which Laser had taken to be "tacit encouragement." Thus, he would not have been shocked if some other candidate had entered the race, but "when it turned out to be Gerri, that truly was a surprise and felt like a betrayal." For her part, Unwin denies giving Laser any encouragement, tacit or otherwise, and is uncertain whether she even knew that he was "definitely running." Both camps, therefore, could with some legitimacy blame the other for splitting the anti-Walding vote. One key Unwin supporter asserted, "Sig should not have come in. Why split the vote? He should have put his efforts on to the executive board and he would have gained more credibility that way." Another observer claimed to have been "extremely shocked when Laser ran. Anyone with half a brain would know that if you run two people, you will split the vote." Yet while Unwin was undeniably the initial official candidate, it seems almost certain that Laser was the first unofficially to enter the race, so his supporters could also feel aggrieved. In the words of one Laser stalwart,

> I was really disappointed. I just could not fathom why she would want to jump in and challenge this nomination. I just could not understand it at all.... I would have thought that the common thrust was to unseat Jim, so her entering the race was baffling and troubling. I thought it was kind of self-serving and I didn't think it was for the good of the constituency or the party.... I can understand Jim. I'm not angry at him at all. He comes from a different background, he felt snubbed, and he didn't believe in bilingualism. But Gerri, what the hell was she thinking of?

How were voters expected to distinguish between the three candidates? As a rule, "policy plays virtually no role in nomination campaigns";[15] convention attendees "are not looking for new policy initiatives, they are looking for winners."[16] In fact, Carty and Erickson discovered that only about one-quarter of nomination tussles they studied had an issue basis.[17] Nevertheless, one might have surmised that the 1986 contest for the NDP nomination in St. Vital would have proven to be an exception to this norm, since disaffection with Walding had been greatly enhanced by his conduct during the French-language crisis. Recall the tense exchange of letters between the premier and the Speaker on 21 February 1984. That evening, Walding had attended a three-hour emergency meeting of the St. Vital executive (including Laser) at Unwin's home. It has been alleged that Walding was "bombarded" by executive members and "cross-examined at length."[18] Notes from that meeting suggest that while Walding believed he was being an "impartial Speaker," he was also "defensive," "definitely bitter," "angry to get letter (from Pawley)," and had "his back up about entrenchment."[19] Unwin's bland summation to the press ("We asked him to clarify his position. We just told him what we felt and asked if he would clarify why people are doing the things they're doing")[20] likely understated the intensity of the views expressed.

Nevertheless, neither challenger opted to resuscitate their differences with Walding over the language issue.[21] When she announced her candidacy, Unwin claimed the matter was "in the past" and would not be a factor in the contest. Of the bell-ringing episode, she merely stated, "Mr. Walding did what he felt was right to do."[22] Laser also declined to highlight the language issue. "People were pissed off that the Pawley agenda had been derailed in a way that played to the worst in Manitoba politics—the racism, the almost Orange, anti-Catholic stuff that came out. The Tories did really bad politics and there were New Democrats who thought that a Speaker who wouldn't let the government govern was playing to this," recalled Laser. "So when we came to the doorstep, we didn't say that, we almost just listened to it and absorbed it, and said, 'Well, you know, you've got an option, and here I am.'" Downplaying the bilingualism issue might seem surprising given not only the historic prominence of French in the community, but also the Pawley administration's specific identification of St. Vital as having a sufficient number of francophones to warrant the provision of bilingual government services. Yet French-speaking voters in St. Vital had been, in 1969, among the first to defect from their traditional Liberal allegiance and had, in subsequent elections, provided strong support for Jim Walding and the NDP.[23] Stirring the embers of the language furor could alienate St. Vital francophones and anglophones alike; it was, therefore, to be avoided by all candidates.

The candidacies of Unwin and Laser (while easily distinguishable from that of the incumbent) had much in common. In contrast to Walding, both could claim to be on the left of the NDP. Also unlike the Speaker, both could emphasize their loyalty to their party. Unwin announced, for example, that she shared "the Pawley government's commitment to strengthening communities and maintaining social services,"[24] while Laser declared, "I'm proud of this government. They're dedicated, honest, and hard-working. I'd be immensely pleased to work with them."[25] The challengers' shared commitment to revitalizing the St. Vital constituency association and providing improved service to all members of the riding (with Laser pledging to open up a full-time constituency association office) provided a further contrast to Walding. Both Unwin and Laser threw themselves single-mindedly into the contest, effectively becoming full-time candidates. Former New Brunswick Premier Richard Hatfield may have been styled as "the man who knocked on a thousand doors" when he first won a party nomination,[26] but both Unwin and Laser easily surpassed that benchmark in the fall of 1985.

All of which is not to suggest that the two challengers were indistinguishable. In fact, Gerri Unwin and Sig Laser could clearly be differentiated by their prior experience, their gender, their strategy and tactics, and their image. As to the first of these, it is worth recalling from Chapter 1 that only those with lengthy records of party or union service are likely to be perceived as credible candidates for the New Democratic Party. At age forty-nine, one year older than the long-serving incumbent, Unwin had been a party member since 1967. Although she and her family had lived in the same house on Havelock Avenue since 1959, her initial years as a New Democrat were in the constituency of Riel, where, for example, she was Wilson Parasiuk's official agent in the 1973 provincial election. She had also, over the years, served as a New Democratic campaign organizer, canvass manager, and returning officer. It was only after the redistribution prior to the 1981 vote that Unwin found herself lodged in the riding of St. Vital. Unwin worked for Walding's 1981 re-election bid, served as his confidante when he weighed the advantages and disadvantages of accepting the speakership, and, shortly thereafter, became president of the constituency association. Over the years, Unwin had also built up an impressive record of community voluntarism, serving as a coordinator of evening programs for the St. Vital School Division, as an executive member of the St. George Home and School Association, and as a volunteer for Brownies and Explorers, in addition to other activities. Finally, it is important to note that through her husband, Fred, a machinist with the Canadian National Railways, Unwin also had active connections to the trade union movement.

At thirty-six, Sig Laser almost inevitably had a thinner resumé of party and community service than his two opponents. As a young man, Laser had gone to northern Manitoba to work as an Autopac claims adjustor, and in 1975, at the age of twenty-six, had decided to run for Thompson city council ("more as a lark than anything"). Since joining the NDP would aid his candidacy by providing access to the party's membership list, Laser signed on in Dick Martin's kitchen with Wilf Hudson as his witness (both of whom would subsequently head the Manitoba Federation of Labour). The NDP connection did not, however, catapult him to victory. With four to be elected, Laser ran against what he claimed was a "council by clique," finishing fifth of six candidates.[27] Returning to Winnipeg, Laser renewed his membership annually, but only became active in the party in 1980 when he moved to St. Vital; three years later, he ran for Winnipeg city council as the NDP candidate in the Glenlawn ward. As we saw in the previous chapter, the 1983 municipal elections were engulfed in the furor over official bilingualism; in fact, Laser's opponent in Glenlawn, Al Ducharme, was instrumental in placing the language question on the ballot. With Conservative voters who might otherwise have stayed home turning out in force to register their symbolic unhappiness with the Pawley government's initiative, it was an unfortunate time to run as a New Democrat. Unlike other candidates for the party, however, Laser was neither "slaughtered" nor "overwhelmed" by the French-language issue,[28] receiving 36 percent of the vote.[29] This defeat against the prevailing tide, coupled with his work as secretary of the municipal NDP, bolstered Laser's reputation, and he was hired in December 1983 as an executive assistant to Howard Pawley, with particular responsibility for the premier's constituency of Selkirk. His first task in his new position, as it turned out, was to hand-deliver to whomever emerged triumphant from the PC leadership convention a note from Pawley requesting fresh negotiations to settle the language imbroglio. For most of the next two years, Laser was somewhat detached from constituency affairs in St. Vital. Four days a week, he worked in Selkirk (to the north of Winnipeg) and, for an interval, even transferred his party membership to that riding. When the opportunity arose to challenge Jim Walding, therefore, Sig Laser had not yet served a particularly lengthy apprenticeship either in the party or in the constituency association. Unlike Unwin, it is true, Laser at least had some experience as a candidate. Otherwise, his record was rather thin, as shown by his 1985 campaign pamphlet, and many long-standing St. Vital New Democrats perceived Laser to be something of a brash upstart, and his candidacy to be premature.

Chapter 1 highlighted the importance of gender equity as particular to the New Democratic Party. Admittedly, the Manitoba branch of the party had been quite slow to follow through on this particular philosophical commitment. Although in most respects the Schreyer victory of 1969 overhauled the composition of the provincial political elite, no such transformation occurred with respect to gender. In fact, in the party's first two decades of existence, not one female NDP candidate was elected to the legislature, an embarrassment that was only partially alleviated in 1981 when five women joined the Manitoba NDP caucus. Advancing gender equity required the party not only to nominate more women candidates, but also to nominate them in "winnable" constituencies. St. Vital, having been in the New Democratic fold for four successive elections, was obviously a "winnable" riding; if Jim Walding was to be replaced as the party's standard-bearer, a movement to draft a female challenger was almost inevitable. With Sig Laser apparently on the verge of entering the race, a group of local women (dubbed "the sisters") actively encouraged the already favourably disposed Unwin to join the fray.

Having both a male and a female challenger to Walding ensured that gender would provide an important subtext to the campaign. At Laser's mid-October candidacy announcement, he emphasized his success at enlisting new members, but acknowledged that Unwin already had "the support of most of the women's groups."[30] Of course, gender considerations also affected male voters. One, who was otherwise favourably disposed toward Laser, found it difficult to make a definitive choice; "to be blunt," he asserted, "Gerri was a woman and that was something of great value." Perhaps not coincidentally the November 1985 edition of the provincial party newspaper featured a lengthy interview with Minister of Education Maureen Hemphill. Her advice to prospective female candidates? "Get in there! Just do it! It's accepted now in the party when a woman challenges a top constituency."[31] The key players on the Laser team (aside from his wife Tannis) were entirely male (David Street, Jim Bardy, Jules Legal, and Michael Stimpson). In contrast, there were several women in Unwin's core group of advisors (including Irene Rossman, Monica Girouard, and Diane Hitchings), and gendered appeals became more apparent as the campaign progressed. Oblique references in Unwin's campaign materials in mid-November to her experiences as "a mother and wife" (see Appendix B) were replaced in early January with this pronouncement:

"The issues are job equity, day care, jobs for children, and family problems."[32] If these were, in fact, the issues of the campaign, it was not because they were the objects of debate, or even disagreement among the three candidates. Rather, these concerns were highlighted to signify who should be perceived as their most effective spokesperson and champion.

Chapter 1 identified an aversion to the enlistment of large numbers of instant members as one further way in which New Democratic nominating practices could be distinguished from those of their Liberal and Conservative counterparts. Canadian political folklore is full of instances where the membership rolls have suddenly mushroomed on the eve of a contested nomination meeting. In 1968, for example, the Liberal constituency association in Toronto Davenport saw its numbers swell from 150 to 5445, with the votes of ten-year-olds and non-residents playing a potentially key role in the final outcome.[33] Similarly, rising Liberal star Donald Johnston was to discover that "it's tough getting nominated to a safe seat."[34] In 1978, Johnston had his eye on Westmount, the bastion of retiring MP Bud Drury. Johnston triumphed, but only after a fierce recruiting war that saw the membership rise from around 300 to over 4000. In some of Canada's metropolitan centres, voters from different nationalities (or from different factions of the same nationality)[35] have been mobilized on behalf of rival candidates; such "ethnic packing" occurs in about one-fifth of all contested federal nominations.[36]

Yet such practices have been relatively uncommon in the New Democratic Party. In some parts of the country, admittedly, becoming the party's standard-bearer is hardly worth the trouble. How else can one account for the fact that, in 1981, a contested NDP nomination in Edmonton was secured by a vote of three to two?[37] Even where the party is a major political player, the enlistment of instant members is discouraged. Such recruits rarely renew their membership; as "tourists" in the party, they manifest little of the ongoing commitment to party goals expected of New Democrats. Indiscriminately selling new membership cards, therefore, is anathema to the NDP's organizational culture.

Sig Laser would have to flout this party norm to secure the nomination. The long-standing members of the St. Vital NDP constituency association were always more likely to gravitate to the candidacies of Jim Walding and Gerri Unwin. Walding could count on the support of most of those whose participation in party life was confined to the annual payment of their dues. These passive members might at one time have canvassed for Walding; most would have publicly declared their support of him through the medium of an election lawn sign, and almost all would have voted for him on one or more occasions. Especially in his early years as an MLA, and with Val's able assistance, Jim would have done much to cultivate their allegiance. To such members, detached from the organizational rot that had infiltrated the constituency association over the preceding thirty-six months, the peremptory challenges to Walding would have been psychologically unsettling; Walding would need to rouse this core group of loyalists from their customary lethargy if he were to retain the nomination.

By contrast, Gerri Unwin could count on the enthusiastic backing of most of St. Vital's more active New Democrats. As president, Unwin would have articulated their frustrations with Walding's seeming indifference to constituency affairs, and she would have come to personify the orphaned riding association's determination to stay afloat. Leaving aside those with familial ties to one of the other candidates, most members of the St. Vital executive were firmly in the Unwin camp.

With Unwin and Walding carving up the existing electorate, Laser's only viable option was to expand the membership rolls. All three candidates had access to the existing membership list as well as to the names of those whose memberships had lapsed at some point over the past several years; getting one's name off the NDP contact list clearly involved more than a straightforward refusal to pay one's annual dues! From the outset, all three candidates sought support from present and past members, but Laser's main focus, as his 1985 campaign pamphlet makes clear, was on enlisting fresh adherents to ensure the party was "truly representative of the diversity" of St. Vital (a subtle dig at Walding's anglophilia). This would not, however, constitute an instance of "ethnic packing"; most of the immigrant groups were second- or third-generation residents of St.Vital and lacked the internal solidarity and deference to community leadership required for such a stratagem. Instead, any potential members (who might previously have felt uncomfortable in an association that, in Laser's words, "was just too bloody white") had to be approached on an individual basis. As well, Laser and his team went after St. Vital's socially marginalized, those living in down-market senior citizens' homes and in public housing complexes. According to Laser, many of these fresh recruits "had bad teeth, wore sweatpants, and lived on welfare." If they actually carried through on their membership pledges, they threatened to transform what had previously been a relatively genteel association.[38]

David Street was a key member of the Laser team. Street, a short, slight, balding, unkempt thirty-year-old, had been recruited out of the navy by NDP patriarch Magnus Eliason and had helped Jim Malloway secure the Elmwood nomination after the departure of renegade MLA Russell Doern. Street was clearly an idiosyncratic character. One confidante claimed Street "was odd and looked odd," and he was no stranger to controversy. During his years in Manitoba, he gave unguarded comments to journalists about skirting the party's membership requirements,[39] organized an inner-city ethnic slate to wrest control of the party's youth wing from suburban "white wine social-ists"[40] and bestowed a very public one-finger salute on a member of the pro-vincial executive. Laser knew that he would get "no credit for having a guy like David Street" involved in his campaign. On the other hand, Street was a friend of Jim Bardy, who had organized Laser's 1983 bid for municipal office, was obviously an adept organizer, and was willing to work for the modest salary of $100 per week. Street had a surprising capacity to connect at the doorstep with the otherwise politically disengaged. Michael Stimpson went door-to-door with Street many times in the fall of 1985 and was impressed by his "magic touch" with people; Stimpson marvelled that Street was able to sell a membership to an individual the other campaigns were reluctant even to approach, "a creepy old man who told us on our first visit that Friday night was his porn movie night."

Sig Laser was also hard at work enlisting new members. "Selling mem-berships is not all that easy," Laser recalled. "In the early weeks of the race, you were lucky if you could sell one a night. In the final week [before mem-bership sales were closed off], you would go out and sell four or five. It was just knowing that you had a goal, you were in a conversation, you were not there to convert or persuade, you were there to sell a membership. And that clarity made it possible." The Laser team's recruitment drive obviously worked; from a base of below 200, the number of members in the St. Vital NDP association had grown to 749 by the 13 December cut-off. The lion's share of this increase, as Laser's 4 January 1986 letter to St. Vital New Democrats tendentiously makes clear, had been enlisted to vote for Sig Laser (see Appendix B).[41]

Running an intensive recruitment campaign requires significant resources. Against about $300 in donations, Laser spent just under $2000 on campaign materials (letterhead paper, large signs, envelopes, Christmas cards, labels, diskettes, postage, typesetting, advertisements, and the like). Seventeen weeks of David Street's services cost about the same (plus $250 for a month's hotel rent and $275 on a pre-Christmas plane ticket for Street). Throw in an additional $220 liquor bill, gas money, a new suit, and assorted other sundries, and Laser spent on his campaign approximately $5000 of his own money (a not insubstantial sum for someone out of work with two young children). To put this amount in context, it is worth noting that in the federal election two years later, the average winning candidate of a contested nomination for any party spent about $2200;[42] isolating just the NDP cases, however, drops this figure to a relatively modest $300.[43]

David Street's vigorous efforts on Laser's behalf were not entirely beneficial. Even Tannis Laser, the candidate's wife, was not enthusiastic about the close link with Street; in mid-campaign, Street was obliged to move out of the Lasers' basement and into a room in the St. Vital Hotel. George Schamber was similarly unimpressed. "Some people might have bought memberships without knowing what they were paying for or why they were paying," he declared. Shortly after the campaign commenced, Colin Trigwell, an organizer for the United Food and Commercial Workers union, recalled receiving a phone call from someone at the NDP provincial office concerned about "the sleazy membership they were getting into the party, not members for what they believe in, but just for the vote." Asked to manage the Unwin candidacy, Trigwell readily agreed, in part because the Laser team's campaign was at odds with party traditions. "The St. Vital executive was full of hard workers, and they should have had the right to determine their candidate," Trigwell declared. "They had worked on every damn election of Jim's. They had all contributed highly. There was not a loafer on the executive board of St. Vital."

Trigwell's presence injected some much needed professionalism into the Unwin candidacy. Her campaign was still not flush with cash, but several members of the executive contributed to the kitty, the odd cheque would arrive in the mail (usually from a woman), and one supporter employed his union connections to score some cheap printing. As a result, Unwin was able to get by spending only about $1000 on her campaign.[44]

Like Walding, much of Unwin's attention was focussed on existing and lapsed members of the constituency association. Unwin did recruit some new members, but claims she only pitched the idea to those who would acknowledge that they were already favourably disposed to the NDP. Because she was outgoing and friendly, had lived in the community for twenty-six years, and had been involved in a wide array of volunteer activities, Unwin had a large group of contacts. Much of Unwin's campaign was focussed on enlisting the backing of this large pool of friends and acquaintances. As a result, Unwin's support, as Figure 4 attests, was highly concentrated in a few square blocks.[45] The home streets of Sig Laser and Gerri Unwin (Egerton Road and Havelock Avenue, respectively) are of comparable length. Yet while Laser had only eight committed supporters from those living on his street, the corresponding figure for Unwin was an astonishing thirty-eight (or 30 percent of all her backers).[46] An additional thirty Unwinites lived within two blocks of Havelock Avenue. Over one-half of Unwin's core supporters lived in the southeast corner of St. Vital; even after eliminating the Winnipeg Canoe Club and the St. Boniface and Windsor Park golf courses, this neighbourhood comprises only about 8 percent of the constituency. In fact, an additional nineteen outliers on Figure 4 were either extended members of her own family or of those already serving with Unwin on the riding executive. Thus, only forty-one members (or 32 percent) of Unwin's core backing were not immediately identifiable as family, friends, or neighbours. By contrast, the support base for both Walding and Laser was far more geographically dispersed throughout St. Vital.

Figure 4: Distribution of Gerri Unwin's 128 Core Supporters, 1986[47]

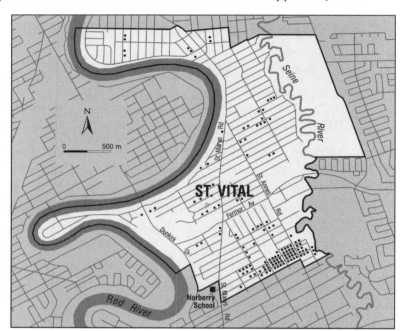

Numerous people interviewed traced their involvement in the contest to a personal tie with Unwin. Irene Rossman urged Unwin to seek the nomination; the two women had been friends since meeting in the hospital while each was giving birth to their first child. Elaine Trudel used to get together once a week with Unwin; at her friend's urging, Trudel joined the NDP in the fall of 1985. Ivy Boutang knew Unwin through her involvement with the local school and was enlisted by a mutual friend.[48] Paul Ritchot and his wife lived just down the street. They signed up to support Unwin whom they knew as "a good intelligent woman"; after the meeting, they let their memberships lapse ("Once was enough"). Unwin's candidacy was genuinely a "friends and neighbours" undertaking.[49]

Well before the 13 December cut-off for membership sales, the Unwin camp's focus shifted from recruitment (enlisting new members) to conversion (persuading existing members). Unwin was an effective door-to-door campaigner, in part because her image contrasted sharply with that of Sig Laser. One Laser supporter had to acknowledge that the two challengers were perceived quite differently: "Gerri was a consensus figure who was good at consensus building. Sig came across as a political operative. It was a false perception, since he had spent many years running a left-wing bookstore. Sig was not as driven as people thought. But because he was a big, well-spoken guy, he was seen as a typical machine politician. Gerri had more of a grassroots image." Another Laser backer agreed that his man "was seen as too nakedly ambitious," while George Schamber perceived Laser as someone who "was young and aggressive and thought he could set the world on fire."

In some ways, Unwin and Laser came to personify the essential duality of Canadian nominating practices: the push for local autonomy versus the pull for central control. On the one hand, local partisans have, since Confederation, "jealously guarded" the prerogative of selecting the party's representative;[50] only if that candidate is their genuine preference will constituency activists work enthusiastically on his or her behalf.[51] Survey evidence from the mid-1980s confirmed that party activists distrust any outside intervention in the process,[52] and there have been numerous conventions where local partisans have quite deliberately flouted the expressed wishes of national or provincial elites.[53]

What is true generally of Canadian political parties is, if anything, even more valid with respect to the New Democratic Party; provincial or national headquarters respect the principle of local autonomy and "interfere only occasionally, and then usually unsuccessfully."[54] In the words of one prominent New Democrat: "We keep our hands off an established riding association."[55] Of course, it may be that there is a happy coincidence of views between local elites and head office. "Given the common cause across different levels of the NDP," suggests Anthony Sayers, it may be that "local outcomes are more consistent with national [or provincial] party objectives and thus obviate the need for direct national [or provincial] intervention."[56] Even so, it seemed to many at the time that Gerri Unwin (or "Genuine Gerri" as she was dubbed by one enthusiast) represented the authentic voice of St. Vital's local activists. She might not have enough votes to win the nomination, but among those constituency members who had done the hard slogging for the party in the past (and would do so again in the future), who had coordinated annual meetings, filled executive positions, organized yard sales, and hosted constituency dinners, she was clearly the majority choice.

On the other hand, any riding association is but one part of a broader network overseen by a provincial or national office. Party headquarters has an obvious interest in what occurs at the constituency level and can usually find the means to express their preferences effectively. At times, such as in the Newfoundland Liberal Party under Joey Smallwood, there has not even been the pretense of local autonomy. In his autobiography, Smallwood claimed to have "selected every candidate in every constituency in every provincial General Election" in which he was the party leader.[57] Réal Caouette as leader of the Créditistes was more subtle but just as disrespectful of local autonomy. His reciprocal arrangement with PC elites to run weak candidates in the 1974 federal election where the putative ally was strong was only exposed when Caouette mistakenly endorsed two official candidates (one strong and one weak) in the riding of Labelle.[58] The electoral requirement that a party leader must formally approve all party candidates gives the brass substantial leverage in constituency nomination contests. Even if the leader's veto is only used occasionally (such as in 1988 when Brian Mulroney refused to endorse Sinclair Stevens), the threat (or even the hint) of same is likely to get the attention of most rank-and-file activists. As Canada's presumptive party of government, the national Liberals have arguably been the most prone to interfere in local nomination contests, with Jean Chrétien's pre-emptive appointment of twelve candidates in the 1993 election only the most visible manifestation of this tendency; that year, in fact, about one-third of Liberal associations reported "outside interference" from the national party in the selection of their candidate.[59] For the 2006 national election, both Liberal leader Paul Martin and his Conservative counterpart Stephen Harper announced that all incumbents would be assured renomination. As a direct result of these decisions, 182 MPs (or about 60 percent of the total) would sit in the subsequent Parliament without having faced a nomination contest.[60]

New Democratic Party elites are by no means immune to this tendency. In 1962, members in the NDP constituency association in Eglington much preferred Liberal Mitchell Sharp to incumbent Tory Donald Flemming. Seeing no chance of securing the riding for the NDP, they opted not to field a candidate in order to avoid splitting the anti-Flemming vote; under substantial pressure from national party headquarters, however, this decision was overturned, and a nomination meeting was duly held.[61] Something similar occurred in 1979 in the dual-member provincial riding of Vancouver South. Two East Indian candidates were competing for a place on the NDP ticket and each had signed up about three hundred new members. The provincial executive, however, "let it be known that only one East Indian should run on behalf of the NDP"; as a result, each of the two leading contenders was obliged to secure a non-East Indian running mate.[62] In short, NDP elites have also been willing to intervene in local nominating contests to promote what they perceive to be the party's best interests.

When Sig Laser announced on 17 October 1985 that he was seeking the NDP nomination in St. Vital, it struck many observers as yet another instance of the party brass meddling in local affairs. Quizzed by reporters about whether his candidacy had the blessing of his erstwhile boss, Laser replied, "The premier has asked me neither to run nor not to run against Walding."[63] An editorialist at the *Winnipeg Sun* was unconvinced. To Laser's claim that "the premier had nothing to do with the challenge," the retort came back, "Sure. And shares in the Northland Bank are a good investment." In fact, noted the paper, if St. Vital was "held by, say, Finance Minister Vic Schroeder, a challenge by a Pawley aide would be looked on as high treason."[64] Two days later, on 22 October, the paper drove the point home with an amusing editorial cartoon (Figure 5). With this kind of media coverage, some members of the riding association inevitably concluded that "there was no doubt that Sig Laser was Howard Pawley's candidate," that Laser was, in fact, "an establishment candidate." Certainly, the *Winnipeg Sun*'s perspective on the matter was shared by Val Walding: "Sig Laser was the one Pawley wanted to run. Oh, of course, he was told to run by Pawley." Happening upon the premier having lunch in the legislative restaurant, Val Walding confronted him with her suspicions. When Pawley denied having anything to do with Laser's candidacy, she retorted, "Which banana boat do you think I came over on?" Pawley did not reply "because he knew I had him." Thus, if Gerri Unwin was widely regarded as the authentic voice of the grassroots, Sig Laser was seen in many circles to be the authentic voice of the premier's office.

Figure 5: Political Cartoon, *Winnipeg Sun*, 22 October 1985[65]

Yet these images were, in some measure, oversimplified caricatures. For one thing, Gerri Unwin was not without influential support. Unwin was "thick with the provincial office," alleged Val Walding. "She was thick with all that gang." Michael Stimpson likewise claimed that Unwin "had an in with powerful people in the party," and it is certainly suggestive that the call to recruit Colin Trigwell to the Unwin camp came from the provincial office. As for Sig Laser, he had been warned against running by Jim Bardy in a mid-September phone call. Bardy was certain that "it was going to be very difficult," and that "it was not going to look nice," because Laser was guaranteed "to get pegged as the guy from Howard's office." Aware of the dangers associated with such a perception, Laser claimed at his campaign launch never to have discussed his candidacy with the premier.[66] In fact, Laser now acknowledges they "had a couple of delicate conversations," but insists Pawley never encouraged him to run. For his part, Pawley confirms this account: "I was certainly not behind Sig's thrust. I called him into my office and said, 'Sig, you cannot continue to work in my office and run.' So he then resigned, but I did not sic Sig onto Jim.... Once he had resigned, it would have been entirely inappropriate on my part to say, 'Sig Laser, even though you are no longer an employee of mine, you cannot run against Jim Walding.' That would have been contrary to everything I stood for organizationally."[67] Bruce Buckley was also working in the premier's office at this time. Over coffee, he advised Laser not to run because it "would make the boss look bad," but Laser "was hell-bound to do it." At the first staff meeting after Laser announced his candidacy, Buckley recalls that Pawley was "not a happy camper. He was worried about the perception of the long arm of the premier's office, so he told the rest of the staff that they weren't to help Sig or anyone else." Laser was stuck with the worst of both worlds. On the one hand, he was tarred with the image of being Pawley's cat's-paw. On the other hand, he was blessed in reality with none of the assistance or resources that would normally flow from such a relationship.

Jim Walding thus confronted two candidates who differed in their gender, experience, strategy, and image. Under normal circumstances, incumbents are able to brush aside any and all challengers. But Jim Walding was not a typical sitting MLA; he lacked many of the advantages usually associated with the position. In Chapter 1, we noted that incumbents can typically rely upon the loyalty of long-time activists, most of whom will have previously donated countless hours of volunteer labour in election and re-election campaigns. In a letter written to an acquaintance in September 1982, Walding observed that the constituency "does not change very much and most of the same people are still active and very dependable at election time."[68] Three years later, however, Walding could rely on few of these active and dependable individuals. In fact, among the twenty-one executive members elected at the November 1985 annual meeting of the constituency association, ten were in the Unwin camp and six backed Laser. With president George Schamber officially neutral, that left only four Walding supporters: himself, wife Val, son Phillip, and Jeanne Griffiths. The latter, despite having little political experience, had been encouraged by Walding to stand for election to the executive. "As a member of my wife's choir," recalled Walding, "she was willing to let her name stand," but "she was the only one."[69] Nor was this an instance in which insurgent candidates had undertaken a hostile takeover of the executive and installed their own slate of nominees. On the contrary, these were the same group of people who had always been involved in constituency affairs, but who were now profoundly disenchanted with their long-standing MLA.

We observed as well in Chapter 1 that incumbents can usually count on the backing of party headquarters. Challenges to sitting legislators are often sufficiently fractious and disputatious as to enfeeble the constituency association. From the perspective of the party elite, who yearn for a united and robust electoral machine on the ground, such challenges are generally to be avoided. The case of the NDP association in St. Vital was different; it was already weak and divided, an unhappy condition largely attributable to the conduct of the sitting MLA. Ousting the incumbent would, in these circumstances, effect the same remedy as lancing a boil, although in their public comments, party spokespersons strove to preserve a facade of party unity. When Gary Filmon announced in late August 1985 that the Manitoba NDP had their sights set on Walding, the co-chair of the party's election planning committee, Jay Cowan, was quick to issue a denial. "EPC doesn't get involved in nomination races," claimed Cowan. "Those motives (to dump [Walding]) are just not there. As far as I know, I or the premier or any other minister has nothing to do with it."[70] In early December, Pawley likewise denied orchestrating the nomination challenge. "I should have put that charge to rest earlier," asserted the premier. "I don't hold grudges against anyone. But, I wouldn't stop anyone from seeking the nomination. Let the best person win."[71] Nevertheless, Pawley's official neutrality in the race belied the fact that he, his staff, and his caucus were hardly indifferent to the outcome. As Pawley recounted, "Well, inwardly, with the feelings of caucus members which was overwhelmingly negative and with all the ill will, I was hoping it would be a new candidate. Whether it was Sig or Gerri, I was neutral on that. There was a lot of ill will towards Jim, and it was actually much more intense among people surrounding me than myself. There would have been no Walding sympathizers inside the premier's office." Nor was Walding making any efforts to ingratiate himself to the party brass. As of 13 December 1985, Walding was one of only three members of caucus (Elijah Harper and the soon-to-be-retired Donald Malinowski were the others) who had paid not a dime of either their $2000 constituency indemnity or their $1000 future fund quota.[72] In fact, contrary to the agreement that had caused so much controversy the previous year, Walding was not even holding his constituency indemnity in trust. To repeat: few, if any, members of the NDP elite wanted Walding to be renominated.

The party's control over the timing of nomination conventions afforded one opportunity to exercise some influence over the outcome. An early date can effectively forestall any challenge to a sitting legislator, while a later date provides insurgents with more time to recruit new members, increase their visibility, and expose the shortcomings of the incumbent. In the 1988 federal election, in fact, two-thirds of those constituency associations with a sitting MP (but only 40 percent of those without) had already held nominating conventions over four months before the vote.[73] The Manitoba NDP's rules for setting nomination dates were weighed in favour of the provincial executive. All constituencies were given membership targets (either 10 percent of the NDP vote in the previous election or 10 percent of the anticipated number of votes required for an NDP victory). In 1985, the St. Vital NDP was given a target of 500; with only 187 members extant, it was one of only fourteen NDP constituency associations in Manitoba that was more than 250 members from its quota. In principle, the EPC would refuse to entertain any nomination date until the allotted target had been reached (and even then the EPC had the discretion to recommend to the provincial executive that a meeting be delayed). In practice, this stringent rule could not be enforced.[74] As of 10 December 1985, the St. Vital NDP was one of only thirteen constituency associations that had come within even 10 percent of their assigned quota. Yet the provincial executive had (on the EPC's recommendation) already approved nomination meetings in Portage (124 members and a quota of 250) on 26 November and in Gladstone (forty members and a quota of 150) on 1 December and was set to endorse a 22 January meeting in neighbouring St. Boniface (despite only ninety-one members and a quota of 500). The membership target, in other words, was a rule if necessary, but not necessarily a rule.

Corroboration that the provincial brass was looking to delay the nomination meeting in St. Vital (and therefore increase the likelihood that someone other than Jim Walding would be chosen) comes from an internal party document. Dated 2 August 1985, it proposes a particular nomination schedule for fifty-five of the fifty-seven provincial ridings (the NDP had already selected candidates in Elmwood and Ellice).[75] What is intriguing about the schedule is that St. Johns and St. Vital were singled out to be held at some unspecified "late" date. Both constituencies were held by the NDP. Both had incumbents who were out of favour with the party establishment. First elected in 1969, St. Johns MLA Father Donald Malinowski, like Jim Walding, had served multiple terms without ever receiving a cabinet appointment and in 1981 had only secured his nomination by polarizing the Polish community with alleged threats of damnation to any who might have been inclined to support his opponent. Most intriguingly of all, both incumbents were about to be challenged by a one-time executive assistant to the premier (although Malinowski eventually chose not to re-offer rather than face almost certain humiliation at the hands of Judy Wasylycia-Leis).

When the provincial executive met on 12 December 1985, they must have been confident that Unwin and Laser had enlisted enough new members to ensure Walding's defeat. Accordingly, they selected 12 January 1986 as the date of the St. Vital nomination convention (from the trio of possibilities proposed by the constituency association).[76] Given that NDP rules deny a vote to anyone who has not held a party card for at least thirty days, the three candidates had only an additional twenty-four hours to register new members with the party office. All of the camps had been holding back some completed forms in order not only to disguise their own strength, but also to lessen the amount of time available for opposing candidates to target these fresh recruits. Thus, the membership rolls rose from 499 on 10 December to 749 on 13 December (with the Laser team registering an additional eighty-one members in just the final forty-eight hours).

Jim Walding may have had few friends on the St. Vital executive and fewer still at the provincial office, but he would not have to fight this challenge alone. For one thing, he could count on the residual loyalty of many he had helped during his fourteen years as an MLA. "They've got to know me and trust me," he claimed.[77] Al Riel was president of the community centre at the time and he recalled that Walding would faithfully attend local functions ("anytime we phoned, he was always there for us"). He and his wife happily joined the NDP just to vote for Jim Walding. Others remembered that when Walding had been made Speaker, he had invited all those who had laboured on his previous campaign to the legislature to see his chambers; "Jim Walding looked after his workers," observed one supporter. As the mother of small children, Sharon Kula had been delighted when Walding had secured her part-time employment in the Speaker's office; she promptly recruited her husband in the struggle against Unwin and Laser. Walding's assumption that he could reactivate old loyalties was not always valid. Admittedly, it held true in the case of Altje Swain, a fellow optician of Dutch descent. According to Swain, Walding had taken her support for granted and when asked point-blank the basis for that assumption had replied, "Because we are fellow Europeans." Swain sardonically retorted that "this was the first occasion she had heard a Brit call himself a European," but she voted for Walding just the same. Others, however, resisted the call to loyalty, and several recalled just how surprised and disappointed Walding had been to discover that they were supporting one of the challengers.

Jim and Val Walding had a particular affinity with St. Vital's senior citizens, and this demographic became the focus of the campaign. Most were either inactive or lapsed members and were, as a result, removed from the anti-Walding grapevine. Most identified with Walding's longevity and experience and resented what they perceived to be a takeover by the constituency's "Young Turks." Many had become New Democrats during the Schreyer years and were pleased to rally around one of the few surviving MLAS from that period. Dave Olinyk was a key data analyst in the Walding camp; it soon became apparent to him that "our supporters had bluer hair than did Sig's."

Walding could also count on receiving a substantial sympathy vote. Walding always insisted that, given the nonpartisanship demanded of the Speaker, it was unfair that he should have been challenged for the nomination by partisans unhappy with his performance in the chair. The *Winnipeg Sun* concurred with this assessment. Warning that a concern for self-preservation would now render future Speakers subservient to government dictates, the paper lamented that this was "not how the game was designed. Nor is it how the game should be played."[78] At least some residents of St. Vital were of the same mind, including a couple who joined the party on their own accord after reading about Walding's circumstances, and who went to the meeting "angry" at Howard Pawley for giving the Speaker "a raw deal" and at Sig Laser for "taking advantage of the situation."

Furthermore, Walding could trade on his reputation as a proven electoral commodity to reassure any potential waverers. When Unwin declared her candidacy, Walding cast doubts upon her ability to hold St. Vital in a general election. "If she's elected," Walding asserted, "it's a gamble."[79] He repeated this sentiment when Laser entered the race. "The people of St. Vital are too intelligent," he suggested, "to gamble frivolously with a seat that we have held for 15 years."[80] Long-time supporter Peter Nolan shared this opinion, feeling that "people should forget about whether they liked Jim Walding since (unlike Laser and Unwin) Walding would win the riding." This theme became ever more prominent in the incumbent's campaign letters from October to December 1985 (see Appendix B).[81] Not everyone responded favourably to such missives; some found the hard sell off-putting. "I felt threatened and I didn't like that," claimed one party member. "I decided to vote for Laser."[82]

The four letters indicate a steadily increasing level of concern in the Walding camp, no mean achievement given the pre-existing signs of stress. How else can one account for the 18 June 1985 letter which Walding, in his capacity as Speaker, sent to the president of Air Canada? Complaining of being assigned a seat in the non-smoking section on an Ottawa-Winnipeg flight, Walding claimed, "This conduct is outrageous and an inexcusable imposition on Air Canada's passengers."[83] Or the 31 October letter to the

Canadian Imperial Bank of Commerce, again sent in his capacity as Speaker? On this occasion, Walding objected to the unwarranted imposition of a $3.64 interest penalty on his Chargex statement and declared, "I can't afford to pay 201% interest per annum."[84] When long-time friends Harvey Bostrom (former MLA for Rupertsland) and Elizabeth Dotrement returned in early January 1986 from a Florida holiday, they found the Walding organization in a state of near panic. The legislature had not been in session in the fall of 1985, so Val and Jim Walding had been campaigning full-time.[85] Yet despite "working like a Trojan," the numbers generated by confidantes Glen McRuer and Dave Olinyk (the team's "computer whiz") were not very encouraging. "The very night we got back," recalled Dotremont, "we got a phone call from the Walding people to get over there." It was decided to place all efforts into pulling the vote; the constituency was divided into districts and individual poll captains were appointed to make certain that all Walding supporters got to Norberry School on the afternoon of 12 January 1986.

Nomination contests are often bitterly fought. Indeed, it has been observed that many candidates "will not receive as rough a ride from their opponents of the other parties as they will get from their friends in the same party."[86] This is especially true in those contests where an incumbent is challenged; these battles are said to "generate the greatest internal conflicts" and to be "the most disruptive."[87] In 1986, this assessment certainly applied to the NDP riding of Inkster where, as in St. Vital and Riel, the sitting MLA was under siege. Challenger Gem Amis had swamped the constituency association with over 700 new recruits, most from the Filipino community and most having paid either the two-dollar membership fee reserved for seniors and the unemployed or nothing at all. When incumbent Don Scott complained, provincial secretary Ron Cavaluce was obliged to admit, "There's nothing wrong, constitutionally anyway, in buying memberships. On an individual basis it's not illegal, a candidate can buy any number of memberships, the constitution is silent on that."[88] Even so, the provincial executive sent a letter requiring the new recruits to indicate their awareness of the NDP's fee structure and to remit any unpaid balance. With both the constituency and provincial executives on side, Scott was able to overcome Amis's countercharge of racial discrimination and hold on to the nomination.[89]

The race in St. Vital, by contrast, had few overt signs of bitterness. David Woodbury, then working out of the provincial office, could not recall "even a hint" of any membership-buying scandal. Only a fragmentary record remains of the membership forms submitted by the three candidates; even so, the data contained in Table 6 are suggestive. Assuming, first, that these recruits did actually pay the appropriate amount, second, that the 149 individuals contained in the table were broadly representative of the other 75 percent of new members for which no data are available, and, third, that St. Vital's unemployed were unlikely to have been captured by the Walding campaign, then Table 6 emphasizes the incumbent's quite extraordinary reliance on the support of senior citizens.

Table 6: St. Vital Memberships Sold by Sig Laser, Gerri Unwin, and Jim Walding[90]

	$20 (Spousal, at least one employed)	$15 (Employed individual)	$6 (Employed student)	$2 (Senior/ Unemployed)
Laser	19	9	4	28
Unwin	6	0	2	6
Walding	4	1	5*	36**

*Includes three sold at five dollars and one at eight dollars, despite the absence of such categories.
**Includes one sold at three dollars, despite the absence of such a category.

This was not a contest in which either challenger indulged in nasty attacks on the incumbent. As Colin Trigwell recalled, "with all the flash and glamour which (the Unwin campaign) didn't have, we stuck clean. We didn't even kick the shit out of Jim." Sig Laser concurred. "There wasn't any slagging," he recollected. "It was not a crass campaign." A Walding supporter confirmed that "Sig wouldn't say anything against Jim." Admittedly, Laser canvassers "let people know that the constituency executive was unhappy with Jim and we probably referenced [his] less-than-stellar sense of loyalty to the party." But when he met the incumbent coming down the steps of a house with a "Laser" sign in the window and flippantly inquired whether Walding was trying to shake the occupant's inclination, Laser instantly regretted the remark.

In fact, some of the bad blood in the contest was to be found in the relationship between the two challengers. There is a subterranean quality to most nomination tussles; candidates and their supporters "can say almost anything they want about their opponent's frailties without a public record of what they have said."[91] Such hearsay is difficult to confirm and easy to deny, but one campaign incident is beyond dispute. Some Laser canvassers were reported to be casting aspersions on Gerri Unwin, in general, and on her ability to win the next election, in particular. This news eventually filtered back to Unwin headquarters, which lodged a complaint with Jim Mochoruk, a member of the executive who was supporting Laser, but who also had ties to Unwin ("It was hard not to want the best for both of them"). Mochoruk lambasted Laser who, although surprised that his ally's "chain had been jerked" over the matter, readily apologized. Each of the two challengers already blamed the other for entering the race and splitting the anti-Walding vote; now, relations between Unwin and Laser grew even chillier. As one long-time member diplomatically observed, "Gerri and Sig were friends, but not the best of friends."

Gerri Unwin was further distressed when the Laser team continued to work the community in the days surrounding Christmas. True, Howard Pawley had endorsed such activity in the December 1985 issue of the party newspaper. This particular holiday season, according to the premier, "is unlike any other during the past four years. This year, we simply don't have the time to stop the work we have been doing. If we are going to be prepared for an election and win it, every minute counts. I certainly hope you enjoy yourselves during the winter break, but I also urge you to continue your Party work."[92]

Unwin categorically rejected this advice. "I can remember being disgusted with Sig for knocking on people's doors on Christmas Eve, Christmas Day, and Boxing Day," she recalled. "I thought at the time that I would never dream of doing that; Christmas is a time when families want to be together."

Much of the tension between the two challengers was rooted in the Unwin camp. In fact, David Street wrote a late-campaign strategy memo to Laser which commenced with the injunction, "Stay away from Unwin people." And the very mention of Street, two decades on, elicited from Unwin a sigh of disgust and the admission, "I didn't like the man. He was rough and gruff."

As a result of this tension, no deal was struck between the two challengers to support the other in the event of a decisive second-ballot showdown with the incumbent. Given that the overarching strategic justification for both the Laser and Unwin candidacies was ultimately to oust Jim Walding, this failure to arrive at some sort of reciprocal arrangement is puzzling.

Certainly, a study of past Canadian leadership conventions would have alerted the two challengers to the perils of delaying these matters. In such contests, the far-sighted candidates have always attempted to make deals and forge alliances prior to voting day. Hence, when an anxious Bill Davis phoned the freshly eliminated Darcy McKeough immediately prior to the final ballot of the 1971 Ontario PC convention, the reassuring reply was, "We settled all that the night before Christmas in my apartment. I'm on my way over."[93] Not all such deals are ultimately consummated (David Crombie thought that he, Michael Wilson, and Peter Pocklington had reached an understanding to move en masse to John Crosbie at the 1983 PC federal leadership convention),[94] and many more do not get beyond the trial balloon stage (such as the proposal that whoever among Paul Martin, Robert Winters, and Paul Hellyer had the most votes after the first ballot in the 1968 Liberal contest would receive the backing of the other two).[95] Nevertheless, many convention accounts underscore the importance of such arrangements even if they are only negotiated with a candidate's subordinates.[96] Robert Stanfield narrowly defeated Duff Roblin on the fifth and final ballot of the 1967 PC convention. While the Stanfield camp had spent the days prior to the vote courting the key players in rival organizations, a weak Roblin team had been relatively inactive. During the voting, none of the eliminated candidates (including such likely allies as Michael Starr and Alvin Hamilton) walked to the Roblin box; "the wheeling and dealing had been left to convention day and that was too late."[97]

Most nominating contests have only one or two aspirants, so such pre-meeting arrangements are less common. Yet only two years previously, in the federal Manitoba riding of Lisgar, Conservative member of Parliament Jack Murta had confronted two challengers who, ironically, were both unhappy with the fourteen-year veteran's support for constitutionally entrenching the language rights of Franco-Manitobans. As it turned out, the insurgents' deal to throw support to each other on a second vote came to naught when Murta narrowly secured a first-ballot victory.[98] Yet no comparable deal was struck between the two challengers in St. Vital. Laser now acknowledges this to have been "an oversight, something that should have been nailed, but wasn't because of coolness between the Unwin camp and ourselves. We should have nailed what was going to happen after the first ballot in the event that one of us was ahead of the other. We probably should have had that discussion. We never did." For her part, Unwin considers the point moot: "No, I would never imply that [second-ballot support] to Sig because I don't think I would have supported Sig, let's put it that way."

As 12 January 1986 approached, there was no obvious favourite to win the nomination. Each of the candidates had demonstrable strengths and weaknesses. Gerri Unwin was well-liked by almost all St. Vital New Democrats, but her chances were compromised by a campaign cadre composed almost entirely of well-intentioned amateurs. Sig Laser had, on paper, enlisted the largest group of backers, but nobody could be certain how many of these fresh recruits would get to Norberry School for the meeting. Jim Walding had alienated the party's power brokers, but he still retained some of the advantages of incumbency and was backed by a veteran team of organizers. Little wonder, then, that when Winnipeggers opened their Sunday paper on the morning of the vote, they read this assessment from provincial NDP organizer Len Roy: "I would say it will be very close."[99]

5

The Vote

NORBERRY SCHOOL WAS THE SITE of the nominating convention chosen by the St. Vital constituency executive. Although annual meetings had previously been held at Nelson McIntyre Collegiate on St. Mary's Road (January 1984) and at the Glenwood Community Club on Overton Street (November 1985), Norberry School possessed a large auditorium and could obviously handle the anticipated crush of members. It was not, however, the only possible site for such a meeting. In fact, Norberry School was not even within the St. Vital boundaries (see Figure 4), which seemed to contradict the Manitoba NDP's injunction that any nomination meeting should be held in a "central" location.[1] Suspicious minds might legitimately wonder whether a constituency executive stacked with Unwin loyalists had opted for a locale that was particularly convenient for Unwin voters, especially given the remote chance that Winnipeg might experience a mid-January snowstorm.[2] Any such machinations were at least partially frustrated, however, when 12 January 1986 turned out to be unseasonably warm. Rather than falling, the snow was actually melting.

In the morning, after having spent "hours and hours on the dumb thing," Jules Legal took his nomination speech over to Sig Laser's house to ensure that the two were on the same wavelength. Although on maternity leave after the recent birth of her second child, Tannis Laser had already been to her office to type her husband's address. Both Legal and Laser had opted for the rhetorical high road; neither would focus on the ostensible shortcomings of Jim Walding. Gerri Unwin was also going over her speech again and again that morning, trying to ensure that the delivery would be flawless. Only Jim Walding had no such concerns; as was his custom, he planned to take only a few speaking points with him to the podium.

In any closely contested nomination tussle, "pulling the vote" can be essential to success. Yet the three candidates took widely divergent approaches to the task. At one extreme could be found the seeming casualness of the Gerri Unwin camp. In the words of the candidate, "We just said if they're going to support me, they're going to support me, and they'll be there. I wouldn't let Colin Trigwell pull the vote because I didn't want those poor people being bugged any more. Colin couldn't believe me, and every time I'd see him forever and ever after that, he'd say: 'Hmm, don't pull the vote. Don't pull the vote.'" Admittedly, members of the Unwin camp had been, for a few days, calling confirmed supporters to remind them about the meeting. But when Irene Rossman phoned up on the morning of the vote to offer her assistance in any capacity, she was told not to worry, that everything was under control. In fact, this assessment was soon exposed to be wildly optimistic; when Unwin's seconder arrived at the auditorium and saw the organizational muscle of the other two camps on display she realized her team had been orchestrating something akin to "amateur hour."

No such appellation could be applied to the Walding efforts. The incumbent had, over the years, realized that there is a "premium" placed on organizational strength, that—in the words of William Cross—the "ability to mobilize hundreds of partisans and bring them to a nominating meeting is valued over party service or mastery of policy issues."[3] In addition to deploying a fleet of private vehicles, the Walding team had rented three twelve-seater vans, plus a handi-van for those in wheelchairs; each of the vans had both a driver and one or two helpers to facilitate the smooth entry and exit of passengers. In this pre-cellular telephone age, moreover, members of the Walding organization were equipped with walkie-talkies to allow for instant communication. A Walding driver may have complained that "it was bloody hard work," but, in fact, the large numbers of senior citizens backing the incumbent greatly simplified the task. Such individuals spend a disproportionate amount of time at home and are, therefore, relatively easy to locate and "capture." The hopes of Jules Legal, for one, plummeted as he witnessed Jim Walding escorting dozens of seniors into the auditorium from a rented bus.[4] One of Walding's regional lieutenants claimed to have pulled every single supporter from her district; in fact, she declared, "if the entire Walding team missed even ten potential voters, it was only because these supporters were half-dead."

The Laser team's approach to pulling their vote lay somewhere between these hands-off and hands-on extremes. Michael Stimpson had been part of a group working the phones, and David Street had organized a team of drivers. Alas, they discovered that many of Laser's recruits had only a veneer-thin interest in his cause. Their enthusiasm had ebbed sometime between the fall of 1985 (when they had purchased a membership) and 12 January 1986 (when they were asked to invest a precious Sunday afternoon listening to speeches in a hot, crowded high-school auditorium as opposed, say, to watching on television the American Football Conference title game between the Patriots and the Dolphins). Colin Trigwell, for one, was not surprised when the Laser team experienced difficulty in pulling their vote.[5] "The instant members didn't come out because they were not good NDPers. 'Here, sign a card, sign a card,' and that's the kind of people he got," Trigwell observed. "Besides, guys who were out partying the night before aren't going to get up to go to a convention. They just won't answer the fucking door." Perhaps Sig Laser should have followed the example of Jean Charest, who, two years previously had defeated a more experienced rival to secure the federal PC nomination of Sherbrooke. According to an organizer for the future Quebec premier, "We had sold cards to people who would go and vote because they'd been promised a beer bash (after the meeting)."[6]

Admittedly, the Laser candidacy did not seem blessed with an abundance of good fortune. Hugh McMeel and his wife were adamantly opposed to Walding. Both would have supported Laser, had they not relocated out of the riding seven months previously. Instead, Madeleine McMeel attended the convention as a visitor, rather than as a participant, while Hugh McMeel served as chair *cum voce sed sine suffragio* (with voice but without vote).

Later in the summer, another Laser backer, Chris Leo, likewise took himself off the voting rolls by moving outside of St. Vital. Rita Cayer, like her husband Reg, intended to vote for Laser at the meeting, but she was taken ill and could not attend.[7] Ronald Buvik had publicly endorsed Laser, but "something happened" and he "didn't make it." Wayne Farmer had happily joined the party to back Laser. But when he was called in to work as a paramedic that Sunday (at triple-overtime pay), he felt that he had little choice but to skip the meeting.

Pulling the vote for Walding that afternoon from a series of apartment buildings on St. Anne's Road were Sharon and Vic Kula. Arriving at Forester's Haven, Sharon hopped out of the van and went in search of the two Walding supporters in need of a lift. In the lobby, she met the proverbial little old lady who inquired, "Are you from Sig Laser? I am waiting for a drive from Sig Laser." Hearing that Sharon was working for Walding, the old lady volunteered, "I like Jim Walding, but the last time he came by, Val did all the talking and I didn't care for that." Sharon reassured her that the Sig Laser driver would likely be along very soon, collected the two supporters, and delivered them to Norberry School. Returning half an hour later to Forester's Haven to pick up another Walding voter, Sharon discovered the little old lady still sitting in the lobby. "I'm not very happy," she said. "Can I come with you?" "No," replied Sharon, "because you are not voting for Jim Walding," and proceeded on her appointed rounds. It was now approaching the time when registration would stop and the doors would be barred in preparation for the commencement of voting. On a hunch, Sharon had Vic swing by the Forester's Haven one final time. A very upset little old lady was still there, lamenting that it was Sunday afternoon, a time when she customarily enjoyed an "outing." "I will take you to the meeting," offered Sharon, "if you promise to vote for Mr. Walding." The old lady readily acquiesced, and they returned to Norberry School just in time. Sharon grabbed Phillip Walding and got him to sit the old lady beside a handsome buffer who was certain to talk up Jim Walding's virtues and thus prevent any potential backsliding.

Registration, which had commenced at 1:30 p.m., was proceeding apace at four tables (divided alphabetically) outside the auditorium. Members had to produce a piece of photo identification in order to receive their thin booklet of ballot papers. Since all three camps had enjoyed access to the complete membership list for the past thirty days, most eligibility challenges would already have been resolved. Still, because this was expected to be a highly contentious meeting, some key members of the provincial office (including provincial secretary Ron Cavaluce and provincial director of organization Becky Barrett) were on hand to deal with any last-minute controversies. David Woodbury, also of the provincial office and much experienced in such matters, was likewise present to serve as balloting chair.

The registration desks had a list of 749 eligible members, but nobody anticipated that many would actually show up to vote. Participation levels at Canadian nominating conventions typically range from one-third to one-half of the eligible electorate;[8] as we have seen, however, those instances in which incumbents are challenged are hardly typical, and, in fact, are generally marked by "very high turnouts."[9] Such was not the case on this occasion; only 431 St. Vital New Democrats (or 57 percent of those eligible) registered for the meeting. Put differently, 318 individuals were either unable or unwilling to employ one of the very few levers of political power available to members of a constituency association.[10]

Not just voting members crowded into the Norberry School that afternoon. Many had brought their families, and numerous kids amused themselves by climbing on and around the balcony. Realizing that their supporters were, on average, significantly younger than those of the other candidates, the Laser team had insisted on the provision of daycare facilities on site, an arrangement of which, despite their avowedly feminist sympathies, the Unwin camp was not particularly enamoured. Even so, the Laser organization would have done well also to line up a squadron of babysitters. Had they done so, the spouses of Joan Pagan, Ross Rowntree, and likely others would have been in attendance to cast votes against the incumbent.

Also present that afternoon were television, radio, and print reporters, as well as an assortment of political junkies, voyeurs, and ghouls gathered to witness the potential end to Jim Walding's political career. In addition to those acting in some official capacity at the meeting, there was an unusually large turnout from the provincial party office. President Brian O'Leary was there to deliver the financial appeal. Cliff Scotton, an éminence grise for Canadian New Democrats was also in attendance, as were Riel MLA Doreen Dodick and Richard Lewco, the NDP caucus research director. Five months previously, Lewco's name had been linked with Norma Buchan's aborted challenge in the riding. "I'm in the party's executive and EPC," Lewco had objected at the time. "I can't take sides. The information that I worked for Norma is just not true."[11] Even so, Lewko seemed unusually engaged in the affairs of St. Vital.

Backers of the three candidates from outside the riding were also crowded into the Norberry auditorium. Eleven of Gerri Unwin's friends had come out for the occasion, as had Magnus Eliason, the patriarch of the Winnipeg NDP (and possessor of six original copies of the Regina Manifesto) who was there with his wife to provide moral support for Jim Walding. One intriguing attendee that afternoon was Lloyd Schreyer. Mention has already been made of the ongoing tension in the party between the "Schreyerites" and the "Pawleyites." Many of the former group (including Sid Green, Bud Boyce, Ben Hanuschak, and Sam Uskiw) had already left the NDP on unhappy terms. Most of Walding's highly professional band of helpers (Harvey Bostrum, Glen McRuer, Dave Chomiak, and John Pimlott) were holdovers from the Schreyer era. Now, an executive assistant to Pawley was trying to take down one of the last MLAs from the Schreyer era. Under the circumstances, therefore, the presence of Ed Schreyer's distant cousin among the onlookers was unintentionally freighted with symbolism.

Conspicuously absent from the spectators that January afternoon was Howard Pawley. Rallying the troops is a key element in any party leader's job description, and Pawley did attend most of the nomination meetings in the run-up to the 1986 provincial election. The election planning committee, however, was determined to keep the premier "away from controversial nominations," and few contests fitted that description better than St. Vital.[12]

"By my presence, and in light of the views expressed by the Waldings that I was favouring Sig Laser, they would have thought my presence there was on behalf of Sig," explained Pawley. "I would have added to the temperature by being there." Perhaps, but the premier was also working on the assumption that the incumbent was likely to be toppled in any event ("Inwardly, I was expecting Walding to lose").[13] Had he thought otherwise, Pawley might have found it more difficult not to provide to Walding's challengers the sort of symbolic legitimation that his presence would have conferred.[14]

Constituency president George Schamber called the meeting to order at 2:35 p.m. and promptly turned the chairmanship over to Hugh McMeel. As per standard operating procedure, the agenda was approved and Ron Cavaluce outlined the protocols for voting (support of 50 percent plus one necessary for election) and for speeches (limit of twenty minutes for each candidate[15] and a predetermined speaking order of Walding, Laser, and Unwin). There would be no invocations of prayer ("Dear Lord in Heaven, help the Social Crediters to success and put their monetary reforms across"[16]) and Jim Walding, Sig Laser, and Gerri Unwin were very visibly in attendance (although "in some parts of Canada even the presence of the candidates at the convention has, in the past, been considered bad form"[17]).

Walding's estrangement from local activists had led to an unusual strategic dilemma: who could he get to place his name in nomination? He ultimately settled on Larry Small, a neighbour who had not been a member of the party until recruited by Walding earlier in the fall. Ironically, Small's only prior political exposure had occurred during the height of the bell-ringing episode when an enterprising *Winnipeg Free Press* reporter had toured the district seeking some "neighbourly advice" for the Speaker. "I can't say what Jim should do because I'm not him," Small had suggested. "But if it were me, I would take a strong hand in the issue and force the legislature to act because it's gone on too long."[18] Small was sufficiently out of the loop that he was uncertain why Walding was even being challenged. Even though it "felt odd" to

Small ("I had a gut feeling: 'Why me?'"), it was still an honour to be asked to nominate Walding. Small agreed, thinking it was a simple matter of standing up in an auditorium and stating, "I nominate Jim Walding." Instead, he was told that he had to write a brief speech and clear it ahead of time with the Walding camp. Small's wife, Catherine, and parents also joined the party and came along to provide moral support, although Catherine's presence was in doubt when one of the couple's children came down with chicken pox. The Walding organization, however, secured a babysitter and thus ensured four votes for the incumbent. A former teacher, Small delivered what he considered to have been "a very organized speech" detailing Walding's history and accomplishments and sat down to listen to his neighbour.

Of the three candidates, Jim Walding was by far the most experienced public speaker. Nevertheless, he seemed nervous as he took to the high stage in Norberry auditorium, and his speech, by all accounts, was shaky and uninspired. Perhaps anxious to dispel the image of being "yesterday's man," Walding spoke of the need for educational research and a more effective adaptation to technological change. Worthy concerns certainly, but a not unfriendly George Schamber concluded that Walding's address "was not much of a crowd pleaser," and there was some low murmuring in the auditorium as he spoke. Even the incumbent's nominator, Larry Small, was unimpressed with Walding's speech, finding it to be "a rambling effort," that was not "well-organized or forceful."

Walding's halting performance may not have been as damaging as his backers initially feared. Most of those in the Norberry auditorium had made up their minds well in advance of the meeting and were not hanging intently on every word of the speeches.[19] In fact, it has been shown, at least with respect to Canadian leadership conventions, that those who are late coming to a decision will often cast a sympathy ballot.[20] With Walding manifestly unwell that January afternoon (the incumbent was variously described as "shaken and exhausted," "failing," and looking "as if he was going to faint"), his poor performance at the podium may have perversely played to his advantage.[21]

Next up was Sig Laser. His nominator, Jules Legal, called on the assembled voters to nominate "a candidate in tune with the philosophy and policies of the New Democratic Party," someone who could "command the respect of colleagues in Government." By implication, but only by implication, these attributes were lacking in the incumbent. After seconder Heather Hunter praised him as "a superior candidate," Laser spoke of the need to re-energize the constituency association ("Let's be clear about it—there was cause for concern") and denied that the nomination tussle had fractured the community ("Quite frankly, friends, there wasn't much left to divide"). Laser did not, however, make any direct references to what he perceived to be the shortcomings of the incumbent. After emphasizing his fealty to traditional social democratic goals (job security, public housing, rent controls, and the like), Laser alluded to the potentially sensitive topic of his "experience in the premier's constituency office." Implying that he had powerful friends at court, Laser called upon the members to "make sure St. Vital gets its fair share of those government programs. I think our community centres and our daycare centres would quickly feel the positive effects."[22] Of the three candidate addresses, Laser's may have been marginally the best. "Sig's a good speaker," acknowledged Colin Trigwell. "After the speeches, I thought Sig was going to win."

Last to speak was Gerri Unwin. She came to the podium after both her mover, Jack Rodie, and seconder, Monica Girouard, emphasized her extensive service record to the party and community. Unwin talked of a life-long commitment to social democracy, of being raised by CCF-minded grandparents from the Isle of Man after her mother died when she was only three years old,[23] and of her continuing fealty to NDP goals (including pointed references to daycare, spousal abuse, and pay equity). Unwin was certainly "composed" on stage, but seemed, from Michael Stimpson's perspective, to be taking "great pains at enunciating her words." It was, acknowledged Colin Trigwell, "a rookie speech"; Unwin did "hit some great points," but overall, it was "not as dynamic" as he would have liked.

——————

From the podium, neither Sig Laser nor Gerri Unwin had specifically highlighted Jim Walding's failures as an MLA. To be sure, there were oblique references to constituency association health and NDP unity, but to an ordinary member, completely detached from the day-to-day affairs of the party, such allusions would not have resonated. As a result, many Walding loyalists were still puzzled that their man was being challenged at all. According to a Laser worker, "What is this all about?" and "What did Jim do?" were common refrains among the "aggrieved" backers of the incumbent. Arguably, Laser and Unwin should have run edgier campaigns; had they done so, all members would at least have been forced consciously to confront whether Jim Walding's performance over the preceding five years merited renomination.[24]

During the speeches, Gil Mignot experienced an epiphany. As a hydro lineman whose union had subsidized one month of his time every election, Mignot had been in charge of constructing, installing, repairing, and replacing Walding's campaign signs almost from the outset. In 1977, Mignot was described as "Just a good solid person—very reliable" in a confidential assessment of his work; in fact, acknowledged his campaign supervisor, Mignot had been "out checking signs at 7:30–8:00 a.m. when I was still in bed!"[25] Mignot had every reason to have developed a strong affective bond with his candidate; after one particularly tense evening watching the returns trickle in, Mignot had embraced an emotionally distraught Walding when victory had finally been secured. Now the incumbent was counting on the fact that Mignot was still "very reliable." As Mignot recalled, Walding had come to his house and said, "Gil, make sure you bring those people in. You know, Gil, I have got to have my pension. I need to win one more election." Mignot had brought "those people in," ferrying several loads of Walding supporters to the Norberry School. But as he looked around the auditorium, he realized that none of his long-standing constituency friends were backing the incumbent, and suddenly he "got the light." When Unwin had finished talking, Gil Mignot—as he recollected—sat down at the back of the hall next to Tannis Laser and said, "Denise [his wife] is up there, but I'm voting for Sig."

After the speeches, George Schamber took a seat beside Gerri Unwin. As constituency president, Schamber had decided on a policy of strict neutrality and he advised Unwin not to interpret his proximity as a signal of favouritism. Nevertheless, in the noise and confusion of a crowded nomination hall, Schamber's choice of seatmates could have provided the sort of visual cue more commonly seen at national leadership conventions. When these work, such as Flora MacDonald's 1976 walk to meet Joe Clark on the PC convention floor (described as "slow, regal, and firm, sad yet proud"[26]), they can be quite evocative. Indeed, John Courtney has argued that such symbolic gestures "are often the safest and fastest way of transmitting information to the delegates."[27] Alas, these signals are easily botched, as when Jean Chrétien steadfastly refused to don Eugene Whelan's trademark green Stetson[28] or when Wallace McCutcheon proudly put his Robert Stanfield sticker on sideways[29] or when Michael Wilson and Peter Pocklington could not find the proper stairway to the Brian Mulroney box. "My God," breathed an agitated Mila Mulroney, "Michael's going somewhere else."[30] Worse yet, for an ostensibly "safe" mode of communication, such visual cues are dangerously vulnerable to manipulation. David Fulton's semi-private endorsement of Robert Stanfield in 1967 was soon transformed when the Nova Scotia premier "moved over to clasp Fulton's hand and seal the bond which Fulton apparently never intended to offer."[31] Two national Tory leadership conventions on, Brian Mulroney executed a similar gambit when he stationed himself near the officially neutral John Crosbie in the stands and "deviously made a polite wave become a handshake and then a grasp, as if an endorsement, all for the sake of the cameras."[32] Perhaps Unwin should have taken advantage of Schamber's seat selection; an apparent endorsement from the constituency's elder statesman might well have swayed a few undecided voters.

Over the years, Peter Nolan had canvassed during elections, organized surveys between votes, and generally "worked his butt off for Jim Walding." When Unwin and Laser had entered the race, Walding had come to Nolan's home complaining that they were "trying to get rid of me after fifteen years" and urging, "We have to get something going, Pete." Nolan had thrown himself into the campaign with his customary gusto. That morning, he had been one of the Walding team's drivers and now he was trying to persuade anyone who would listen that "nobody in the constituency knew Sig or Gerri, but you could run a dog with a Jim Walding sign on it, and the dog would win." As the first ballot was being counted, Nolan was approached by another Walding driver, a local family lawyer. Everyone had been issued a booklet of multicoloured paper slips upon registration; voting entailed detaching a ballot of the designated hue, writing down the candidate's name, and depositing it in the ballot box. The lawyer, however, had merely marked his coloured slip and dropped the entire booklet in the box (thus disqualifying him from participating in any subsequent ballots). Now he was wondering what he should do. Nolan glared at his hapless co-worker, shouted, "You're a fucking idiot," and stalked off.

After the ballots had been taken away to be counted, chairman McMeel introduced Wilson Parasiuk, minister of energy and mines with responsibility for the *Manitoba Hydro Act*, as guest speaker. In 1973, Gerri Unwin had served as Parasiuk's official agent in Riel, and in 1981 Parasiuk had secured the cabinet position that, after his successful stint as Hydro critic, Walding had assumed would be his. Parasiuk regarded Walding with neither affection nor respect, considering him to be the "weakest and laziest person" he had ever met. During the 1979 session, Walding had purportedly confided to his fellow backbenchers during a lull in the House's business: "This is a wonderful day for me. I now qualify for my pension." To Parasiuk, this remark betrayed an entirely inappropriate perspective on the purposes of political activism, and Walding's inexplicable absence from the emergency meeting at the Fort Garry Hotel during the 1981 campaign had solidified Parasiuk's view. Being asked to serve as guest speaker by the St. Vital association struck Parasiuk as "passing strange," since he did not "hang out with Jim Walding at all and had been very upset with him." Nevertheless, Parasiuk agreed and gave a lengthy analysis of Manitoba's improving economic prospects and a spirited attack on the sins of the national government. After all, someone had to serve as guest speaker and "nobody else wanted to go because they knew it was bound to be a contentious meeting."

During Parasiuk's speech, key members of the Unwin camp were caucusing. The large turnout and the response to the speeches had convinced them not only that they were running last and would soon be eliminated, but also that neither Walding nor Laser had enough support to secure a first-ballot victory. Accordingly, Unwin would soon be confronted with a momentous decision. At Canadian leadership conventions, it is the norm for eliminated candidates to signal their preference for one of those still in the hunt.[33] The case of Sinclair Stevens is typical. When he withdrew and supported Joe Clark after finishing a disappointing seventh on the first ballot of the PC national leadership convention in 1976, he gave no thought to receding quietly into the stands of the Ottawa Civic Centre. According to Stevens, "a withdrawing candidate ought to name his own preference publicly. It was consistent with any candidate's pretensions to leadership that he try to lead, even as his own cause faltered."[34] Yet no such norm has emerged with respect to Canadian nominating conventions, and Unwin's first inclination was to give no signal whatsoever.

Nevertheless, the Unwin camp began carefully to consider their options.

As Parasiuk rambled on about the iniquitous Mulroney administration (closing a research station in Gimli, trying to de-index pensions, not funding infrastructure in Winnipeg, cutting transfer payments, and the like), Laser worker Jim Bardy spotted two elderly women wearing "Laser" buttons leaving the high school. Giving chase, Bardy caught up with them in the street and beseeched them to stay around for a likely second ballot. The two women (Barb Perkin and Verna Sinclair) had both been recruited by the Laser campaign. In fact, Perkin was the regular care provider for the Laser's two young children, and, to this day, is still close to the family (the Laser kids continue to receive birthday cards from "Gramma Barb"). Although Perkin had not previously been active politically, she was quite prepared to take out a senior's membership "on behalf of the party she loosely supported and the guy whose kids she took care of." Alas, late Sunday afternoon was Barb and Verna's regular time to play bingo, and, despite repeated entreaties, they could not be induced to return to the auditorium. Instead, they thrust their two ballot booklets at Bardy and left. Placing the unmarked voting slips in his pocket, Bardy returned to Norberry High School.

———

Across the hall, Colin Trigwell was intently watching the door to the counting room. The Unwin scrutineer, Diane Hitchings, had taken a coloured ribbon with her. If Unwin was still in the race, Hitchings planned to enter the auditorium wearing the ribbon; if Unwin had been eliminated, no ribbon would be visible. After what seemed like an inordinately long time, the door opened and the balloting party filed out. As Trigwell had feared, there was no sign of a ribbon. Now the Unwin camp would have a difficult choice to make.

Manitoba NDP secretary Ron Cavaluce had, at last, been given the results of the first ballot, and he took to the stage to make the announcement. There had been 430 votes cast; the magic number to secure a first-ballot victory, therefore, was 216. The results were:

Walding: 163
Laser: 136
Unwin: 129
Spoiled: 2

After the tumult had died down, Cavaluce declared that there would be another vote, but inadvertently instructed the crowd to mark their pink ballot slip for the second round with either "Unwin" or "Walding." Cavaluce corrected his gaffe shortly thereafter ("Laser" or "Walding"), but some confusion remained.

———

The results of the first ballot must have been disappointing to Sig Laser. He had, after all, sold 330 new memberships and enjoyed, as well, a smattering of support from St. Vital New Democrats of longer standing. Yet Laser had received only 136 votes (or something less than 40 percent of his potential electorate). Given that the overall participation rate that afternoon was 57 percent, it is apparent that, between them, the Walding and Unwin camps had been roughly twice as successful in getting their voters out to Norberry School. Unwin's team may have despaired of her unwillingness to drag reluctant supporters to the polls (and there were undoubtedly some who could and should have been "pulled"), but relying on the personal attachment of friends and neighbours had left her just eight votes short of advancing to a decisive final ballot.

The irony is that neither Walding nor Laser could have defeated Unwin in a simple showdown. Irrespective of his efforts to get out from under the premier's long shadow, Laser was doomed to be regarded as a Pawley surrogate. Thus, at least some of the bad blood that had developed since the 1981 campaign between Pawley and Walding was transfused to Laser and Walding. As the more consensual figure, Unwin was perfectly situated to capture either the "anybody-but-Walding" sentiment of the Laser team or the "anybody-but-Laser" conviction of the Walding camp. Jim Mochoruk has confirmed that, had Unwin beat Laser for second spot, "all of Sig's supporters would have gone to Gerri." And, Unwin recalls, she surveyed the crowd before delivering her speech, "thinking of all these Jim supporters that were sitting out there and [realizing] that if he didn't win on the first ballot that maybe they would support me." Yet as John Crosbie had discovered three years previously at the PC national leadership convention, being everyone's second choice is of no consequence if you are unable to squeeze into the final showdown. Laser's seven-vote lead after the opening ballot almost certainly cost Unwin the nomination.

Now she had to make a decision. Would she publicly endorse one of the two remaining candidates? After a brief deliberation, Unwin confirmed her original impulse. She would remain officially neutral on the final ballot. At Canadian leadership conventions, those eliminated candidates who have declined to signal a preference to their supporters seemingly have had a variety of motivations. Some have been merely paralyzed by their failures,[35] others have been moved by more pragmatic considerations,[36] while some candidates who remain neutral after their elimination from the contest have seemed genuinely to be animated by honourable motivations.[37] Brian Mulroney's aloofness after being eliminated on the third ballot of the 1976 PC leadership contest illustrates that these widely differing motivations can easily coexist. At the forefront, of course, was Mulroney's vaunted ambition. "I'm not going to be king-maker," he pronounced. "I'm going to be king."[38] As well, Mulroney was aware that his delegates would likely cleave on ethnic lines, irrespective of his endorsement. Moreover, Mulroney held a personal grudge against front-runner Claude Wagner. In the nasty trench warfare at Quebec delegate selection meetings, a Wagner slate had been organized to deny Mulroney delegate status in his own constituency; thus, when Wagner emissary Roch LaSalle approached Mulroney before the final ballot, he was brusquely reminded that Mulroney "had no vote to deliver."[39] On the other hand, Mulroney was also anxious "to avoid the appearance of screwing anybody." After all, recounted Mulroney: "If I supported Clark openly, it would have looked like a conspiracy against a French-Canadian."[40] Given that Mulroney himself had felt victimized by an anybody-but-Brian coalition (famously dubbed by CBC television reporter Charlotte Gobeil as a "gang-bang" by the other candidates),[41] it is no surprise that Mulroney sat on his hands during the final ballot.

So it was with Gerri Unwin. She, too, was being cross-pressured by a confusing mixture of motivations. On the one hand, she had entered the contest explicitly to oust the incumbent and she was still aware "that some might have seen the need to get rid of Jim Walding" as the top priority, so a visible shift in his direction was effectively ruled out. On the other hand, unlike many on the executive, Unwin harboured no malice towards the incumbent; "Gerri didn't want to hurt Jim," recalled George Schamber. As well, Unwin's negative affect towards Sig Laser and his campaign seemed to preclude a move to his side. "I wouldn't have done that," confirmed Unwin, "because I don't think I would have promoted Sig." One Unwin confidante spoke of a "personal grudge" between the two challengers, while, more diplomatically, a second observed that "Sig and Gerri were not the type to hold hands."

From Unwin's perspective, it was Laser who had been a late entry into the race, it was Laser who had prevented a woman from securing St. Vital for the NDP, it was Laser who had been oblivious to the need for years of involvement in the constituency before seeking nomination, it was Laser who symbolized the heavy hand of central office control, and it was Laser whose recruitment and canvassing practices had seemed both personally offensive and contrary to party traditions.

One final factor was at play in Unwin's decision to stay officially neutral. Understandably, she also had political ambitions to safeguard. Colin Trigwell recalled telling Unwin, even before the first-ballot results had been released, "You have got to think of your future, Gerri. We didn't work this hard not to run again, and the worst thing we could do is not run again. If Sig gets in, you are not going to have a chance again." Looking at Jim Walding, however, it was impossible to imagine that, win or lose, he would seek the NDP nomination in St. Vital for a seventh time. A Laser operative retrospectively agreed that it was "not bad logic" to assert, "Well, Walding will never hurt us as much as Sig." At least one of Unwin's confidantes, however, was horrified by such talk. "I was very disillusioned," she recalled. "I thought Gerri was in the race entirely for idealistic reasons. I was very upset."

She was not the only one distressed by what was unfolding in the chaotic interval between the two ballots. Except for those such as Jim Bardy, who mistakenly believed that Unwin had endorsed his man,[42] most members of the Laser team were flabbergasted by her inaction. "I was surprised and disappointed that Gerri didn't declare for Sig," observed Jim Mochoruk. "Everyone should have seen that both candidates were better alternatives than Jim Walding." Not surprisingly, Sig Laser's feelings on the subject are even stronger: "We assumed she would naturally, visibly throw her support. But she didn't; she made no move at all. She let her people do whatever they wanted to do. Did nothing herself to validate the entire effort. Our previous discussions, the campaign mine, the campaign hers, did nothing to finish it off, did nothing, just said: 'Well, they'll vote however they'll vote.' Just did nothing."

Well, not quite nothing. Unwin and her key advisers still had to decide what to do on the second ballot. Almost to a person, they opted to back Jim

Walding. Although Unwin herself is somewhat hazy on her recollection ("If I voted, I'm sure I would have voted for Jim"), several of her confidantes confirmed that she had, in fact, backed the incumbent. Unwin did not declare her preference, noted Colin Trigwell, "But she voted for Jim ... what we did do then was work with the executive board. I met with the executive that were on our side. I feel that it was pretty well all of them [who voted for Jim]. They were a tight group."

Thus, constituency stalwarts Aurore and Ed Sawka moved from Unwin to Walding; "he was already our MLA," they rationalized. "We decided to give him another chance." Likewise, Diane Hitchings recalled, "I talked with Gerri between ballots and I decided to vote for Walding. Gerri said she would not support anyone publicly, but privately indicated she was going with Walding. I wouldn't go against Gerri."

This movement to Walding among most members of Unwin's inner circle was effectively subterranean. Twenty years on, neither of the other two candidates was aware of what had taken place. According to Val Walding, Unwin had "probably told all her people to vote for Sig." As for Laser, the revelation that Unwin had voted for Walding brought him up short: "I never thought of that. That doesn't add to my sense of the day. It just makes me wonder what the whole damn thing was about."

With the second ballot about to get underway, the Laser camp had a brief strategy session. Jim Bardy removed the voting slips of Barb Perkin and Verna Sinclair from his pocket. Amazingly, something similar had occurred to David Street, and he produced two further sets of ballots. What were they to do with these four booklets? They had been obtained neither by force nor by fraud, and the original owners had intended them to be used in support of Sig Laser. Actually casting these votes would require only a modicum of manual dexterity. As the ballot boxes were passed along the rows, palming a number of slips prior to placing them in a box would have been relatively straightforward. Nor would the deception leave any trace, as the ballots had been legitimately issued to registered voters, and in the confusion it would have been impossible to ascertain through a head count how many members had decamped. In fact, one month previously at the NDP nomination meeting in Ste. Rose, 306 ballots had been cast, despite there having been only 298 eligible members in attendance;[43] even then, the result had stood. At the time, Bardy and Street were regarded as something akin to outlaws by the provincial party establishment; Colin Trigwell, for one, did not consider them to be a "legitimate" crew. "Bardy and Street would not do anything with the party," Trigwell recalled. "They stayed away from the party and did their own thing." On this occasion at least, they kept to the straight and narrow path: "We didn't stuff them," recalled Bardy. "We did not try and get other people to place them for us. It's something that's always bothered me. Of course, the votes were ineligible, but I would be less than honest if I said it never happens. It happens. It's not that hard to do, but we didn't do it and we didn't try to do it." The four ballots remained uncast—and Sig Laser still has them (see Figure 6).

Figure 6: Unused Second-Ballot Slips, 12 January 1986[44]

Active in the civil rights and anti-Vietnam War movements of the 1960s, Carol and Jay Goldstein emigrated from San Francisco shortly thereafter and joined the Manitoba NDP as "philosophical socialists." Neither had been particularly active members of the party, and although Carol knew Gerri Unwin as "a nice person" from frequent meetings at the St. Vital Library and Jay liked Sig Laser's persona (he "came across as very enthusiastic, young, inexperienced and sincere"), neither had arrived at the meeting committed to any particular candidate. Such indecision had put them very much in the minority that January afternoon. Tom Brook has estimated that an "undecided factor of even 10% would be high for most nominating conventions," since any member who is still unsure by voting day will generally just stay away from the meeting.[45] After listening to the speeches, the Goldsteins had plumped for Sig Laser on the first ballot. Yet now Jay was having second thoughts as he considered which candidate was more likely to hold St. Vital for the NDP. Walding, after all, "had a track record, while Sig was a young fellow without too much experience." Her husband's vacillation before casting his second ballot alarmed both Carol and the woman sitting to her other side, and they jointly importuned Jay not to switch his vote. Their pleading was to no avail. "When it came to the crunch," Jay recalled, "I went against my personal feelings and voted for Walding. I decided to play it safe and go with the proven candidate and not take a chance with the neophyte."

———

Walding's long-time sign man, Gil Mignot, may have defected before the first ballot, but his wife, Denise, would not be so easily swayed. "I had given my word to Jim in the front hall of our house that I would vote for him," recalled Denise. Still, she was reluctant to advertise her loyalties by putting on a "Walding" button, knowing that she would come under pressure from those anxious to oust the sitting MLA. Yet button or no, Denise was not going to escape being lobbied. Gil was still sitting at the back of the auditorium, while Denise was at the front with her sister, her brother-in-law, and three others, all five of whom were intending to back Laser on the second ballot. Denise recalls that they importuned her, "Don't vote for Jim; don't be crazy." Her reply ("But I gave my word") was recognized by friends and family alike as the final word on the matter. "Oh shit," muttered her brother-in-law. Denise Mignot would support Jim Walding on the second ballot.

———

116

After casting his second ballot, one Laser backer realized that the result was likely to be close. He could easily have recruited a friend to come and vote for Laser. Why had he not done so? Perhaps, he reflected, his enthusiasm for the cause had been significantly dampened when he saw Tannis Laser behind the wheel of a car with a pro-choice bumper sticker.

The two contenders were now a study in contrasts. Sig Laser, by all reports, appeared composed and assured. Admittedly, Laser had been concerned not only by his surprisingly meagre vote tally in the first round, but also by Gerri Unwin's unexpected failure to endorse his candidacy. Even so, he was only twenty-seven votes adrift of Walding heading into the showdown, and there seemed to be obvious parallels between the incumbent's situation and that which had faced Joe Clark three years earlier in his doomed attempt to succeed himself as national PC leader. Clark, like Walding, had been well ahead after the first ballot, but had already tapped into all of those who might, at any stage, have been inclined to provide support. With no growth potential, Clark had been inexorably overtaken by Brian Mulroney on the final round. Was not Jim Walding now confronting a similar circumstance? Had not Unwin's 129 backers already decided that the incumbent had to be replaced? Even aware of the dangers of hubris, Laser nonetheless found himself saying, "I think Walding's toast."

Judging from his appearance, the incumbent seemed to have arrived at the same conclusion. Already shaky at the outset, Walding's condition had visibly worsened over the course of the afternoon. To friend and foe alike, Walding appeared very unwell. One observer noted that Walding looked "terrible, as white as a sheet," a second suggested that the incumbent appeared "wan and haggard, with no colour in his face," and a third summarized his condition as "catatonic." One newspaper account related that, for "most of the meeting," Walding was "clutching his wife's arm and wringing his hands."[46] Denise Mignot stayed loyal to the incumbent, but from his pallor, she deduced that Walding "thought he was losing the convention," an impression confirmed by confidante Elizabeth Dotremont, who provided both emotional and physical support throughout the wait for the results of the second ballot. Indeed, Dotremont's partner, former MLA Harvey Bostrum, was to be ribbed the following day for "working to get a guy elected who couldn't even stand up on his own." Concerned that Walding was about to have a stroke, Dotrement expended much of her energies in shielding the beleaguered incumbent from Winnipeg's paparazzi.

———

Jim Bardy was awaiting the results of the second round when he was approached by another Laser backer. It was too bad, noted the newcomer, that a woman backing Laser had lost her voting slips and had been unable to participate in the second ballot. Bardy was dumbfounded. "No one told us!" he recollected in exasperation. "I would have given her one of the extra ballot books. I wouldn't stuff it through some other method, but I would have given it to her in a second. Of course, it didn't happen."

———

Heading into the counting room, Glen McRuer, the Walding scrutineer, had shot a look that Val interpreted as saying, "This is going to be very tight." And so it turned out to be. The ballots, which had been collected in several boxes, were dumped into the centre of a large table and then separated by David Woodbury of the provincial office into three piles: Laser, Walding, and spoiled. This was, by all reports, not a contentious exercise. Yet at least a few of the remarkably high total of eleven spoiled ballots must have occasioned some discussion, especially those featuring an ostensibly indecipherable scrawl. According to Fred Zastre, the Laser scrutineer, these "could have been from some kid scribbling on a piece of paper." Zastre acknowledges that he was "very jittery," but maintains that nothing untoward got by him ("I was like a hawk on it"). Zastre was, however, relatively inexperienced (having been recently recruited by David Street to assist in the Wolseley constituency). In contrast, Glen McRuer was an experienced and tough political operative who was always going to be an effective advocate for his candidate's interests. "Glen McRuer has substantial force of will," claims one of his acquaintances. "He is not someone to be taken lightly." As it turned out, Woodbury's decisions on vote validity were not appealed by either scrutineer. With the issue of spoiled ballots effectively resolved, the two piles of valid votes could now be counted. And counted again. And counted a third time.

———

As the time crawled on, the crowd became understandably restive. On several occasions, chairman McMeel dispatched someone to the counting room to get a progress report. On each instance, the same reply came back; the result was close, and they were being very careful to get it right. "It's coming, it's coming," McMeel assured the agitated members. "Just be patient."[47]

———

As part of his stance of official neutrality, president George Schamber had not participated in either ballot. Schamber realized that the results were likely to be exceedingly close and believed that he might be called upon to cast the deciding vote. Schamber was, he recalled, profoundly uncertain as to his preferred outcome:

> I would have voted for Gerri Unwin if she had been on the final ballot, and there had been a tie. But the final choice was between Jim and Sig. I might have been tempted to follow the Speaker's rule and vote for the continuation of debate and, therefore, vote for Jim. On the other hand, I knew the writing was on the wall. I was unhappy with Jim's speech and I knew the party was unhappy with Jim and I am a party man. Jim had been a true constituency man, but he wasn't well and he had a wife who was nattering all the time. Over the years, Jim had asked his friends in the constituency to lobby Pawley to put him in the cabinet, but he never asked me because he knew I was a party man. On the other hand, Sig was young and egotistical. He was not then an easy person to like, although he has mellowed in recent years. And Sig had taken advantage of being in the premier's office; some would say that he could take time off to campaign for the nomination whenever he liked. So I really don't know how I would have voted.

———

In fact, Schamber was likely mistaken about the tie-breaking procedure; chairman McMeel was unaware that Schamber had not voted and, in any case, he would have broken a tie by calling either for an entirely new round of voting or, if too many members had already decamped, for an entirely new meeting.

———

Finally, the door to the counting room opened, and the balloting committee walked out. Everyone had a grey, ashen appearance. Fred Zastre, the Laser scrutineer, recalled Dave Olinyk, "looked like someone had beaten him up." Olinyk also managed to catch the eye of his friend, Glen McRuer, the Walding scrutineer. When McRuer gave him a half-wink ("somewhere between a wink and a twitch"), Olinyk knew their man had won. With Val Walding, who was waiting anxiously in the aisle, McRuer was more direct; he smiled and held up one finger. Val hastened back to her husband and whispered the news in his ear, but Walding felt no elation, only "a sort of relief."

Fred Zastre was likewise spreading the word discreetly. He found Jim Bardy and whispered, "One vote." Bardy looked at him in shock and Zastre reiterated, "We lost by one vote." Bardy then had the unhappy task of going over to where Sig Laser, David Street, and Jules Legal were sitting together. "It's one vote," Bardy said. "They recounted. It's not there."

———

On stage, Ron Cavaluce had finally been given by the balloting committee a piece of paper containing the second-round vote breakdown. As per established protocol, however, Cavaluce merely announced that Jim Walding had secured the nomination without releasing the actual vote totals. It mattered not. Besieged by the media, Fred Zastre blurted out the final numbers: 203 for Walding, 202 for Laser, eleven spoiled ballots. "I counted it twice, to be sure," added Zastre.[48] Like a tsunami, the news quickly engulfed the auditorium.

———

In the bedlam that followed, one Laser worker started shouting at a pair of executive members who he (correctly) divined had switched from Unwin to

Walding on the decisive ballot. Another Laser supporter, perhaps fearing from his choice of seatmates that the president had abandoned his stance of neutrality, accosted George Schamber and demanded proof that he had not participated in either ballot. Schamber calmly pulled from his pocket an unused booklet of voting slips.

———

Carol Goldstein turned to her husband: "See, Jay. It's your vote."

———

Sharon Kula thought, "Ah ha, that little old lady."

———

In the noise and confusion, a delighted Dave Olinyk was able to pick out both of the defeated challengers. To his eyes, "Sig looked shell-shocked," while "Gerri looked happy."[49]

———

As the results sank in, Sig Laser realized that he would not be reading his acceptance speech. In it, he had intended to thank his opponents: "Mrs. Unwin" and (the Hydra-headed candidate) "Mr. and Mrs. Walding," who by their "dedicated participation" had shown themselves "to be loyal New Democrats." Laser had also planned to express his gratitude to his wife, to his nominator, to his workers, and to David Street for having "always insisted on an upfront and dignified process." That particular speech was doomed to remain in Laser's pocket, and he moved (seconded by Gerri Unwin) that Jim Walding's nomination be made unanimous. "I am nothing," noted Laser subsequently, "if not the loyalist." The agenda called for the delivery of the "candidate's acceptance speech"; this address, in which the victor customarily acknowledges the contributions of the vanquished and invites them to make common cause against partisan enemies, can be a crucial "vehicle for healing."[50] Walding, however, was in no condition to offer same. Instead, the meeting adjourned.

The nine accredited members of the local media now swarmed the principal players. Sig Laser had regained his equanimity. "Gerri and I are both long-time executive members and it was time for both of us to run," he observed. "It was time for a contest." Ron Cavaluce rejected suggestions that the party brass had been anxious to replace Walding. "I think that's false," insisted Cavaluce between clenched teeth. "I think the (challenge) is very healthy and I think it's super."[51] As for the winner, he agreed that many voters wanted him out ("I won't argue with you"), and his only comment to the news that he had triumphed by a single vote was an enigmatic "Really?"[52] Walding denied that he had been stunned by the strength of Laser's challenge: "Stunned was not the right reaction. I saw it coming. But the tension of such an afternoon is really tremendous and the strain was beginning to tell on me. We've been working all along to get the nomination on the first ballot, that was our intention but it didn't work out that way."[53] Finally, Walding warned observers against the tendency to count him out. Paraphrasing Mark Twain, he declared, "In '71, I wasn't expected to win the election. In '73, St. Vital was written off. In '77, they said it was gone and in '81, the same sort of thing was said. The reports of my political demise are greatly exaggerated."[54] Greatly exaggerated, indeed.

Jim Walding at Election Victory Party, 1971. *Winnipeg Tribune*, 6 April 1971. (UMASC)

Your St. Vital New Democrat, Jim Walding, will continue to work with Ed Schreyer on matters of concern to you and your neighbours.

An MLA does not become familiar with the rules of the Legislature and government procedures quickly. Jim has experienced your government firsthand. He has served as the Chairman of House Standing Committees. He has spoken to your government for you.

Re-hire Jim Walding as your MLA.
Re-hire Ed Schreyer as your Premier.

Jim Walding Campaign Pamphlet, 1973. (AM)

Jim Walding and Ed Schreyer, from Jim Walding Campaign Pamphlet, 1977. (AM)

Howard Pawley with his wife Adele after winning the NDP leadership in 1979. (UMASC)

For ten years, the people of the St. Vital - Norwood community have trusted Jim Walding.

- **Jim Walding lives here . . . with us.**
  Jim, Val, and the family live at 26 Hemlock Place.

- **Jim Walding works here . . . for us.**
  Jim listens to his constituents and things get done.

- **Jim Walding speaks for us . . . in the legislature.**
  Chairman – NDP Caucus
  Chairman – Public Accounts Committee
  Opposition Spokesman – Hydro & Telephones

In ten years of service as Ombudsman to his constituents, Jim has received thousands of letters and phone calls. He has developed the knowledge, experience, and contacts to deal promptly with a wide range of problems. A proven investment in representation can continue to benefit the people of St. Vital and all Manitobans.

An Enviable Reputation for Service, Stability, and Responsibility.

Jim WALDING

Jim Walding Campaign Pamphlet, 1981. (AM)

Jim Walding, Speaker's Portrait. (AM)

Sig Laser Campaign Pamphlet, 1985.

The three candidates: Gerri Unwin, Sig Laser, and Jim Walding. *Winnipeg Sun*, 12 January 1986.

An anxious Jim Walding, together with wife Val (right) and supporter
Elizabeth Dotremont, awaits results of second ballot at St. Vital NDP
nominating meeting on 12 January 1986. (*Winnipeg Free Press*)

Jim Walding remains seated when members of the legislature are asked to stand to vote against a non-confidence motion on the Pawley government's budget, 8 March 1988. (*Winnipeg Free Press*)

Jim Walding, on 11 March 1988, meets reporters for the first time after the non-confidence vote. (*Winnipeg Free Press*)

6

The Aftermath

LATER THAT EVENING, the victor and the vanquished hosted markedly different gatherings for their workers. Sig Laser had rented the Glenwood Community Centre for the day. Prior to the meeting, it had served as the staging point for the camp's drivers, while afterwards, rather than the anticipated victory celebration, it was the locale for something akin to a wake. All in attendance (including members of the party brass and one of Pawley's aides) were attempting, in Jim Bardy's words, to ensure "that Sig wasn't going to go a little bit screwy." Inevitably, the search began for a scapegoat. But when Michael Stimpson began to remonstrate against Gerri Unwin's perfidy, he was brought up short by David Street. Had Stimpson not noticed that some people he had been expected to get to the meeting had not, in fact, been present? Nor was Stimpson alone in this failing. Laser himself pulled from his pocket a couple of names of people who had needed a ride to Norberry School, but who had been overlooked in the hubbub.[1] As for Jules Legal, he made the distressing discovery that eighteen was not the age of majority for the New Democratic Party.[2] Two decades on, it is obvious that the oversight still rankles: "I didn't know that, and my daughter had just turned sixteen. Shit. She was born on March 4, 1969. She would have been eligible, and I had no idea. I thought it was eighteen, the same as the regular voting age. Oh Lordy, Lordy. That one blew me away. That's awful." Anxious to provide moral support to her father, sixteen-year old Paula Legal had actually spent the day at the Norberry School, but as a non-voting visitor, rather than as an enfranchised member. It also came out that Joe and Jeannette Zakaluk (and their son Brad), friends of the Lasers who lived only two doors down, had not been in attendance. Tannis Laser's sister had at least tried to pull them out, but they simply could not be bothered. As Tannis has sardonically observed, "all our friendships are cemented by guilt." In fact, the candidate's wife had her own feelings of remorse. "If you are looking for the one vote, it was me," she recently observed. "We had two young children, and I would say to Sig: 'Could you please wait until the kids are down in bed before you go out canvassing?' I was the one vote." There was, in short, more than enough guilt to go around.

One might have anticipated that the mood at the Walding house that evening would have been markedly more upbeat. In fact, anger was the dominant emotion among the incumbent's inner circle. "Everyone was very stressed," recalled one confidante. "It was a very sombre mood: tense and wound up. Everyone was relieved, but also disappointed, since we had hoped for a bigger victory. For Jim, even winning by one vote was a shock; he felt unappreciated." Only those on the periphery of the Walding camp, such as Larry Small and his wife, were able unabashedly to revel in their team's victory. For those at the core, by contrast, there may have been a grim satisfaction at having "pulled it out of the fire," but they also felt "angry, bitter and betrayed."

Many of those both at the Glenwood Community Centre and at the Walding home gave some thought to deconstructing the second-ballot results. A common belief was that many of Gerri Unwin's backers had gone AWOL after the first round, that if they could not vote for their friend and neighbour, they would simply decamp. Provincial NDP director of organization Becky Barrett received several expressions of concern after the meeting was over (presumably from disgruntled Laserites) about the premature exodus of Unwin supporters. In fact, the numbers do not support this interpretation. Counting spoiled ballots, only fourteen fewer people participated in the second round (416 as opposed to 430). When one recalls from the previous chapter that at least four Laser backers left the auditorium before the second ballot commenced, that another Laser supporter had misplaced her voting slips (and assuming that some unscrupulous individual did not find the packet and vote twice), and that a Walding driver had already mistakenly deposited his entire booklet in the ballot box, then it seems that no more than eight of Unwin's 129 first-round backers failed to vote on the decisive ballot. What may have given rise to the contrary impression was that many Unwinites were not present when the final results were announced. Lacking an emotional investment in the outcome, they had simply left for home after casting their second ballot.

The eleven spoiled ballots from the second round also occasioned much comment. A valid vote had to satisfy three criteria: it had to be legible, it had to be on the slip of the appropriate hue, and it had to be cast for one of the two remaining candidates. That only two ballots had been disallowed on the first round suggests that it was the last of these conditions that was most frequently violated in the decisive count; at least nine of those whose votes were disqualified had already displayed both adequate penmanship and a comprehension of the colour-coding scheme. We are left, therefore, with the likelihood that many of the spoiled ballots on the second round were cast for Gerri Unwin. How are we to account for this phenomenon? One possibility is that these votes were deliberate acts of protest, although immediate departure from the auditorium might well have made the point more effectively than waiting out the lengthy interval between rounds in order to make a meaningless vote. It seems at least as likely, therefore, that any Unwin ballots on the second round were simple mistakes, especially given that many of Unwin's backers were political neophytes who might well have been unaware that the rules called for their champion to be dropped from the final showdown. This explanation becomes even more plausible when we recall both Cavaluce's initially erroneous instructions from the podium and Unwin's subsequent failure to provide to her supporters any visual cue as to her preference. Monica Girouard confirmed that at least one Unwin supporter who would have backed Laser in a showdown with Walding cast a useless second ballot for Unwin. There may well have been others.

Finally, much was made of the breakdown of Unwin supporters on the final ballot. Working on the assumption that eight of these people left Norberry School without voting in the second round and that nine more cast invalid ballots, this still left 112 Unwin backers up for grabs. If we further assume that there were very few defections between the Walding and Laser camps on the final round,[3] then the arithmetic is relatively straightforward. For Walding, the addition of Jay Goldstein effectively cancelled the loss of the lawyer who had inadvertently dropped his entire booklet into the box. Walding's move from 163 to 203 on the second round meant, therefore, that the incumbent had won the support of approximately forty Unwinites. Sundry defections and misadventures had reduced Laser's first-round tally by six from 136. His final total of 202 votes indicated that he had picked up around seventy-two Unwin supporters. Needing to entice two-thirds of those available members to secure victory, Laser had fallen just short of that goal.

Given what was uncovered in the previous chapter, it is possible to tease further insight from these numbers. If we group together Gerri Unwin, her extended family, her executive backers, and other members of their households (spouses and children), it is possible to account for twenty-six of Unwin's first-round votes. If all of these individuals participated in the second ballot, the best estimate is that twenty of them supported Walding, with only six backing Laser.[4] Thus, Laser achieved far more than the necessary two-thirds level of support among the Unwin rank-and-file (outpolling Walding in this cohort by approximately sixty-six to twenty). Given the existence of the secret ballot, a precise breakdown of these numbers would have eluded even a contemporary observer, and these difficulties have clearly not lessened in the intervening two decades. Nevertheless, one fact seems unassailable: there was a remarkable disjunction inside the Unwin camp. Those in the candidate's inner circle disproportionately backed Walding; those on the fringes overwhelmingly supported Laser.

Walding's anger over the nomination contest did not dissipate quickly. On the following day, neophyte MLA Marty Dolin dropped by Walding's legislative office to acknowledge the nomination victory. After sharing a pot of tea, Walding observed: "You're the only person who has been in to congratulate me after fifteen years as an MLA." Three days later, on 16 January 1986, he crafted a letter signifying his intention to resign as Speaker at the commencement of the next session of the legislature, although delivery of same was delayed a further six days while Walding contemplated his options (see

Appendix B).[5] Walding's ostensible rationale for quitting the speakership was perplexing; it was hardly self-evident that participation in intra-party politics precluded impartiality in the adjudication of inter-party politics (unless Walding was implying that a bias *against* the NDP now disqualified him from the position!). Nor was Walding's status effectively altered by the announcement, since he continued to perform the Speaker's administrative duties and receive the Speaker's stipend. With the Pawley government now into the fifth year of its mandate and enjoying a healthy lead in public-opinion soundings,[6] there was little likelihood of the Manitoba legislature being reconvened prior to a provincial election. There was, as one editorialist observed, "more symbolism than substance" in Walding's announcement.[7]

But if the letter's substance was both inconsequential and impenetrable, its symbolism was neither of these things. The announcement reflected Walding's anger over five years of perceived mistreatment by the premier. Walding gave Pawley no advance notice of his intentions and the accompanying press release contained this barb: "I have carried out the job assigned to me by the Premier and now I can resume my political career in speaking out for the people of St. Vital."[8] In a single sentence, Walding managed to suggest, first, that he had been a loyal foot soldier to the party, second, that Pawley had only himself to blame if he did not care for Walding's conduct as Speaker, and, third, that it had been unfair for Pawley to countenance a nomination challenge while Walding's political career had been, at the premier's behest, in abeyance. When asked by a reporter whether the nomination fight had been "unusual," Walding drove the point home. "Let's put it this way," he observed. "It probably wouldn't have happened in Schreyer's time."[9]

The entire affair was obviously an embarrassment to the government. "Mr. Walding would have been doing his party a favor by saying nothing," noted one editorialist, since the announcement gave "the Opposition a chance to point to the disagreements everyone knows exist."[10] In fact, Gary Filmon took every advantage of this opportunity to expose yet "another example of division" in the NDP.[11] "If they can't get along with themselves," chortled the Opposition leader, "they can't get along with the people of Manitoba."[12] In vain, the premier's office issued a brief statement that Pawley "wholeheartedly endorsed" the decision and noted that Walding would now be able to campaign actively as a New Democrat without "being shackled or encumbered by the role of the Speaker."[13] Pawley's private reply twelve days later merely acknowledged receipt of Walding's letter, before offering this rather stilted encomium: "I would like to take this opportunity to congratulate you on your winning the St. Vital Constituency nomination and wish you every success in the upcoming election."[14] Although Pawley did subsequently pen a more personal note (thanking Walding for assisting some Selkirk students with their mock parliament),[15] it was clear that the fences between the two men would not easily be mended.[16]

With his nomination secure and his responsibilities as Speaker confined to a few administrative matters, Walding could now wrap up his controversial trust agreement of October 1984. Recall from Chapter 3 that Walding had placed his two thousand dollar annual constituency indemnities for both 1983 and 1984 into an interest-bearing account, a practice he pledged to continue until such time as he either returned to a more conventional political role or left politics altogether. After rejoining the NDP caucus on 3 February 1986, Walding instructed the trustee, Glen McRuer, to disburse $4314.27 to the party, a sum which signified that the 1985 constituency indemnity had not been paid. This shortfall must have provoked some consternation at NDP headquarters, because it would be three months before Ron Cavaluce would even acknowledge receipt of the monies. Ultimately, it must have been decided that there was much truth to the "bird in the hand" epigram, for the provincial secretary merely thanked McRuer for his "cooperation" and let the matter rest.[17]

Walding may have believed that publicly embarrassing Howard Pawley carried few political risks, that his relationship with the premier was already ruptured beyond repair. At the local level, however, Walding had to reach out both to Sig Laser and Gerri Unwin and to those St. Vital New Democrats who had backed one of the challengers. Certainly, it has not been uncommon in Canada for ongoing frictions from a contentious nomination meeting to torpedo a subsequent electoral campaign. In 1937, for example, future British Columbia premier W.A.C. Bennett lost a bitter fight to Tom Norris for the Conservative nomination in South Okanagan; afterwards, "neither Bennett nor any of his supporters made an effort to see Norris elected," and the Liberal candidate squeaked in by fewer than 300 votes.[18] Similarly, one of Eugene Whelan's early electoral forays was scuppered when, even though the two "were pretty close friends," his nomination opponent boycotted the campaign,[19] while in 1988, the notorious Jag Bhaduria lost the otherwise winnable riding of Markham after being "abandoned" by the local executive, who resigned en masse to protest his candidacy.[20] St. Vital's location astride Manitoba's political diagonal meant that the election of a New Democrat was anything but automatic; several of Walding's victories (as well as his initial defeat) had occurred by relatively narrow margins. Walding might not have been so solicitous of his challengers if St. Vital had been a safe NDP seat. As it was, he beseeched the constituency association to come together behind his candidacy in order to vanquish their common foes in the Conservative and Liberal parties (see Appendix B).[21]

That battle was soon to begin. On 11 February 1986, Premier Pawley dropped the writ for a vote on 18 March. The five-week campaign was unusual by Manitoba standards. The free enterprise versus socialism dialectic, which had dominated political discourse during the Lyon years, was abandoned as the two major parties converged on the political centre. For his part, Gary Filmon was determined to wean his party from "the hard right";[22] as a result, the Conservatives declared their support for rent controls, promised a 6.5 percent hike in social-service spending,[23] pledged additional funds for separate schools,[24] and even promised to double the number of visible-minority employees in the provincial civil service.[25] In fact, after hearing one of the Tory leader's speeches, a Brandon University professor was moved to comment: "I don't see much difference between that statement and what Tommy Douglas was saying."[26]

For their part, the NDP also contributed to this peculiar role reversal by promising little that was either controversial (aside from an ill-defined pledge to institute pay equity in the private sector) or expensive (since the party's tab for its electoral promises was only about one-quarter of the Conservatives' total).[27] Instead, the NDP was reduced to complaining that the

Tories were irresponsible spendthrifts,[28] and touting, in a fashion eerily reminiscent of Sterling Lyon's 1981 campaign, how such megaprojects as the Limestone hydroelectric station and a new potash mine would ensure the province's prosperity.[29] To add to the confusion, both parties employed vapid slogans (with the NDP's "Stand Up for Manitoba" countered by the PC's "Let's Give the Future All We've Got"),[30] and the televised leader's debate was characterized as a "dismal" encounter between Filmon's "vagueness" and Pawley's "mind-numbing banalities."[31]

Only two features sharply distinguished the campaigns of the New Democrats and the Conservatives. First, the former took some pains to tar the latter with the sins of their federal counterparts. Brian Mulroney's national government was, at this time, hugely unpopular with Manitobans. Having to suffer one Tory administration was bad enough, suggested Howard Pawley; to endure a second would be intolerable. In fact, there was much speculation that the NDP had timed the election call so that a presumably nasty federal budget would be delivered in mid-campaign.[32] Aware that the prime minister was an electoral liability, the provincial Tories flatly turned down Mulroney's offer to make some personal appearances.[33] Noted long-time MLA Harry Enns, "Regrettably, my federal party isn't being of great assistance to me in this campaign."[34]

Second, the two major parties could be readily differentiated by their willingness to revisit the heated language wars of 1983 and 1984. For the New Democrats, the matter had been definitively settled by the Supreme Court and was now a non-issue. The Tories, by contrast, were quite prepared to poke at the political embers if some advantage could thereby be achieved. Thus, the Conservative candidate in Springfield (despite being a Franco-Manitoban!) constantly reminded voters of NDP House leader Andy Anstett's key role in the controversy,[35] while his counterpart in Gimli took out a huge advertisement asking, "Who stood up for YOU on the French-language issue?"[36] As for Filmon, his repeated claims that he was not going to bring up the matter were, to put it mildly, disingenuous.[37]

In Chapters 2 and 3, we noted the traditionally close correspondence between the NDP's vote province-wide and its share in St. Vital. Given that the government had called the election with a five-point lead in the polls and that the campaign had seemingly done little to provoke the electorate to reconsider its preferences, one might have surmised that Jim Walding was in little danger of defeat. The Conservatives, however, thought otherwise. At the outset, St. Vital was included among a list of seven NDP-held constituencies that "the Tories have their eyes on,"[38] and similar comments were still being heard on the eve of the vote.[39] The Conservatives recruited Paul Herriot, a former president of the Winnipeg Chamber of Commerce, and poured resources into the race; province-wide, only sixteen candidates (from the total of 219) spent more than Herriot's campaign tab of $18,079.[40] Yet, Herriot's campaign rhetoric was somewhat out of step with Filmon's attempt to move to the political centre. In one speech, he claimed that the NDP "want to establish by law what kind of salaries our employers should pay us; they want to tell us what we're worth, and if that's not bordering on communism, I'd like to know what is."[41] Whatever their personal feelings about Jim Walding's renomination, those at NDP headquarters realized the importance of retaining St. Vital and supplied both money and organizers to Walding's campaign. Even then, the incumbent's budget of just under $13,000 was significantly less than that of his principal competitor. In fact, Sig Laser, who had landed back in Pawley's office as an advance man on the premier's election tour (a jaunt that conspicuously avoided any appearances in St. Vital), was put back into his home riding to energize his nomination backers on Walding's behalf.[42] Those labours met with some success, although party sources did "confide" to the media that Walding was "having trouble getting workers and volunteers,"[43] a few high-profile local New Democrats (such as Jules Legal) opted to sit out the election and there was less support than usual from organized labour. Nevertheless, most members of the association did rally around Walding, albeit with a perceptible absence of enthusiasm. "What was I going to do?" was Michael Stimpson's plaintive summary. "I still wanted a New Democrat to win." Anthony Sayers has highlighted that a broader commitment to party goals is central to the NDP's organizational culture; after a hotly contested tussle for the 1988 NDP nomination in Fraser Valley West, for example, the vanquished was appointed as the victor's campaign manager "because he was considered to be the best person for the job."[44] So it was in St. Vital. Both Gerri Unwin and Sig Laser swallowed their pride; the former became a campaign manager assistant and the latter served as one of seven zone captains. That Laser's assigned posting on election day was in the Walding home (on aptly named Hemlock Place) only made his misery complete.

On 18 March 1986, the Manitoba NDP squeaked back into office. Although most public-opinion polls before and during the campaign had given them a healthy lead over the seemingly floundering Tories, the two parties ended up in a virtual dead heat at 41 percent of the popular vote. For the NDP, this decline of six points from their 1981 total was generally attributed to a Liberal resurgence, although there were several constituencies where the rebound in Liberal popularity occurred principally at the expense of the Tories.[45] Ultimately, thirty New Democrats, twenty-six Progressive Conservatives, and a lone Liberal (party leader Sharon Carstairs) were elected. It would have to be, in the words of industry minister Eugene Kostyra, a "cautious" majority.[46]

One of the victorious New Democrats, for the fifth successive occasion, was Jim Walding. At the outset, Walding had acknowledged to long-time campaign manager Pat Portsmouth that he was still recovering from a stroke, and she quickly discovered that his memory had become quite unreliable. Worse yet, Walding fell and violently struck his head while out canvassing. A concerned Portsmouth asked the provincial office: "What happens if your candidate dies?" Back came the reply: "Why, are you going to kill him?" A British Columbia resident, Portsmouth had managed Walding's victorious campaigns in 1977 and 1981, and the incumbent had again requested her services in 1986.[47] Nevertheless, the two were at loggerheads near the campaign's end over a Walding leaflet proposal that Portsmouth and the rest of the local team were convinced ran contrary to party policy. A tense standoff was only defused when Portsmouth concluded that there was not enough cash in the kitty for anything more elaborate than an election-day "door-knocker."[48] Ultimately, Walding's share of the popular vote was shaved by seven points to 45 percent; yet he was still 550 votes clear of Paul Herriot, with the Liberal candidate a further 2400 votes adrift. Given the disfavour with which he was regarded by large segments of his party, Walding could, with some justifica-tion, claim that his re-election was largely attributable to his "personal appeal."[49] Still, it would never have been achieved without the grudging labours of many of his erstwhile opponents, most of whom were in no mood to celebrate the poll-by-poll arrival of the St. Vital results. When Paul Herriot dropped by to congratulate the victor, he was surprised to discover a reserved Jim Walding in an almost deserted hall. "I had more people come out for my defeat than he did for his victory," recalled an amazed Herriot.

The election results confronted Howard Pawley with a delicate problem of constructing a new cabinet. After the 1981 election, Pawley's exclusion of Henry Carroll and Russell Doern had ultimately led those individuals to bolt from the NDP caucus; since the NDP at that time enjoyed a nine-seat majority, the defections were embarrassing, but little more. This time, the appoint-ment of a Speaker would reduce Pawley's government to a working majority of only two votes (twenty-nine to twenty-seven), so seriously bruised egos on the NDP backbenches were a luxury the premier could not afford. Further complicating Pawley's task was the influx of talented and ambitious fresh-men MLAS, and the fact that only one cabinet minister (House leader Andy Anstett) had lost his seat. And, once again, there was the matter of what to do with Jim Walding, who, perhaps naively, had "great hopes of going into the cabinet" (although this time at least, he acknowledged, Pawley had made no such promise).[50]

Shortly after the election, media commentators began suggesting that it was imperative for Pawley to find some sort of ministerial appointment for Walding. One noted that the member for St. Vital had "been snubbed too many times by his party colleagues" and that, if he were again excluded from the cabinet, Walding "might at some suitable moment settle his moral accounts with his party by voting against them."[51]

A second suggested that widespread defections were unlikely since with "the possible exception of former Speaker Jim Walding, there are not nearly as many loose cannons on this particular NDP deck" as previously.[52] Walding's status as an unsecured armament was soon in evidence. Two post-election meetings with the premier brought no promise of a ministerial post, although at the second of these, Pawley had offered not only to return Walding to the Speaker's chair, but also to raise the annual stipend by $3000 to make it equivalent to that of a cabinet minister. Alas, Walding had made it blindingly clear in both his May 1985 address to the legislature and his January 1986 resignation from the post that he considered the institution of the speaker-ship to be fundamentally flawed. Had the premier been prepared to consider Walding's pet project of establishing a separate constituency for a continu-ous and non-partisan Speaker, then events might have hurtled down a differ-ent path, but Pawley was, as yet, unprepared to countenance such a dramatic reform. As a result, an obviously agitated Walding hand-delivered an extraor-dinary letter to the premier on 3 April 1986, outlining the rationale for his inclusion in the cabinet (see Appendix B).[53] By any standard, the tone and language of the missive was intemperate, with its warnings against "precipi-tate action," its talk of "an insult to St. Vital," and its allusion to Walding's singular role in the NDP's re-election. Worse yet, the epistle's contents were soon in the hands of the media, although Walding refused all calls to comment on what he termed a "confidential" communication ("I won't nego-tiate through the press"[54]), and Pawley likewise denied being the source of the leak ("We wouldn't release the letter"). What seems most likely is that someone close to one of the two principals perceived that public disclosure would ratchet up the pressure on the other.[55] If that individual was in the Walding camp, he or she made a serious miscalculation, for the contents had "really offended" the premier. Pawley insisted that, prior to this incident, he was still actively considering a cabinet position for Walding: "The letter was something that upset me, but the next day, the *Winnipeg Sun* published parts of it and I thought to myself: 'He can't be trusted.'"

Of course, another leader might have been guided by the Arabian proverb to "keep your friends close and hold your enemies closer." Or, as Lyndon Johnson once said, in characteristically colourful language, of J. Edgar Hoover, "Better to have him inside the tent pissing out, than outside pissing in." Yet Howard Pawley's leadership approach was dramatically different from that of the former American president. One business publication noted at the time that Pawley had "refined an often under-estimated yet highly rated consensus, team building management style."[56] To Pawley, the possibility that Walding would be a disruptive force inside the cabinet strongly militated against his inclusion. "The premier may be too consensual in some ways," noted a government source. "But there is one area in which he is very tough indeed. If you want to get into a Pawley cabinet, you have to be a team player."[57]

On 14 April 1986, Howard Pawley unveiled his new twenty-one-member cabinet; to the media, the "only surprise" was that Jim Walding had again been left out.[58] Walding had apparently been offered a variety of other positions, but had been "adamant" about being included in the cabinet. "No premier can function with someone holding a gun above his head," asserted one Pawley spokesman,[59] while another claimed that the premier had "decided at the outset that he had to meet this head on. If he were to give in once, there would be no end to it. You can't run a government on that basis."[60] Support for this decision had come from most members of the NDP caucus. In the four weeks after the 18 March vote, Pawley had discussed the shape of the new administration, including the role to be played by Jim Walding, with each of his MLAs. While a few suggested to the premier that the member for St. Vital should be included in the cabinet, that seniority in and service to the party should be rewarded, the majority sentiment was clearly to the contrary. One cabinet minister claimed that Walding could not be trusted: "If he blackmails you now, he will blackmail you when he is in cabinet." In fact, Vic Schroeder had indicated to the premier that he and several other ministers were unprepared to serve in any cabinet that included Walding (although the qualitative difference between this threat and those intimated by Walding in his 3 April letter is not immediately apparent).

Even so, Pawley must have known that there would be repercussions from his cabinet announcement. Myrna Phillips had been tapped for the speakership, a controversial selection given her reputation for bellicosity; she had, in fact, on one occasion threatened to take a blowtorch to the nether regions of the bison statue at the entrance of the legislative assembly.[61] That left only eight lonely souls on the government backbenches. When asked by the press about Walding's exclusion, the premier's "voice went dry and he grabbed for a drink of water." The member from St. Vital was no different from the others left out, he explained. "Every MLA will be involved to the fullest extent.... I have a number of capable individuals who are not in the cabinet."[62] The premier curtly concluded, "I don't expect Mr. Walding to leave the party because he's not included in the cabinet."[63]

Perhaps not, but others were less certain. With sources close to Walding characterizing Pawley's announcement as "an insult to the St. Vital voters"[64] that had left the former Speaker "very bitter," it was no surprise when Tory leader Gary Filmon chimed in, saying, "I'm certainly interested in talking to him."[65] Meanwhile, Walding did nothing to discourage his prospective suitor: "I'm reassessing my position and I'll announce my decision before the session (beginning May 8). Yes, leaving the party is one option."[66] In a frank television interview, Walding decried the fact that the premier had elevated three rookie MLAs to the cabinet. "I feel slighted," he declared. "After fifteen years, well, I've served my apprenticeship."[67] Aides to the premier had attempted to soften the blow of his exclusion by claiming that "no doors are closed to Mr. Walding"[68] and that "the letter was a serious mistake, but he, like the other backbenchers, has the opportunity to work for a cabinet position."[69] Walding, however, was unconvinced that Pawley would ever change his mind. "That would be up to him, but I would doubt it, he observed. "Loyalty is a two-way street; you can't keep giving and giving and giving."[70]

Walding seemed particularly vexed that his 4 April missive had been interpreted as threatening, especially when the premier personally informed him that the communication had been the main reason for his exclusion. "Of course, I didn't threaten anyone. That's not my way," he insisted. "I always use reason and logic. I wrote that letter just to make my feelings clear to the premier."[71] Subsequently, he was to characterize the missive merely as "sort of a job application."[72] Thus, when *Free Press* columnist Frances Russell suggested that the letter was tantamount to blackmail and extortion, Walding, first, demanded an apology (see Appendix B)[73] and, subsequently, attempted to have her called before the legislative committee on privileges and elections for questioning and a potential reprimand. Nothing came of either of these initiatives; the managing editor of the *Free Press* found Walding's demand to be "barren of any merit,"[74] while the Speaker could uncover no prima facie case that there had been a breach of privilege.

In the end, Walding opted to remain in the NDP. After having skipped the first two post-election caucus meetings, he showed up at the third in late April and subsequently accepted the party's assignment of a large office. Not surprisingly, members of his constituency association had vigorously lobbied Walding during the period to remain a member of the NDP caucus; whatever their roles in the nomination contest, no one wanted the incumbent to take any action that might simultaneously threaten the government and orphan the riding. "It looks like the whole thing is going to be blown out soon," noted constituency spokesperson Sig Laser. "And I'm happy he is staying with us."[75]

On 29 April, Walding made it official. He told press representatives that he would be remaining in the NDP caucus, but that he was reserving the right to dissent on matters of conscience. "I think you can be a loyal caucus member," asserted Walding, "but no member can commit himself to vote for anything no matter what it might be." Reaction to the announcement ranged from the premier's delight (since Walding was a "valued" member of caucus) to Gary Filmon's regret (since it reduced "the opportunity of the government going down more easily on a vote")[76] to the bemusement of the *Free Press* (since it was difficult "to understand why a government backbencher should call a press conference to announce that he will indeed sit in the legislature as a government backbencher").[77] The most revealing part of the accompanying press release (Figure 7) was the concluding sentence. "In arriving at this decision," it read, "no inducements have been offered nor undertakings made." Unlike the other seven backbenchers, Walding would not avail himself of any of the other postings at the premier's discretion (such as caucus chair, which went to Steve Ashton). He would not be a legislative assistant to a minister, nor would he sit as the government's representative on the board of Manitoba Hydro. His participation in, and support for, the Pawley administration, therefore, was hardly unqualified. Walding acknowledged that the party brass might feel "some relief" at his announcement, but when asked directly if he might do something that would lead to the defeat of the government, he replied, "That's always a consideration."[78] Walding had effectively put the Pawley government on probation. "I won't speculate on what might happen in the future," he concluded. "What is going to happen tomorrow, next week or next year, I don't know. I would have to judge that at the time."[79]

Figure 7: Jim Walding press release, 29 April 1986[80]

About two weeks ago I made a public announcement that I was re-assessing my position, following the statement by the Premier that he saw fit not to include me in his government.

Since then, I have received a great many telephone calls and letters, mostly from St. Vital constituents, but also from across the city and from several country locations.

I appreciate the support and loyalty I have received and am thankful for the opportunity to listen to the advice of many constituents.

After giving deep and careful thought to all aspects of this matter, I have concluded that it is time to end further media speculation in making this statement.

In view of the support and confidence given me in the last five elections, I can best serve the interests of St. Vital by remaining in my present position.

The flexibility of the backbench will permit me to speak out for St. Vital and provide full representation for my constituents.

In arriving at this decision, no inducements have been offered nor undertakings made.

In fact, twice within the next six weeks, Walding signalled his independence from his party. At his 29 April press conference, Walding had observed that as a backbencher he could "speak out freely on any topic";[81] now he was determined to take full advantage of that silver lining. When finance minister Eugene Kostyra tabled a budget calling for a half-billion dollar deficit, Walding accused the government of fiscal irresponsibility. Shortly thereafter, he posed a seemingly innocuous question to the premier: was it government policy to exclude people from employment on boards and commissions on the basis of language, ethnicity, and gender? When Pawley replied that it was not, Walding then inquired why NDP caucus members had received a memo asking specifically for the nomination of a Native, a francophone, and two women to fill some vacant positions. The response to this intervention was electric. Conservative MLAS thumped their desks with glee, while those on the government benches appeared surprised and downcast. Outside the legislature, Walding complained that the government's memo "didn't seem quite consistent" with Section 15 of the Charter of Rights and Freedoms.[82] "If you're in favor of the so-called equality provisions," declared Walding, "then I don't see how you can be in favor of this discriminatory action, which this clearly is."[83] One editorialist noted that the former Speaker's objections to affirmative action echoed Russell Doern's beliefs that "hiring a francophone was akin to marrying your mother," and speculated that perhaps Walding's body had been occupied by Doern's "ghost."[84] In fact, Russell Doern was, for the moment, very much alive; in a political commentary, he praised Walding's "zinger on official discrimination" and predicted, "From this point on, when D.J. Walding speaks, people will listen!"[85]

There was, inevitably, a price to be paid for such outspokenness. In August 1986, NDP House leader Jay Cowan offered Sharon Carstairs one of five spots in the Manitoba delegation to the Canadian Parliamentary Conference. As her party's sole elected representative, Carstairs was loath to accept; if she was absent from the legislature, then the Liberal Party of Manitoba was likewise absent. Grateful to the St. Vital MLA for helping her "learn the ropes, which very few others had done," and knowing his love of all things parliamentary, Carstairs instead offered both her place and a "pairing" commitment to Walding (so that the voting balance between Government and Opposition in the legislature would be unaffected in his absence). Jay Cowan, however, refused the proposal.[86] On another occasion, when Carstairs persuaded the two other House leaders that the government should pick up the tab for her secretary's salary, the key proviso was that such monies could only be made available to a party leader, and not to an independent MLA. "Obviously," concluded Carstairs, "Jay Cowan was not going to make this an option available to Jim Walding."[87]

It may be difficult to credit, but the relationship between Jim Walding and his party worsened perceptibly in 1987. At the year's outset, Walding mailed to his constituents his first "Report from the Legislature" since the electoral triumph of the previous March. In it, Premier Pawley was paid the backhanded compliment of finally "recogniz[ing] the unacceptability of the large deficits of the past few years." As well, Walding bluntly criticized the government's plan to freeze teachers' wages. "Not only is the proposal unfair," asserted Walding, "it undermines the principle of free collective bargaining, a principle that the NDP and the CCF have fought for throughout their history."[88] No doubt this communication made a refreshing change from the customary dollop of predigested pap, but at least some of Walding's constituents must have been bewildered by its contents.

Privately, Walding's dealings with the government also deteriorated. In mid-February, Walding discovered, after the fact, that he had been appointed to the legislature's urban affairs committee. An enraged Walding fired off a formal note (addressed "Dear Mr. Pawley") to the premier: "It would have been a matter of common courtesy to seek my acquiescence of this appointment before enacting this Order in Council. Since no permission was requested, I am unable to accept the position. Kindly revoke the appointment immediately."[89] Pawley attempted to mollify Walding (tellingly, his note was addressed "Dear Jim") by pointing out that all urban NDP MLAs had been appointed to this committee, and that participation would afford Walding "direct input to discussion and policy decisions relating to your constituents."[90] Walding, however, was undeterred. "While readily understanding the point of your letter," he responded, "I would ask for the same understanding of the principle involved in my letter of resignation of Feb. 18th. Kindly revoke the appointment without further delay."[91] A full two months would pass before Pawley finally conceded the point and reversed Walding's posting to the urban affairs committee.[92]

In the interval, Walding had become notably more obstreperous in the legislature. Always a stickler for the rules of parliamentary procedure, Walding had grumbled but acquiesced in early March 1987 when the government had telescoped first and second readings on a bill to limit store openings on Sundays. Walding had cautioned the House, however, that should a similar attempt be made to suspend the rules in future, "they may well not have the same unanimous consent that is being given to this bill on this day."[93] Apparently, nobody on the government side got the message. Ten days later, they attempted, with the agreement of all Opposition MLAs, to perform precisely the same manoeuver on a measure to extend the assessment appeal deadline for Winnipeg property owners. To their (unjustifiable) surprise, Walding refused his consent, an action that effectively pushed back the bill's passage by a fortnight. Walding's justification was straightforward: "I might be a member of a team, but I'm also a member of the Legislature which has rules developed a long time ago. When those rules are followed, you get the best legislation possible. When you rush things through you get bad legislation. It was a matter of principle."[94] Whatever the merits of this high-minded rationale, Walding's veto was a source of considerable embarrassment to the government. "There has been some pressure," Walding observed the next day. "A number of members talked to me."[95] Caucus whip Marty Dolin indicated that Walding could well face some disciplinary action: "We do act in concert and collectively, and one of the problems here is what you do with people who don't do that."[96] Sig Laser, now the president of the local constituency association, echoed this unhappiness. "It's something New Democrats in St. Vital would want to disassociate themselves from," claimed Laser. "It certainly was never discussed at any of the riding meetings."[97] Media observers were generally more sympathetic towards Walding, although a scathing editorial appeared in the *Winnipeg Sun* claiming that the maverick MLA had forgotten that the letters "NDP" were responsible for his election: "Now, however, Jimbo figures they stand for Nothing Doing, Pawley. Walding has shown his disdain for the party by refusing to give approval to quick passage of an assessment bill that the city needs ... If Walding can muster enough moral outrage over such a simple issue, one wonders where he's going to come down when matters of substance start crossing his desk. Simply, he's a loose cannon, crashing and banging around the legislative deck."[98]

By their nature, loose cannons command attention. "Why do you have so many microphones pointed at me?" Walding coyly inquired when he stepped into the lobby after Question Period to confront five TV cameras and twenty expectant journalists.[99] Still, he took full advantage of the media spotlight to muse at length about his feelings of rejection after being denied a cabinet post:

> Since then, I [have been] quite dispirited and disillusioned. I have been a team player for more than fifteen years. I did more than any other backbencher, I have more experience than two-thirds of the members of the cabinet. I have lost all excitement. Sometimes I wonder what it would take to earn my rightful place, especially when political rookies get elected right into cabinet. You expect to advance as years pass by. But, sixteen years after, here I am back as a backbencher ... I feel a sense of unfairness in all this. I guess you cannot have everything you want in life. But I am still a New Democrat.[100]

For now. Poised on a precarious three-seat majority and slipping in the opinion polls, it now seems obvious that the Pawley administration should have tried harder to appease Walding, although the premier was clearly in a difficult bind. On the one hand, the former Speaker was still insisting on nothing less than a ministerial position. On the other hand, his unguarded comments during the furor over the property assessment appeal bill ("I would have perhaps done the same thing if I were in cabinet. It's a matter of conscience and principle"[101]) would have done nothing to convince Pawley that Walding was prepared to be a team player. Yet if embracing Walding was difficult, threatening him was madness, and Dolin's bluster about expelling Walding from caucus could not be countenanced, a fact duly recognized by the *Winnipeg Sun*'s editorial cartoonist (Figure 8). Even so, the relationship between Walding and the NDP continued to spiral downhill. As party whip, Dolin was understandably frustrated by Walding's cavalier dismissal of caucus meetings as unproductive. "It really is a token experience," claimed

Walding. "You get an awful lot of information on paper which is actually a waste of time. It's a bureaucratic exercise."[102] Yet it had been at a caucus meeting where the proposal to extend the property assessment had been fully vetted prior to its introduction into the legislature. Walding had absented himself deliberately from this discussion; for him then to object in the House that he had not had sufficient time to study the measure ("This afternoon, about 15 minutes ago, is the first time I saw this bill. I don't know what's in there."[103]) must have been particularly galling. By the end of April, Dolin's patience had expired. On 28 April 1987, he sent a lengthy letter to all members of the St. Vital NDP executive documenting the "negligent" conduct of their MLA and urging them to take unspecified steps to convince Walding to take his responsibilities more seriously (see Appendix B).[104] Since both Jim and Val were also members of the riding executive, they also, perhaps inadvertently, received this missive. Howard Pawley has speculated that "Val would have been wild" at getting the letter, but we are certain that her husband saw nothing amusing in being requested "to try to convince your member Jim Walding" to be "a cooperative member of the government caucus."

Figure 8: Political Cartoon, *Winnipeg Sun*, 13 March 1987[105]

Walding's biting response (see Appendix B), in which he asked members of the government caucus to reflect on whether Dolin's intervention had "enhanced or detracted from the security of tenure of the Government" was mailed on 4 May (although some of the language implies that the letter was actually composed a few days previously).[106] This date is highly significant. On 3 May 1987, the St. Vital NDP had their major annual fundraiser, the Family Dinner. A number of party dignitaries, including Howard Pawley and Marty Dolin, were in attendance after having been invited by the constituency executive. Jim Walding took this occasion to announce that he would not be a candidate in the next provincial election. "It's 16 years now, and 19 years at the time of the next election, and I think 19 years in politics is long enough," he subsequently explained. "Rather than leaving it until a time closer to the election, I'm telling them now so they have three years until the next election to make arrangements to conduct a candidate search."[107] Alas, Walding's announcement provoked an unfortunate reaction. Marty Dolin's response, recalled Howard Pawley, was to say "something smart-alecky and start clapping and Jim was quite obviously offended. I was sitting at the same table so I was sure that it would be guilt by association.... At that time, it would have done nothing for the Walding peace of mind. I know I was really uncomfortable because I was at the same damned table, and Marty is getting this clapping going." If Walding had been having second thoughts about mailing his blistering reply to Dolin, this incident would surely have hardened his resolve.

The entire affair dramatically reduced the chances of any reconciliation between maverick and party. Walding's determination not to re-offer had effectively removed one of the party's few remaining checks on his behaviour. Two days after his retirement announcement, Walding criticized rookie minister Judy Wasylycia-Leis in the House for rejecting a St. Vital sports club's grant application. "I suppose that there are now no constraints and I don't have to be indebted to anyone for a renomination or a re-election,"[108] Walding observed. Worse yet, the angry exchange of letters between Dolin and Walding soon found their way into the media. "I don't know why Mr. Dolin sent the letters or released it to the press," Walding noted ominously, "but it's bound to have the exact opposite effect."[109] Most distressing of all, the affair effectively ruptured relationships between Walding and his riding executive. In the thirteen months after the March 1986 election, Walding had been a regular, albeit somewhat detached, attendee at constituency meetings. The Dolin letter, however, provoked both of his nomination challengers to weigh in on the matter. Gerri Unwin was quoted in the press as being puzzled by Walding's behaviour. "I worked very hard to help Mr. Walding and the NDP to get elected here in St. Vital and we expect him to perform his duties," Unwin asserted. "I feel if you are an MLA you should be attending caucus meetings and I don't understand why he's not."[110] As for Sig Laser, his status as the president of the riding association obliged him to respond formally to Dolin's communication. In his 7 May 1987 letter, copied to Jim Walding, Laser indicated that members of the executive had effectively washed their hands of their MLA; the parliamentary party was free to "take whatever actions you deem necessary" (see Appendix B).[111] For his part, Walding merely stated that he would neither retire prior to the next election nor, in the interval, discuss his performance with the riding executive.[112] Jim Walding's isolation from the Manitoba New Democratic Party was now effectively complete.

The remainder of 1987 merely solidified this circumstance. When the government introduced a new Human Rights Code, Walding voted with the Opposition on second reading. In his judgement, the measure contained a clause (later modified in committee) that equated homosexuality with heterosexuality. "Since I regard homosexuality as a deviation from normal human activity," stated Walding, "I could not support it."[113] Pawley had insisted on including matters of sexual orientation in the code, and would have been particularly irked by this stand. Walding was also separating himself physically from the government. Aside from attending sittings and answering his mail, he was rarely spotted at the legislature. At one point, Pawley aide Bruce Buckley perceived that Walding seemed to be experiencing vision or balance difficulties, but his offers of assistance were politely refused. Joyce Scotton, the director of the government caucus, had similar suspicions about the state of Walding's health; whenever she had something for him to read or sign, the St. Vital MLA invariably took the document back to his office rather than attend to the matter straightaway. Walding's attendance at caucus meetings became even rarer, and after an unfortunate incident, ceased altogether. Notwithstanding the ubiquity of cigarette smoking among their allies in the trade union movement, the Manitoba NDP had, in the summer of 1987, zealously joined the anti-smoking crusade. Aside from the members' lounge and special sections of the cafeteria and dining room, smoking had been banned everywhere in the legislative building (and, indeed, in all government buildings).[114] Thus, the NDP caucus room had become off-limits for smoking, and several MLAs (notably Harvey Smith) had been slow to adjust to the new regime. On one occasion, whip Marty Dolin (himself a smoker) detected a caucus member taking an illicit drag and good-naturedly reminded him, "I have said it not once, but half a dozen times. No smoking!" Jim Walding, sitting in the opposite corner smoking a pipe, believed the comment had been directed at him. He got up, left the room and never attended another caucus meeting.[115]

Although unhappy and isolated, Walding may have taken a perverse pleasure in witnessing the tribulations of his successor as Speaker. Given her propensity for partisan invective (Sterling Lyon was famously characterized as "a slimy little pig"[116]), the Tories had regarded Myrna Phillips as an inappropriate choice for the job and had refused to second her nomination. That task had fallen to Sharon Carstairs, and "Blowtorch Myrna" had returned the favour by recognizing the Liberal leader at every opportunity and by maintaining what one columnist labelled a "personal vendetta" against certain Conservative members.[117] Indeed, an exasperated Jim McRae, MLA for Brandon West, was at one point moved to complain, "Madame Speaker, if for once I could get to my feet and finish a complete thought without being interrupted by you, I'd appreciate it."[118] Imagine the Tory delight, then, when news leaked out in October 1987 that Phillips had attended a four-day strategy retreat for government MLAs. This conduct was particularly troublesome, given that, at the time of her appointment, Phillips had been awarded the unprecedented allocation of a $30,000 per year executive assistant to relieve her of her partisan and constituency duties.[119] Neither Jim Walding, nor his predecessor, Harry Graham, had attended even out-of-session caucus gatherings, and the former was only too pleased to lecture Phillips on the etiquette of the position. "The

Speaker's job is to appear as much as possible, entirely if possible, to be independent of both sides," declared Walding. "The tradition in parliamentary
government is the Speaker cuts any association with partisan politics at all."[120]
Phillips eventually rode out the controversy, although at the end some MLAs
claimed that her two-year tenure as Speaker seemed "more like ten."[121]

The 17 November 1987 annual meeting of the St. Vital NDP association
provided further testimony of Walding's detachment from ongoing political
responsibilities. The only motion of consequence passed at the gathering
called upon Walding "to make full use of his franking privilege by way of
sending out caucus information material to St. Vital constituency and that
any remaining or unused print/mailing franks be released to caucus for
additional informational mailings."[122] After almost two decades, Val Walding
abdicated from the social coordinator's responsibilities; even contemplating
a different occupant seemed surreal, so the post remained vacant. The
agenda called for the delivery of an "MLA's Report," but the meeting's minutes
make no mention of same. When Walding did release a "Report from the
Legislature" to his constituents, few government initiatives were deemed
praiseworthy and much space was given over to a chart documenting that
under the previous five years of NDP stewardship, spending on "Government
Services" and "Civil Service" had grown at a rate almost four times greater
than that for "Housing" and "Education."[123]

Jim Walding might have concluded his political career with two further
years of service as an embittered backbencher, but for an abrupt change in
the voting balance in the legislature. Despite some short-lived resignations,
Howard Pawley had managed to keep his cabinet personnel essentially intact.
Thus, Wilson Parasiuk had resumed his ministerial post (after being cleared
of conflict of interest allegations), while the same beneficence was extended
to Elijah Harper (despite being convicted of refusing a breathalyzer test and
leaving the scene of an accident).[124] At one time, Walding might have contemplated being drafted as even a temporary ministerial replacement, but he no
longer entertained such aspirations.

Larry Desjardins's departure from cabinet, however, was of an entirely
different order. Enticed by Ed Schreyer to cross the floor from the Liberals in

1969, Desjardins had nevertheless remained aloof from the NDP's philosophical mainstream on a range of issues (including sexual orientation, abortion, and aid to separate schools). Now he was beset by problems that were physical (he was recovering from quadruple bypass surgery), professional (he had testy relations with the head of the Manitoba Lotteries Commission), political (the premier's office had been interfering with his staff appointments), and personal (a family member had been ensnared in a legal imbroglio). After a twenty-seven-year run as the MLA for St. Boniface,[125] Desjardins's political career was winding down.[126] In August 1987, Desjardins resigned from cabinet and hinted that he would soon be leaving politics altogether, a prospect so alarming to the NDP government that they "begged him to remain at least as an MLA, offering him any position he wanted."[127] Alas, what Desjardins actually coveted (and what he accepted in November 1987) was a highly paid job as executive director for Manitoba Health Organizations (a consortium of private health providers). Worse yet from the government's perspective, Desjardins intended to retain his seat in the legislature until immediately prior to the opening of the next session. This scenario conjured up a range of ethical issues. Was it appropriate for a long-time minister of health abruptly to become a health-care lobbyist? Was there not obvious potential for conflicts between the interests of his constituents and those of his employer? Was it fair to the people of St. Boniface to delay his resignation to the point that they would be denied any representation in the forthcoming legislative session? Consideration of such matters impelled local editorialists to conclude that it was "time to say goodbye, Larry,"[128] and that Desjardins's constituents should not have to suffer such "contemptuous treatment."[129] Desjardins was unmoved by this widespread condemnation; he would not officially resign until 9 February 1988, a scant two days before the reopening of the House.

The arithmetic for the 1988 session had been fundamentally transformed. The government's three-seat majority on election night, 1986, had been effectively reduced to two (twenty-nine to twenty-seven) with the appointment of Myrna Phillips as Speaker. Even so, Jim Walding (or any other rebellious New Democrat) had been powerless to defeat the government. A vote with the Opposition members (assuming perfect attendance) would have simply produced a twenty-eight vote tie, which Speaker Phillips would then assuredly have broken in the government's favour. Desjardins's long goodbye, however, had reduced Pawley's majority to a single vote (twenty-eight to twenty-seven), and had thus empowered a vengeful Jim Walding.

What is astonishing was the government's apparent equanimity in the face of this change in legislative arithmetic. "If there were any weak links in the chain, they would have broken by now," claimed a spokesman for the premier in early September. "There's no real concern or panic."[130] There was also no attempt to accelerate Desjardins's early-February departure; it was observed, without contradiction, that "Mr. Pawley entirely agrees with that timing."[131] The former premier now acknowledges, however, that this was a strategic blunder, that he should have "forced Desjardins's hand" by getting his resignation in August 1987 and holding an immediate by-election. "We could have won the seat in the fall of 1987," laments Pawley. Even a hypothetical defeat in an equally hypothetical by-election in St. Boniface would not have altered the government's situation. A twenty-eight to twenty-eight balance would have been no worse than twenty-eight to twenty-seven; in either circumstance, a single defection would have been sufficient to topple the government.

It was not long before Walding started to employ his new-found leverage. During the Throne Speech debate that commenced the new session, he accused the government of profligacy and mismanagement. "People are not sure who's in charge of the store—or more frighteningly, is anyone in charge of the store," Walding told a startled House. Pawley may have downplayed the remarks as "constructive criticism,"[132] but when Walding refused publicly to announce his voting intention on the Opposition's motion of non-confidence, speculation grew that he would bring down the government. "We believe this is just Jim being Jim," noted one NDP official. "But we can never tell. He can be pretty cranky."[133] On 22 February 1988, the legislative gallery was packed, and all fifty-seven MLAs were present for the crucial vote, including one recovering from a broken ankle who hobbled into the chamber on crutches. "I'd get off my death bed to defeat this government," declared Tory Jim Ernst.[134]

His heroic efforts were to no avail. While a nervous Pawley covered his brow with his hand, Walding slowly removed his earpiece and stood to oppose the Tory motion.[135] Afterwards, the premier claimed to have been unconcerned. "No one really expected Jim Walding not to support the government on our side," asserted Pawley,[136] although the lengthy applause that erupted from the government benches after Walding's vote seemed to indicate otherwise. Merrily whistling past the graveyard, the premier concluded, "Jim Walding's a loyal committed New Democrat that may have some differences of view."[137] Opposition leader Filmon, who had visited Walding earlier in the day to lobby for his support, was obviously disappointed in the outcome: "I think you can cry wolf so often and get all the attention before people say, well, it's just the publicity you're interested in."[138] But Walding insisted that he had seriously considered bringing down the NDP and that only last-minute discussions with a few trusted advisers had persuaded him that it was "too early" to kill the government.[139] "No one should take it for granted because I'm giving the government my support this time, that it's going to be that way for the rest of the session," he warned.[140] "I support good legislation and I will support good measures. If it's bad legislation I will oppose it."[141]

With a new provincial budget next on the order paper, Walding would soon get another opportunity to hold the government to account. In the interim, a dispirited band of Manitoba New Democrats gathered for their annual convention. Over the previous year, the party had been rocked by a series of management scandals in provincial Crown corporations as well as by public unrest over spiralling taxes and auto-insurance premiums; opinion polls consistently showed the government trailing the ascendant Tories by twenty-five points. Citing "personal business," Walding was conspicuously absent from the 4 to 6 March meeting, but he told reporters that he was unimpressed with the party's apparent unwillingness to consider new policy directions. "It could be I'm the only one who sees anything to criticize and everyone else sees that everything is pretty in the garden," he complained.[142]

Yet Walding gave no indication on 7 March that he was considering a vote against the government's budget. On the contrary, he seemed to be revelling in the respect with which he was suddenly being treated by members of the cabinet. "They come over and sit down and chat with me now," claimed Walding. "Before, it was the other way around—I had to try to corner a cabinet minister or even make an appointment to talk to one." After years of feeling like a "trained seal," Walding seemed pleased that now he could "perhaps influence things a little."[143] When asked directly about finance minister Eugene Kostyra's budget, Walding was cautiously supportive: "I rather like the general tone of it."[144]

Nevertheless, Premier Pawley wanted reassurance that the maverick backbencher was still on side. In the previous week, he had dispatched ministers Len Evans and Billie Uruski to sound out Walding over dinner, and they had reported back that nothing seemed amiss. On 4 March, Marty Dolin asked Walding directly about his voting intentions. As the caucus whip subsequently reported to Pawley, Walding had danced around the question, before acknowledging that his "inclination" was to support the budget. Even so, on 8 March, Pawley requested that Dave Chomiak go for lunch with Walding. Chomiak, it will be recalled, was a close ally of Walding who had been instrumental not only in setting up Walding's 1984 trust-fund agreement, but also in securing victory at his 1986 nomination meeting. Pawley recalls Chomiak returned from lunch to report, "I am 98 percent sure that everything is okay with Jim."[145] Certainly, Sharon Carstairs was of the same opinion; she sent her staff home early on the assumption that nothing untoward was going to happen.[146]

Nevertheless, the Conservatives seemed strangely confident. As far back as late February, a "backroom Tory" had phoned a *Winnipeg Free Press* reporter with instructions to "circle March 8. The government is going to fall.... I've been doing a lot of work."[147] That morning, when Pawley aide Bruce Buckley slipped out for a cup of coffee, he came across a pair of Conservatives who taunted, "Hey Bucko, you're going down today." This ebullient mood was also apparent as Conservative MLAs filed into the House for the late afternoon vote on the Opposition amendment to the budget.[148]

Wilson Parasiuk noted, with some concern, the Tories' sense of eagerness, while Gerard Lecuyer was similarly troubled to see the smiles on the other side of the chamber. Raising the alarm among his seatmates, Lecuyer told them to watch out. Even more distressing to those on the government benches was the sudden influx of Conservative wives who, like *citoyennes tricoteuses* from Revolutionary France, crowded into the public gallery in anticipation of an execution. As the vote commenced, Gary Filmon was unable to take his eyes off Jim Walding. "He was the person to watch," recounted Filmon. "I followed every move he made from the moment the vote started. I watched every shuffle. I saw him move his glass of water."[149] Walding was palpably nervous. Early in the afternoon, he had gone AWOL and neither the party brass nor his cohorts on the "buddy" list[150] had any idea as to his whereabouts. Such absences were hardly unprecedented, however, and Walding's entry into the legislature had been largely unremarked. Now, with everyone watching, Walding stood up, his face "twitching,"[151] and voted for the Opposition motion. He had brought down the government.

The aftermath was electric. According to a deputy clerk of the Manitoba legislature, a "strange hush—followed by what can only be described as pandemonium—engulfed the House."[152] Sharon Carstairs was jolted from her letter-signing reverie by the Tory MLA to her front: "Walding voted with us!"[153] Across the aisle, government members "swiveled in their chairs in horror" to stare at Walding.[154] When the count was complete, the Opposition motion had passed by twenty-eight to twenty-seven; in the confusion that followed, some New Democratic MLAs even voted for the main motion as amended, thus inadvertently joining in the denunciation of their government's budget. The sitting then adjourned.

Amidst the tumult, Walding drifted out.[155] "It's time for the people of Manitoba to decide whether the government still has a mandate, and I don't want that decision to be all on me," he told reporters in a voice shaking with emotion. "It's too much of a strain. I can't do it anymore."[156] When asked about his earlier praise of the budget, he replied, "I changed my mind. I have no further comment."[157] With that, Walding walked alone down a legislative corridor and into hiding.[158]

For many Manitoba New Democrats, Walding's act has been seared into their consciousness. Gerri Unwin was driving in her car when the news came over the radio. "I can't believe this," she recalls thinking in shock. Another remembers, first, her mother running out of the house to tell her what had happened, and then receiving instant confirmation from Howard Pawley's ashen face on the television. Without wishing to exaggerate the importance of the event, it is still striking how many St. Vital New Democrats can recall precisely what they were doing at the moment they heard about Walding's vote.

For the next three days, the Waldings disappeared from public view. As reporters staked out their home, rumours circulated that they had flown out of the country to Britain, or even to South America. The reality was rather more prosaic. Jim and Val had simply checked into the Holiday Inn on Pembina Highway, where they were able to decompress in blissful anonymity. "We felt better for it," observed Val. "I didn't want to come back, to be honest." In the interim, Manitoba's political landscape had dramatically shifted. On 9 March, Howard Pawley announced, before a teary-eyed group of supporters, that there would be a provincial election on 26 April 1988. "Clearly this would not be the time of my choosing," he observed.[159] As well, Pawley informed Manitobans (on what he subsequently characterized as "the saddest day in my life")[160] that he was retiring from provincial politics; the NDP would require a new candidate for Selkirk and, more importantly, a new leader. "The events of yesterday precipitated the decision.... As leader, I must take ultimate responsibility for what happens. It is my personal judgment that a change in leadership is desirable."[161]

Two days later, Walding emerged from hiding to hold a remarkable news conference. He expressed no regret for his 8 March vote. "I'm not sorry one little bit," he claimed. "What I did is abdicate the personal responsibility to prop up this particular government."[162] More controversially, Walding mused at some length about his future employment prospects: "Can I say I'll never work for anybody again ... whether that offer is from a federal Government or a sympathetic Conservative employer or someone else? I see from the press that the Conservatives are very happy and may well be grateful. I don't know what is going to happen in the future. If I get an offer, I would consider it on its merits. I'm only 50 and certainly not at the end of my working life."[163] He added, "I have a wife and family to support. I have a future to support. My income ceases on April 26. I have no other income except my pension which is modest."[164]

When pressed for details, Walding insisted that he had not struck a deal to bring down the government, but admitted, in distressingly opaque language, that he had been party to some delicate conversations on the subject: "I don't want to mention any names, but, you know, suggestions have been made ... I've been told that people would be grateful ... Oh it was not any one person or any one time ... Probably since the session started ... I can't give you a firm answer (about where the conversations occurred)."[165] Asked point-blank whether he could be "bought," Walding replied, "I don't think so. Start at $5 million and work your way down, and we'll see."[166]

The tenor of these remarks did nothing to reassure New Democrats that they had not been cheated out of government. In fact, it remains today an article of faith for many New Democrats that "the fix was in," that Walding "was paid off," and that he "took something with him" when he subsequently left Manitoba. Amateur sleuths at the time were not averse to sifting the Walding household garbage, and a number of professional journalists have likewise striven to uncover evidence of corrupt practices (including an unsuccessful attempt to access Walding's telephone records). Three days after the Walding news conference, *Winnipeg Free Press* columnist Frances Russell wrote a lengthy article on the "pattern of unusual events" that surrounded the fall of the government, before noting that "political rewards or inducements, of any kind and offered in any way, are a serious criminal offence."[167] Seventeen years later (!), she returned to this theme with a column complaining generally that political corruption "is notoriously difficult to prove" and specifically that "allegations" that Walding had been "bribed by the Official Opposition Conservatives have never been fully investigated."[168] Admittedly, the RCMP did look into the Walding affair in the mid-1990s and interviewed a number of the principals, including Howard Pawley. In 1996, however, the inquiry was terminated.

The evidence of corrupt behaviour, however, seems remarkably circumstantial. Much has been made of the fact that the Waldings sold their home on Hemlock Place for $77,000 in 1988[169] before purchasing a decidedly more upmarket bed-and-breakfast in Victoria. Suspicious minds have wondered how the payments on a six-figure mortgage could be maintained, although it is not difficult to imagine a range of perfectly legitimate explanations.[170] Much has also been made of the Consevatives' naked avarice for power in 1988. It has been claimed that it was a Tory employer who enticed Larry Desjardins to leave public life and thereby reduce the government's majority to one (although those able to offer such positions are rarely avid New Democrats). It has also been claimed that two other backbenchers had been offered ill-defined inducements to bring down the government. Harvey Smith (NDP, Ellice) reported being told that "arrangements could be made that I would benefit," while Don Scott (NDP, Inkster) likewise heard that "they would be able to find something for me" (although at least one of the Tory contacts alleged that he had only been "teasing").[171] It has further been claimed that there is abundant evidence that the Tories had advance knowledge of Walding's act, that the shouts from the Conservative front benches immediately prior to the vote of "you guys are dead,"[172] revealed a complicity in corrupt practices (although one party can be tipped off without the other having been bought off). At least some members of the Walding inner circle had been notified when, that morning, he had reached a final decision. "The Throne Speech and the budget are votes of confidence in the government," Walding recollected. "So if not then, then when?"[173] Later, Elizabeth Dotrement had received a phone call from Val Walding: "Elizabeth, he is going to do it!" Having come to this fateful decision, it would have been madness not to have passed the news on to the Tories as well, so that all their members would be in attendance for the vote.

Unless new evidence comes to light, the case for corrupt behaviour in this affair (at least on Walding's part) seems remarkably insubstantial. Inducements may well have been offered to the maverick MLA; in fact, one Conservative source acknowledged at the time that Walding had rejected a private-sector job offer in British Columbia in return for backing a previous non-confidence motion.[174] Walding's press conference musings, which occasioned so much alarm among Manitoba New Democrats, are thoroughly inconsistent with the tight-lipped indignation one would expect from someone guilty of a criminal transgression. On the contrary, his remarks appear, in retrospect, to be those of someone who discovers part-way down that he has not donned the appropriate safety harness before leaping into the void.

It is also noteworthy that, to this day, none of the long-standing executive members of the St. Vital NDP association believe that Jim Walding was paid off. Certainly, these individuals were shocked by the actions of their MLA, as Gerri Unwin indicated at the time: "He didn't actually promise us he wouldn't do something like that but there certainly was a strong feeling that he wouldn't. We knew the way he was feeling but we were all very surprised by what he did. And some members do feel betrayed because he was nominated by the NDP as an NDP member and that's what he was supposed to be."[175] But feelings of surprise and betrayal did not catapult into suspicion. Most executive members knew Walding intimately from years of doing political battle (initially, always on the same side; latterly, sometimes not). Their sense of his character was inconsistent with his behaving in a corrupt fashion. Even Sig Laser and Gerri Unwin, who might understandably have been inclined to think the worst of their rival, shared the view that "Jim Walding was not paid off." Or as Jules Legal put it, "I didn't believe the rumours. I think he had more integrity than that. I thought that he had a lot of integrity, even if he was wrong-headed."

It is understandable that New Democrats in the legislature and at the provincial office thought otherwise. Accusations of underhanded dealing could serve both as a stick to attack the Tories and as a rationalization for their own mishandling of the situation. If the government had worked harder at keeping Larry Desjardins happy, for example, Walding might never have been provided the opportunity to cast a decisive vote. Pawley acknowledges, "Larry would have thought that he did not have enough support from me." To his credit, Pawley also accepts responsibility for not having come to some sort of arrangement with Sharon Carstairs, although in her memoirs, the Liberal leader makes it abundantly clear that even the prospect of a cabinet seat in a reconfigured New Democratic ministry was less appealing than the opportunity to contest a fresh provincial election.[176] Yet discussion of Desjardins and Carstairs diverts attention from the central issue: the government's failure to keep the loyalty of a seventeen-year caucus veteran. As one St. Vital New Democrat wryly observed, "Any party that could put up with Joe Borowski in the cabinet should have been more accommodating with Jim Walding."

For the two years after the 1986 election, the Manitoba NDP consistently underestimated the threat posed by an unhappy Jim Walding; he would, they assumed, do nothing to jeopardize the accumulation of additional credits to his legislative pension. Walding, it will be recalled, had abandoned his career as an optician shortly after his initial electoral success, and having "no intention" of "re-entering optics," had let his membership in the Association of Dispensing Opticians lapse in 1984.[177] Walding, therefore, had no obvious employment prospects outside politics, and, when he balked at being again left out of the cabinet in April 1986, one NDP source had been openly dismissive. Walding was just "raising red herrings"; since he needed additional years to maximize his pension, it was "in his own self-interest not to unseat the government."[178] Two years later, the party was still operating on this premise. "So this surprised us when he jeopardized his pension plan," Pawley now recollects with some chagrin. "We wrongly assumed ... that he would want to serve out the term." Such assumptions, of course, had ever-diminishing utility as Walding moved closer to his pension ceiling.

Not that the government was relying entirely on Walding's pecuniary inclinations. In a 3 March letter, Walding indicated that he was again astride one of his favourite hobby horses. "I am still hopeful in seeing parliamentary reform introduced as it concerns the Speakership, and to this end I have written to both Mr. Pawley and Mr. Filmon," Walding reported to a member of the public. "I hope that their response will be a little more enthusiastic than it was four years ago."[179] For their part, the NDP at least appeared to take Walding's proposal seriously. In a five-page "personal and confidential" memo to the premier on 2 March 1988 (the pertinent parts of which are reproduced in Appendix B), House leader Jay Cowan laid out the government's strategic principles.[180] There are a number of interesting features to this document. First, it betrayed doubts about Walding's trustworthiness;

there were obvious concerns about being blindsided either by a question in the House or by a public announcement. Second, there was a distinct preference for an all-party consensus; any enthusiasm for significant institutional reform would vanish if it was doomed to become the object of partisan contestation. Third, the apparent urgency of Walding's request was minimized; as Cowan noted, they received "similar requests for early responses all the time." Finally, the government imagined a straightforward swap. Some attractive perquisites were dangled in front of Walding (chairmanship of the review committee, the prospect of junkets to other jurisdictions); in return, the government would be buying valuable time (since nothing could be altered until at least the subsequent session of the House). Pawley and Cowan did, in fact, meet with Walding and advance this proposal. "I didn't feel comfortable about doing this," recalled the former premier, "but, on the other hand, I realized the precarious situation we were in." Walding, waiting to hear what the Tories had to offer, was noncommittal. A few days later, Pawley happened to come upon Walding ducking into the caucus room to pick up his mail and inquired whether the MLA had yet heard back from Filmon. An annoyed Walding rejoined, "If he knows what's good for him, he'll get back to me." Filmon's eventual reply on 7 March must have been disheartening, since it signalled that there was little prospect of all-party agreement on the subject (see Appendix B).[181] None of this manoeuvering would have surprised a political cynic. On the one hand, the Conservatives were unlikely to support any initiative that, in mollifying Walding, would decrease the likelihood of the government's ouster. On the other hand, the NDP were not actually offering anything of substance, only the prospect of further study. It seems safe to conclude that the day before he voted to bring down the government, Walding realized that his quest to reform the Manitoba speakership had become entirely quixotic.

How, then, can we best understand Jim Walding's decision on 8 March 1988? Part of the explanation can be found in philosophical differences. Walding was a fiscal conservative; he had been happier in the Schreyer era when, he claimed "there was a common sense outlook on fiscal responsibility."[182] In his February 1988 Throne Speech intervention, Walding had launched a broadside attack on the Pawley administration's willingness to countenance large budgetary deficits. "We've been doing well in this province, but are we doing well on borrowed money?" he thundered. "The day of reckoning will come whether it's next year or the year after."[183] Ultimately, Walding had supported the Throne Speech, claiming that the government should be allowed more time to turn around the ship of state. But only four days separated that pronouncement and Eugene Kostyra's budgetary address on 26 February. Such documents are months in the making and few, if any, changes of consequence could have been made at that late stage. Even so, Walding took this inaction as proof that the government was incorrigible. "I made a speech during the Throne Speech debate that was very critical of the government," he recounted. "I saw no movement in the two weeks following that to rectify things."[184]

Walding's social conservatism also had placed him at odds with the government. The NDP, he claimed, had drifted away from the CCF's venerable motto "Humanity First" in order to reward "specific interest groups."[185] It is particularly instructive to contrast the post-mortem observations of Pawley and Walding. The former emphasized his pride in the NDP government's record on "fairness" issues: "We've provided more equal opportunities for minorities, [N]ative people, the handicapped and women. We have begun a program of pay equity that has already gone some distance in the public service."[186] Three days later, Walding offered quite a different perspective on these initiatives; human rights codes, affirmative action, and pay equity were singled out as symptomatic of a misguided approach.[187] "The laws that were passed (in the Schreyer era) were the same for everyone," he claimed. "Since then, we've started developing policies for particular linguistic, cultural, and ethnic groups. I think it's an abdication of what the party believed in when I joined it."[188]

Fiscal and social conservatism aside, Walding's vote on 8 March 1988 was deeply personal, animated by his health, his spouse, and his pride. Reference has already been made to Walding's physical decline subsequent to his 1982 stroke, a decline exacerbated by the mounting pressure of holding the balance of power. After the vote, in fact, Gerri Unwin pointed immediately to this factor: "I think everything was beginning to affect his health and that may have had something to do with his decision."[189] Walding acknowledged as much on 12 March: "It was so much of a strain that I couldn't continue."[190] Far from revelling in the unaccustomed spotlight, the maverick backbencher found it increasingly burdensome. Walding described to reporters how the "hardest minutes" passed as he sat waiting to vote, how "an emotional void" opened as he stood up, and how his "quavering" voice and "unsure" step as he left the legislature were reflective of his feelings of "panic."[191]

Under the circumstances, it is not surprising that Walding declined to flag his intentions to the government. "I thought Walding and I had an understanding," acknowledged Pawley. "Even a half an hour before the vote was called, I never expected we did not have his vote."[192] Two decades on, it is obvious that this deception still rankles. "We thought that Walding had the decency and integrity to announce first his intention, and then we could have taken corrective steps," recalled the former premier. "This is where we miscalculated. We did not expect to be ambushed, to be stabbed in the back this way." Yet permitting these "corrective steps" (which presumably would have included a full-court press from the other twenty-seven members of the NDP caucus) would only have served, certainly in the short-term and likely for a longer interval, to ramp up the debilitating pressure on Walding. One week after his vote, Walding spoke of his new-found feelings of well-being: "There is a sense that a great weight has been lifted, and the strain I was feeling just evaporated away.... I'm not fully recovered from my stroke, and it slows me down and puts a crimp on what I can do. Retirement is not out of the question. Now that the strain (of politics) has drained away I feel much better."[193] By election night, a tanned and relaxed Walding was singing the praises of retirement: "I'm feeling better than I have done for years."[194]

Walding's behaviour in this affair was also profoundly shaped by his relationship with his wife. Val Walding had been a formidable presence throughout her husband's almost two decades of public life. Val had strong opinions and she articulated them forcefully. In private, Val was certainly Jim's closest political confidante, and, in public, she often seemed to have a more prominent persona than her husband, the MLA. It is not surprising, therefore, that many St. Vital New Democrats who had been closely acquainted with the couple looked first to Val to explain Jim's vote. "Val got him to bring down the government," declared one long-standing executive member. "No question, Val was responsible. As far as Val was concerned, Jim should have been in the cabinet." Many others concurred with this analysis. One suggested that Jim had been "pushed by Val," a second indicated that Val was "in his ear like this all the time," while another claimed that Jim "had a wife telling him he was right, right, right." Elizabeth Dotremont is one of a handful of New Democrats who remained on amicable terms with the Waldings. She, too, perceived the critical part played by Val Walding: "Jim was bitter and Val was even bitterer [sic]. Val kept saying: 'The party set it [the nomination challenge] up. Make them pay.' She never quit. Val nattered and nattered at Jim to make them pay." This casting of Val Walding in the role of a Lady MacBeth may not be fair. Contemporary press reports revealed that she used her influence in the opposite direction when her husband was contemplating a vote to oust the government over the Throne Speech;[195] "I talked him out of that," she recollected, "but I couldn't the next time." Yet whatever her role as a final precipitant, Val Walding's vocal unhappiness was certainly one of the preconditions for her husband's 8 March vote.

Finally, there was the matter of Jim Walding's personal pride. As we have seen, he had experienced numerous stinging rejections: the cabinet disappointments of 1981 and 1986 (when political neophytes had vaulted over him into ministerial posts), the French-language crisis of 1983 and 1984 (when the entire NDP front bench had been visibly disgruntled as he delivered a ruling), and the 1986 nomination challenge (when his opponents seemed to have the blessing of the party establishment). Even to the end, this perception of mistreatment continued. Walding took some umbrage that Pawley often relied on intermediaries rather than dealing with him directly as a senior colleague. Moreover, while appearing on Peter Warren's talk-radio program in mid-February 1988, Walding was subjected to a loud and lengthy harangue from a member of the St. Vital NDP executive who lambasted the MLA for his disregard for party principles and his disloyalty to those supporters who had "worked countless hours getting him elected and re-elected."[196]

Shortly thereafter, the party whip confided to reporters that he did not par-ticularly care for Walding ("I don't find much in him to like") and threatened to "kick his ass" if he voted against the budget.[197]

It would have taken a particularly saintly individual not to harbour some desire for revenge, and many in St. Vital interpreted Walding's 8 March vote as a straightforward payback for seven years of abuse from his party. "Jim was just being vindictive" and "he was just getting back at people" were common refrains. Even Sig Laser, whose nomination challenge had been one of the prime irritants to Walding, was able to empathize with his rival's state of mind. Implicit confirmation came from both Val ("It's not an easy life being in politics, especially if you're stabbed in the back a few times") and Jim who "poured out some deeply felt emotions" and "admitted to hurt feelings" when he attempted to explain his vote to reporters.[198] On election night, Walding acknowledged that the atmosphere inside the party had not been "enjoyable or welcome. That's the trouble with people who get elected. They think that being elected confers some sort of wisdom. It doesn't."[199] Nevertheless, the MLA always insisted that his action had not simply been a matter of tit for tat, of betrayal for betrayal: "I'm only human. I tried to put all that aside. I did what I did for the people of Manitoba. Call that a rationalization if you will."[200]

Thus ended Howard Pawley's second administration. Jim Walding's vote on 8 March 1988 marked the first time in Canadian history that a majority government had fallen from a defection of one of its members.[201] Jim Walding's act, however, would have repercussions far beyond the par-liamentary record book.

7

The Fallout

THE 1988 PROVINCIAL VOTE was a disaster for the NDP. The party had grown accustomed to winning Manitoba elections; it had, after all, been in office for fifteen of the previous nineteen years. In 1969, the NDP's success had begun when Ed Schreyer had secured the leadership only seventeen days before the election. The trick, however, could not be repeated in 1988. Two years earlier, Gary Doer and Leonard Harapiak had been rookie MLAS vaulting past Jim Walding into the cabinet. On 30 March 1988, having outlasted three other rivals, these two faced off on the final ballot of another mid-campaign leadership contest. By the narrow margin of 835 to 814, Doer defeated the "Ukrainian Bobby Kennedy"[1] to succeed Howard Pawley and commence a twenty-one-year (and counting) run as leader of the Manitoba New Democratic Party.

In the short term, however, Doer faced a Herculean task of turning around his party's standing, which according to polls was languishing at 19 percent. At that level, suggested Angus Reid, it was "questionable (whether) they would elect a member."[2] Characterized by Filmon, presumably negatively, as "a very slick individual,"[3] Doer was obviously anxious to distance himself from Pawley's unpopular regime. The Manitoba NDP had "new leadership," "new ideas," "new directions," and "new and interesting people" running as candidates; there would therefore be "a lot of changes" if he formed the next government.[4] This optimistic scenario was, however, dashed on election night; the party held on to only 24 percent of the popular vote and elected only twelve MLAS.

Under normal circumstances, this would have signified a resounding victory for the Conservatives. True, the prime minister was an albatross;

both John Turner and Ed Broadbent campaigned vigorously for their provincial cousins, but in Doer's telling jab, "Mr. Mulroney's not allowed in town."[5] Otherwise, all seemed well for the Tories. In contrast to 1986, they had a well-focussed message: they pledged to be better guardians of the public purse than the spendthrift socialists who, in one particularly egregious example, had permitted the Manitoba Telephone System to blow $27 million on an ill-considered venture in Saudi Arabia. When Filmon performed well in the leaders' debate, the Tories seemed destined for a majority government.[6]

Instead, they were frustrated by the resurgent Liberals. In early January, Sharon Carstairs had allowed that her ambition was to capture at least four seats in the next provincial election.[7] The party's fortunes were soon lifted dramatically by dissatisfaction with the other two alternatives, by a determinedly centrist platform ("competence with a heart"),[8] and by the popularity of their leader. One poll showed that 40 percent of Manitobans thought that Carstairs, whose "weird squeaky voice (had) become her trademark," would make the best premier of Manitoba; the corresponding figures for Filmon and Doer were only 24 percent and 19 percent respectively.[9] On election night, the Liberals with twenty seats (from 36 percent of the vote) were only a step behind the Conservatives' total of twenty-five seats (from a 38 percent share). Gary Filmon would head a minority administration.

But if this result was bittersweet for the Tories, it was positively unpalatable for the New Democrats. Their portion of the popular vote had been halved in only seven years, and they had salvaged only four seats in metropolitan Winnipeg. Marty Dolin interpreted this massive rebuke as a straightforward signal that the party had strayed too far from its roots. "We kicked the working and middle classes with Autopac and taxes and they kicked back—hard," asserted the defeated caucus whip.[10] Former Attorney General Roland Penner, however, preferred to point the finger of blame outward, specifically at Jim Walding. "It's unfortunate that because of a treacherous individual, who betrayed the trust that had been placed in him, this happened," Penner lamented. "If we had been allowed to complete the four-year mandate we had, things would have been much different."[11] As for the alleged culprit, Walding declined to reveal his voting intentions ("I don't think that I'm going to answer that"),[12] although his earlier ruminations that "a time out of power is a time when a party rejuvenates itself"[13] provided a clear indication as to where his vote was not headed. On election night, Walding served as a local radio analyst; reputedly, he had been the station's fourth choice (behind Peter Fox, Larry Desjardins, and Howard Pawley).[14] The electoral crash of the NDP evinced no gloating. "It's always a little sad to see friends and colleagues defeated, but that happens all the time in politics," Walding observed. "What I did, I did to benefit Manitoba. If some people have to suffer or go down in defeat, so be it."[15]

Walding had evinced a desire to slip quietly out of the limelight (although serving as a political commentator and granting interviews to the media may not have been the optimum method to effect same). "If I've been forgotten, that's fine," he claimed on the day of the election. "That's how I wanted it."[16] Forgetting Jim Walding, however, would be a mistake. The chain of events documented in the preceding four chapters had a variety of important consequences. Like a diving cormorant, Walding's sneak attack sent ripples outwards. The immediate impact was felt in people's personal lives and in the NDP's decline. Yet all Manitobans and, arguably, all Canadians were ultimately influenced by Walding's conduct.

Personal Consequences

In the short term, many people's lives were upended by the non-confidence vote and subsequent election.[17] MLAs from the class of '81 (who had been re-elected in 1986) were still one year short of the minimum pensionable service when the government fell. The Conservative member for Assiniboia, Ric Nordman, was sixty-eight at the time; despite fourteen years of public service (seven as a city councillor, seven as a member of the legislature), he was left without a pension when defeated by the Liberal candidate in 1988. Feeling "cheated," Nordman took on part-time accounting work in the family travel agency;[18] he died eight years later.

Not just MLAs found their life circumstances dramatically altered. When the party crashed to third place, many NDP apparatchiks were suddenly unemployed. George Ford had been clerk of the executive council under

Pawley; he and his partner Agnes Ananichuk (ironically, an anti-Walding member of the St. Vital executive) were obliged to relocate to British Columbia in search of work. Bruce Buckley, one of the premier's aides, happened upon Walding in a parking lot some time after the government fell. "Thanks, Jim," said Buckley sarcastically. "I'm out of a job now." Walding replied: "You'll thank me for it someday." Not yet, apparently.

Admittedly, the opportunities and advantages lost by some were gained by others, and a sufficiently sensitive and wide-ranging scale might, at least among those not intimately entangled in the Walding affair, detect no net individual losses effectuated by the maverick MLA's actions. For the principal players, however, the aftershocks were overwhelmingly negative. Consider the case of Howard Pawley. Even leaving aside the unceremonious end to his seven years as premier and his nineteen years as the MLA for Selkirk, Pawley was deeply affected by Walding's act. During his resignation announcement, Pawley claimed he was neither angry nor resentful towards the renegade backbencher. "I'm not looking back to yesterday, but forward to the campaign and the re-election of my colleagues," the premier maintained. "Jim Walding is not our opposition. Gary Filmon and the Conservatives are the opposition."[19] On election night, however, when the full magnitude of his party's collapse became apparent, Pawley's guard dropped. As the "visibly shaken" premier sped off to party headquarters, he delivered a parting shot: "Walding is history. He belongs to the ashtrays of history."[20] Nor did the matter soon fade from his consciousness. On "many" occasions after the government fell, Gerri Unwin's path would cross that of Howard Pawley. Invariably, the former premier would ask, "Gerri, what do you think?" Unwin recalled that "it was just tearing him apart." The RCMP's aborted inquiry into the Walding affair in the mid-1990s did nothing to ease Pawley's mind on the matter, especially when his access-to-information applications yielded only newspaper clippings. As recently as 2005, Pawley characterized the non-confidence vote as "the most traumatic thing in my life and it continues to be. Certainly it troubles me that this has never been answered, never explained."[21]

For most St. Vital New Democrats, the stakes were manifestly lower; even so, the bitter feelings have continued to linger almost two decades later.

Admittedly, a few have been able to enjoy some closure; two executive stalwarts claimed that they had "buried all hatchets" long ago. As well, a few were able to make a wry joke about the affair; pointing to a telephone booth and claiming it had been the site of "Jim Walding's retirement party." And at least one remained on good terms with the former MLA; George Schamber and his wife visited the Waldings when they were living out of the province- and thereafter enjoyed occasional telephone contact.[22] For most, however, the anger towards Walding is still remarkably close to the surface. Even his name is regarded as something akin to a swear word, although the highly localized and partisan nature of this phenomenon will prevent Walding from joining the pantheon of those (including Machiavelli, Boycott, and, most pointedly, Quisling) whose political notoriety has become embedded in the language. One St. Vital New Democrat expressed his "deep bitterness" about Walding's behaviour; upon discovering that the former MLA had returned to live in Winnipeg, there was "surprise that no one had got out the tar pot." Chapter 3 documented Hugh McMeel's role in Jim Walding's rise to prominence. McMeel openly acknowledges that the bitter feelings towards his former protegé have not abated with time: "Some years back, my wife and I came across Jim and Val at a funeral. We were seated at the same table as them. I wouldn't talk to them. I wouldn't look at them. Whenever I have seen Val in the supermarket, I have looked the other way. And this, even though at one point I knew the Walding kids as well as I knew my own."

It would be extraordinarily difficult to be the object of such contempt, not least because it was emanating from neighbours who had, for many years, also been friends and supporters. Denise Mignot, it will be recalled, stuck with Jim Walding on the second ballot despite overwhelming familial pressure to the contrary; when the government fell, she phoned Walding to convey her distress. "If we had wanted a Conservative government, we would have worked for them," she pointed out. "How could you do this to all the people who worked so hard to get you elected?" He replied, "Yes, I know."[23] In the fall of 1988, few were surprised when the Waldings announced plans to sell their home and leave Manitoba. "Moving to Victoria is something we've been half-planning for a long time," Walding explained. "It's a very nice part of the country that a lot of prairie people retire to. I've decided to join them."[24] The following spring, the couple opened a four-suite bed and break-fast in a Victoria suburb, and Jim also took a part-time job as an instructor with a local optical company. He continued to express no "regret" for his action: "It's something that happened, something that's in the chapter before this one. We've passed that now."[25] Two years later, however, the Waldings sold (for a modest profit) their bed and breakfast. "It was just getting too much for us," claimed Walding. "We were up early in the morning and it was seven days a week."[26] The couple then opened a flower shop, and Val contin-ued to work as a fragrance demonstrator in a local department store. The charms of the West Coast, however, soon began to fade, especially living so far from their extended family. In 1995, the Waldings moved into a modest bungalow in the Winnipeg northeast, far from their former stomping grounds in St. Vital.[27]

The Waldings could not have imagined that reconciliation with their former friends and colleagues in the NDP could be easily achieved, even with Jim insisting that he did not "feel any animosity towards anyone."[28] Some years previously, they had returned to the Manitoba legislature for the unveiling of Walding's portrait in the Speaker's gallery. Although Liberal and Conservative MLAS were out in force for the ceremonial event, there were no representatives from the NDP caucus. As House leader Steve Ashton explained, "After the events of 1988, I have no reason or intention of attending an event with Jim Walding. I sat next to him. I talked to him. I trusted him. I don't know what I could say to him. It would not be pleasant. The great betrayal continues and I know many people in the NDP who feel the same way."[29] Echoed Flin Flon MLA Jerry Storie, "Jim Walding isn't a hero of mine, that's for sure."[30] To Gary Filmon, the NDP boycott was "regrettable," while Sharon Carstairs deemed it "childish," but Walding seemed unaffected: "They're busy people. You'll have to ask them if they had a motive."[31] Nor were there many in attendance from the St. Vital NDP, although George Schamber and Gil Mignot put in an appearance.[32] Walding's long-time "sign man" took the opportunity to upbraid his former champion: "I'm willing to let bygones be bygones, but that was a very despicable thing you did." Walding offered no reply. In short, it was a sombre, rather than a celebratory, occasion for the one-time Speaker. As one editorialist summarized, party members "might have turned out to see Mr. Walding hanged, but not to see him hung."[33]

Worse yet, the rumours of illegal or improper behaviour never seemed to disappear. By election night, 1988, Walding was clearly vexed by media questions about his integrity. Suggestions of a deal with the Tories were "offensive"; added Walding, "It was asked once and I answered it. The answer is still the same."[34] Even so, the questions continued. An exasperated Val Walding finally addressed the charge. "If there was a deal, I wouldn't be working 10-hour shifts," she objected. "I'd be lying in the sun in Hawaii."[35] For years after, journalists continued to pick at these allegations.[36]

For almost twenty years, the Waldings' existence revolved around the Manitoba NDP. The party was at the centre not just of their political life, but also of their social life. All that was changed irrevocably by the vote on 8 March 1988. For his part, Walding was "prepared" to live with the enduring enmity of his erstwhile comrades. "I'm not surprised," he once observed. "There's a lot of people who lost their jobs, so they are bitter."[37] Nevertheless, even his old-time adversary, Sig Laser, admitted to feeling some sympathy with Walding's circumstance: "Walding cut himself off from his family, his class, his people. And whatever triggered it, he's cut himself off. The action is too despicable to call him a tragic figure, but it is sad, it sure is sad. You don't wish that kind of isolation and cutting off from friends and associates on anyone."

Party Consequences

Entering the 1988 campaign, the Manitoba New Democratic Party had high hopes of retaining St. Vital. The party had held the seat for the previous seventeen years, and, in 1986, even a wounded Jim Walding had been able to fend off a strong Tory challenge. Speaking on behalf of the constituency executive the day after the fall of the government, Gerri Unwin put on a brave face. "I know a lot of people here are mad at the NDP and may agree with what Mr. Walding did, but if they stop to think rationally, they'll still support us," Unwin maintained. "There's strong support for the NDP here. I think we can win it."[38] Unwin also claimed that there was "no shortage" of possible contenders for the NDP nomination. With hindsight, it is apparent that she enjoyed inside information; Unwin soon announced her own candidacy. Les Campbell, a relative newcomer to the constituency, likewise joined the fray, as did, inevitably, Sig Laser. The St. Vital NDP was thus one of the few constituency associations not to acclaim its candidate in 1988. Like Howard Pawley's bastion of Selkirk (another riding that the NDP "hoped to retain")[39] and Inkster (where, in a disturbing instance of déjà vu, another Pawley aide was challenging another rebellious backbencher),[40] there would be a contest in St. Vital.

With the nominating convention date set (on 12 March) for 20 March, there was no opportunity to initiate a fresh recruitment drive, so all three candidates concentrated on rekindling the flagging enthusiasm of the existing members. This time, there was more "overt animosity" between Laser and Unwin than had been the case two years previously. The neophyte Campbell was brushed aside on the convention's opening ballot, and in the decisive showdown Unwin narrowly prevailed over Laser by ninety-two to eighty-three.[41] "Life must go on," declared the victor afterwards. "Life for the NDP must go on."[42] Walding's betrayal was now just a "sad memory" that would not affect her chances of retaining the seat. "I think that people are just at the point right now where they're really trying to forget what's happened," Unwin insisted. "I think people are going to say: 'It's history; let's get on with it.'"[43]

She could not have been more wrong. The NDP campaign in St. Vital was a disaster. Many long-standing workers refused to get involved. Those that did campaign for Unwin confronted a Catherine wheel of anger (against the NDP's record, against the party's treatment of Walding, against Walding's defeat of the government, and against having another election). One party worker recalled going door-to-door attempting to hand out Unwin literature. Many householders took the pamphlet and attempted to strike the hapless volunteer; some of the less irate just refused it altogether, preferring to let the leaflet slip to the ground. It was, in short, a "bloody brutal" campaign. As the holder of the poisoned chalice, Gerri Unwin took the brunt of the abuse.

Unwin recalled that she was frequently greeted with, "Get out of my yard. I know who you are. Get out of my yard." To its credit, the party continued to pour resources into the campaign; Unwin, like the Tory challenger, spent approximately $20,000, while Liberal expenses were just over $13,000. Alas, the NDP money was not employed to maximum effect. One pamphlet misspelled Unwin's name no fewer than six times; after the campaign, boxes of unused Unwin material had to be landfilled (which at least had the salutary effect of eliminating the middleman).

Paul Herriot, who was back for a second try as the Tory candidate in St. Vital, could have been excused for assuming that victory was at hand. The NDP campaign was imploding and the Liberals were starting from so far back (only 15 percent of the constituency's vote in 1986) that media pundits dismissed their chances.[44] As a result, St. Vital Tories simply set their sights on replicating the total from the previous election. "The last time it was a tough fight and we thought we could win, so we plugged in everything we could," observed Herriot in mid-campaign. "But there is not a great deal we can do more than we did the last time."[45] The Conservative vote in St. Vital actually dropped marginally in 1988. But while the NDP vote was cut in half, the Liberal share essentially tripled, and, to the surprise of many, Bob Rose was elected as part of the red tide that rolled across metropolitan Winnipeg.

The 1988 result was a calamity for St. Vital's New Democrats. Not since the election of 1962 had an NDP candidate in the riding received a lower share of the vote than the 22 percent garnered by Gerri Unwin. What made the result in St. Vital particularly dire was the collapse of the NDP in its traditional heartland. In 1986, as Table 7 makes clear, Jim Walding had relied upon the approximately 70 percent of his electorate that lived east of St. Mary's Road to overcome the Tory lead in the more socially advantaged west-side neighbourhoods. In 1988, by contrast, Gerri Unwin finished a poor third even in her party's supposed stronghold. In spite of the difficult campaign, Unwin expressed surprise at the decisiveness of her defeat: "Right to the end I thought it was a race between the NDP and the Conservatives." St. Vital's status as a bellwether had again been confirmed; the provincial NDP's meagre total had been only two points greater.

Table 7: St. Vital Vote Breakdown, 1986 and 1988 (%)[46]

| | 1986 | | | 1988 | | |
	PC	Lib	NDP	PC	Lib	NDP
West of St. Mary's Road	49	14	37	42	42	16
East of St. Mary's Road	36	16	48	32	44	24

Nor did New Democratic fortunes improve markedly when yet another provincial election was held in 1990. True, the NDP rebounded to Official Opposition status with twenty seats from a 29 percent share of the popular vote. In this, they were manifestly aided by the vagaries of the single-member plurality electoral system; the Liberals collapsed to seven seats despite winning a healthy 28 percent of the vote. At this point, the allure of winning the NDP nomination in St. Vital had essentially vanished. A para-chute candidate, Kathleen McCallum, was nominated by Sig Laser and acclaimed to carry the NDP standard. McCallum improved the party's share of the vote to 26 percent (only three points below the province-wide mark), but still finished a badly beaten third. During this period, the St. Vital NDP association's financial free-fall, which had been precipitated by Walding's withdrawal from constituency affairs in the mid-1980s, continued unabated. After fighting three provincial elections in five years, the association was encumbered by an accumulated debt of over $20,000. One member who moved into the constituency in 1988 and soon found herself on the execu-tive was struck by the strange combination of "desperation" and "lethargy" that seemed to pervade the association. Something had to be done to reduce the financial burden, but the task seemed too monumental even to com-mence. Eventually, twelve executive members co-signed a loan, although the treasurer had to devise a different route to walk his dog to forestall the credit union manager banging on the window as they went by. Through a punitive regime of self-taxation (elaborately disguised as bake sales, con-stituency dinners, and the like), the debt was gradually reduced. When the amount reached $3000, the pretense of raising external monies was entirely abandoned; ten members of the executive reached into their wallets for

$300 apiece. Only at this point was there a reversal in what had been dubbed "the NDP's declining St. Vitality."

By 1995, the party's nomination in the riding was again a prize to be coveted. Several aspirants came forward, and, at last, victory went to Sig Laser. Unfortunately, Laser spent four days in hospital after hitting his head while ice-skating and did little door-to-door campaigning. Even so, Laser was ahead early in the count, but the Conservative incumbent eventually prevailed by just over 600 votes. At 35 percent of the vote, Laser had outpaced the provincial NDP average by two points. It was not until 1999 that the NDP came to power both in St. Vital (when Nancy Allan swept out the Tory incumbent) and in the provincial legislature (where, on his fourth try, Gary Doer finally replaced Gary Filmon as premier).

One pundit had speculated, shortly after the government fell in 1988, that the Manitoba NDP might one day "thank" Walding for obliging the party "to revive and renew itself." Under Doer's leadership, it was suggested, the Manitoba NDP might even steal the 1988 vote; at "the very least, the NDP will be well off for the next election."[47] It did not prove to be that straightforward. Walding's act crippled the party in the key constituency of St. Vital and left Manitobans with long-lasting memories of high taxes and mismanagement. It would be over a decade before Manitoba's "governing party" would return to office.

Provincial Consequences

The budgetary defeat and the subsequent provincial election dramatically shortened the tenure of the final Pawley administration. Had Walding not pulled the plug (then or subsequently), there would likely have been at least two further years of NDP government. Were the lives of ordinary Manitobans significantly altered during the 1988 to 1990 interval when the Progressive Conservatives suddenly found themselves sitting to the Speaker's right? Had this been the Tory party of Sterling Lyon and had they held a majority of seats in the legislature, the answer would almost certainly have been in the affirmative. But neither of these conditions obtained. During his first five years at the helm, Gary Filmon had attempted to craft a more moderate and

centrist alternative to the NDP. And as premier of a fragile minority government, he was unlikely to tilt dramatically to the right. Variations between the
final Pawley and the first Filmon administration, therefore, were always likely to be matters of nuance.

Admittedly, symbolic differences were easy to detect. The nameplate on
the door of Manitoba Hydro's chief executive officer was pointedly switched
from "chairperson" to "chairman." One cabinet member opted to redesign
her ministry's letterhead by replacing a line of NDP green with a more appropriate hue of Tory blue.[48] Another shook hands with demonstrators wearing
Ku Klux Klan hoods; his later partial apology left the impression that he
could not "fathom" what he had done wrong.[49] Yet another minister advised
Liberal Gulzar Cheema, a Sikh, to "Sit down, boy."[50] All of which arguably
paled beside the extraordinary appointment of Grant Russell to sit on the
Manitoba Intercultural Council. Since Russell had served as the vociferously
anti-bilingual spearhead of Grassroots Manitoba, this move was characterized as "throwing raw meat to the dinosaurs on the party's right wing."[51]
Symbolic politics are anything but trivial. Each of these actions sent clear
messages to Manitobans about the Conservatives' conception of tolerance
and equality, and each provoked strong reactions from those (including
most NDP MLAS) who harboured a different understanding.

Yet at the substantive level of budgets and legislation, sharp differences
between the Pawley administration and their immediate successor were
much harder to detect. The Filmon government introduced its first budget
on 8 August 1988. Ironically, it bore a remarkable resemblance to the document that, five months earlier, had precipitated the ouster of the NDP. Finance
minister Clayton Manness may have railed against the "unsustainable level
of public sector spending" under the New Democrats, but in both budgets,
total expenditures were projected to be $4.56 billion, and the proposed
mining, gasoline, and cigarette tax increases were also identical.[52] In fact, the
only major difference could be found in the Tories' projection of a significantly lower deficit (thanks principally to windfall mineral royalties and
sharply higher equalization payments). At this stage, the Manitoba NDP was
not anxious to fight another provincial election; they were undoubtedly

delighted to discover that they could support the first Conservative budget without betraying any strongly held beliefs.

Much the same could be said about the minority government's second (and final) budget of 5 June 1989. The 1987 NDP budget had ramped up some taxes in anticipation of enjoying a much improved fiscal circumstance at the end of their mandate; the unexpected change of government, however, meant that it was the Tories who were taking advantage of spiralling revenues. In fact, Manness was able to lower the deficit still further, while reducing taxes for middle-income families and hiking the education and health budgets by 7 percent. Once again, the NDP found relatively little to quibble about; the proposed cuts were, as Gary Doer acknowledged, "almost the exact same tax breaks" on which the NDP had campaigned fourteen months previously.[53] Less than a day after its introduction, Doer announced his party's support for the budget.[54]

Nor did Filmon's first government transform the provincial statute book. The premier claimed to recognize "the strength of the legacy we have inherited," and insisted that Manitobans were not "looking for a revolution—turning the province upside down in a fit of ideological zealotry."[55] Cutting back social programs was a favourite project for neo-liberal governments of that era, but in neither words nor deeds did Filmon's minority administration display such an inclination, and provincial expenditures in health and education catapulted upwards. Some social groups were delighted when they did not suffer at the hands of the incoming regime. Franco-Manitobans, for example, had bitter memories of Filmon's conduct early in his stewardship and were understandably "fearful of what would happen to French-language services and minority rights." Instead, they discovered that the government was prepared to follow "primarily the same policy" as the NDP by expanding services for francophones and moving bilingual civil servants to areas of high French demand.[56] In fact, in a November 1989 speech, which drew a standing ovation from Franco-Manitobans, Filmon pledged to extend French-language services to a wide range of government agencies, hospital boards, and Crown corporations. Complained Grant Russell, his erstwhile ally in the language wars of 1983 and 1984, the premier was pandering to Manitoba francophones' "delusions of grandeur."[57]

Having experienced the cutbacks to northern communities under the Lyon administration (and having consistently sent a block of New Democrats to the legislature),[58] Manitoba's Aboriginals were also trepidatious about a Filmon government. They, too, were pleasantly surprised. The Conservatives doubled the budget of an inquiry into the treatment of Natives under the justice system, advanced $10 million to reserves damaged by provincial hydro development, and allowed a band in The Pas to set up their own gaming commission. According to the president of the Manitoba Métis Federation, the Tories had been prepared "to sit down with us and deal straightforwardly. We get through, we get listened to."[59]

That Manitobans experienced two years of remarkably mainstream government after the ouster of the NDP cannot be denied. Nevertheless, one must not push this argument too far. The first Filmon administration was not indistinguishable from their immediate predecessor. There were no cutbacks to education under the Tories, but within that spending envelope, there were sharply higher grants to private schools.[60] Daycare spending was likewise maintained, but, again, more of the funds were funnelled to private operators, precipitating demonstrations in front of the legislative buildings by public-sector child-care workers.[61] Rent controls were not scrapped, but tenant organizations were still upset when the government refused to proceed with legislation that would have obliged slum landlords to make needed repairs.[62] There was no wholesale purge of the civil service, but the Conservatives did move on deconcentration; 692 public-sector jobs were moved out of Winnipeg into rural Manitoba, the vast majority to constituencies held by cabinet ministers.[63] Widespread privatization of provincial Crown corporations did not occur; the Tories did, however, sell off the general insurance portion of the Manitoba Public Insurance Corporation, just as that division was starting to become profitable.[64] The provincial labour code was not gutted, but the Tories' attempt to scupper final-offer selection only failed when the Liberals insisted on an amendment unacceptable to the government.[65] The Filmon administration did, however, eliminate a $200,000 annual grant to the Manitoba Labour Education Centre,[66] and, until public protests forced a backdown, amended safety regulations to permit higher levels of carcinogens in workplaces.[67]

None of these initiatives would have come forward under a New Democratic government. Conversely, much of the Pawley administration's planned legislative agenda (including measures to establish a public health trust fund and to extend pay equity to school boards) disappeared without a trace.[68] Government reaches deeply into many aspects of our social existence; it is likely that all Manitobans were, in some fashion, influenced by the replacement of a New Democratic with a Progressive Conservative administration.

National Consequences

That Walding's vote affected himself, his family and neighbours, his party, and even his province is not especially surprising. That his action may have irrevocably altered the Canadian political community is, on the face of it, a more implausible claim. Yet even contemporary observers were aware that the consequences of Walding's vote could be felt well beyond Manitoba's borders. It was suggested, for example, that the ouster of the Pawley government would "likely affect national debates on such issues as free trade and abortion."[69] Without minimizing the importance of these particular discussions, we shall here look exclusively at the consequences for the Meech Lake Accord. Much has been written about this ill-fated constitutional deal and most of it is not directly relevant to our concerns. Here, we will provide only a brief, Manitoba-centric chronology before turning to the key question: can the fall of the Meech Lake Accord be linked to the fall of the Pawley government?

The *Constitution Act, 1867* (a.k.a. the *British North America Act*) begat the *Constitution Act, 1982*, which, in turn, begat the Meech Lake Accord of 1987. Canada's founding constitutional document was a simple act of the British Parliament and contained no mechanisms for subsequent generations of Canadians directly to alter its provisions. Neither of these features was particularly problematic for the fathers of Confederation, but both became more irksome as Canadians increasingly took for granted their autonomy from Britain. After many years of intense bickering, the constitutional logjam was finally broken when Prime Minister Pierre Trudeau orchestrated the *Constitution Act, 1982*. In addition to entrenching the Charter of Rights and

Freedoms, the Act provided for the patriation of Canada's constitution from Westminster and the inclusion of a domestic amending formula.

Resolving two long-standing problems had not come without a price. Over the preceding two decades, many Quebecers had begun to question their attachment to the Canadian political community; in fact, in 1980, fully 40 percent of the participating electorate had voted in a referendum to give their provincial government a mandate to negotiate some sort of sovereignty-association with the rest of the country. Yet even if the Charter ultimately proves to be a force for national reconciliation, it is clear that, in the short term, the *Constitution Act, 1982* only served to magnify Canada's English-French divide. None of Quebec's traditional political demands (such as greater powers or a veto over future amendments) found their way into the document, and the process by which it emerged (with the Quebec delegation sleeping across the river in Hull while representatives of the federal government and the nine English-speaking provinces cobbled together a deal) was a godsend for those Quebec nationalists intent on breaking up the country.

Bound by constitutional provisions to which it had not consented, the Quebec government expressed its displeasure over the next few years in ways that were both practical and symbolic. To newly elected Prime Minister Brian Mulroney, this rent in the national fabric was unacceptable (not least because Quebec's reintegration offered the prospect of both political gain and historical one-upmanship).[70] To Ottawa's envoys, Quebec Premier Robert Bourassa outlined his terms:

1. Quebec wanted the right to nominate three of the nine judges on the Canadian Supreme Court.
2. Quebec wanted the right to opt out with full compensation from future national shared-cost programs.
3. Quebec wanted a veto over a wider range of constitutional amendments.
4. Quebec wanted to be given special powers over immigration in order to protect the province's francophone character.
5. Most contentiously, Quebec wanted its distinctive status enshrined in the Constitution.

Perhaps because his administration was ideologically opposed to an interventionist central state, Mulroney was not particularly troubled by any of these demands, and multilateral discussions with the remaining provinces were also quite encouraging.[71] Accordingly, the prime minister invited the ten premiers to constitutional discussions on 30 April 1987 at his retreat in Meech Lake, Quebec.

Prior to the meeting, Howard Pawley had expressed his unease about two particular items on the table. First, the federal government was proposing to increase the necessary level of support under the general amending procedure from seven provinces having 50 percent of the country's people (as mandated under the *Constitution Act, 1982*) to seven provinces having 80 percent of the population. The net impact of such a change would be to satisfy Quebec's request for a constitutional veto; even more populous Ontario would obviously get one as well. Pawley was unimpressed: "We're opposed to any blanket veto for any province, whether it be Quebec or Ontario, or any other particular province."[72] Second, the federal government was also proposing, as per Quebec's demand, to rein in its spending power by making it easier for provinces to opt out, with compensation, from federal initiatives in areas of provincial jurisdiction. According to Pawley, this could create a "patchwork across the country, and prevent the development of major new social programs like medicare."[73] Given the apparent chasm that existed between his position and that of Robert Bourassa, the Manitoba premier was skeptical that a deal could be brokered, rating the chances at "less than 50 per cent."[74]

Howard Pawley's pessimism, however, was unfounded. After a marathon negotiating session, the eleven heads of government were able to reach an agreement through the simple expedient of extending to all ten provinces most of the rights and powers demanded by Quebec. Thus, all provinces received increased opportunities to veto future amendments, all received the power to nominate Supreme Court justices and (in a late addition) senators, all received greater control over immigration, and all received the right, under certain conditions, to opt out of federal programs with compensation. Quebec's exceptionality was acknowledged only in a clause that bestowed upon its provincial government the power "to preserve and promote" its "distinct society." Both of Manitoba's concerns had been addressed; the province would have the same rights as Quebec and Ontario to veto future amendments and, in what Pawley labelled as a "major breakthrough," those opting out of federal initiatives would only receive compensation if they implemented a similar program meeting national objectives.[75] After the meeting, the Manitoba premier was unusually ebullient. He declared that he was "thrilled" with the deal and looking forward to "the happy job" of holding public hearings on the Accord.[76] "Personally," concluded Pawley, "I feel a better and prouder Canadian."[77] The Manitoba premier's bonhomie extended even to his long-time antagonist, Brian Mulroney. According to Pawley, the prime minister "showed good leadership,"[78] and "deserved special praise."[79]

Pawley's euphoria quickly abated. The eleven heads of government had only come to an agreement in principle; a second meeting, scheduled for 2 June 1987 would be required to sign off on the written document. Within three days of returning to Winnipeg, the Manitoba premier began to fret that the "major breakthrough" on the federal spending power would not be completely reflected in the legal text. "If I was persuaded that federal power would be weakened, I would oppose [the Accord]," warned Pawley before suggesting that provinces that opt out of federal programs would only be compensated if they meet national "criteria" as well as "objectives."[80] Pawley clearly did not foresee such a change as a likely deal-breaker. "I have no hesitation in saying there will be no problem with the wording," he declared. "If there is any looseness, it will be fixed."[81] As the 2 June meeting approached, Pawley continued to insist that he was only seeking "some minor and some technical wording changes" to the spending-power clause,[82] perhaps by stipulating that national objectives must be defined by the federal Parliament. At this time, Quebec was likewise seeking a change to clarify and strengthen the distinct-society clause,[83] but neither dissident evinced much sympathy for the other's proposal. When Pawley upped the ante by also asking for some movement on Aboriginal rights and for Canada-wide hearings on the deal,[84] and when federal officials were unable to draft a pre-meeting text acceptable to all parties,[85] the Accord was clearly in some jeopardy.

Once again, however, the doubters were confounded. After a marathon nineteen-hour negotiating session at Ottawa's Langevin Block, the eleven heads of government were able to agree to the legal text of the Meech Lake Accord. Pawley had enlisted Ontario's David Peterson as an ally,[86] and as the price for their signatures, the two premiers had extracted concessions over Aboriginal rights, multiculturalism, the distinct-society clause, and the spending power. It was the latter point which Pawley stressed, when, at 5:30 a.m. on the morning of 3 June, he emerged from the meeting. "I'm satisfied that the national objectives are tied into that program," insisted the Manitoba premier. "There was a lack of clarity. I believe that clarity has been improved in this document."[87] When Pawley returned to the Manitoba legislature two days later, he was greeted by applause from both sides of the chamber. While expressing regret that the Accord might make it more difficult for the northern territories to achieve provincial status, Pawley offered a glowing assessment of the deal. "It is historic because of what it contains and because of what it symbolizes—renewed spirit of good will and reconciliation across Canada," he summarized. "I am particularly proud of the contribution Manitoba was able to make in creating this new accord."[88]

Quebec was the first to ratify the Accord. Anxious to forestall any proposed changes, Premier Bourassa pushed the package through the national assembly on 23 June 1987—sixteen years to the day after he had sunk an earlier constitutional initiative, the Victoria Charter. Canada's three-year amendment clock thus began to tick; unless ratified by the national Parliament and the legislatures of the other nine provinces before 23 June 1990, the Meech Lake Accord would expire.

In Manitoba, no such haste was apparent, although unbeknownst to Pawley, his government had only nine months left in office. Manitoba was legally required to hold public hearings on the Accord, and although the Conservatives wished these to commence in the autumn,[89] the premier demurred. "There is no rush," he claimed, and suggested that the hearings would be held in early 1988.[90] During the final months of his premiership, Pawley's public support for the Meech Lake Accord rarely wavered. In September 1987, he indicated his pleasure when the parliamentary committee charged with scrutinizing the deal issued a favourable recommendation. According to Pawley, the MPS had backed his view that "despite some problems" (which could be addressed in subsequent constitutional rounds), "the accord is worth supporting."[91] Shortly thereafter, the Accord was approved by a tally of 242 to sixteen in the House of Commons, with all fourteen Manitoba MPS (from all three parties) voting with the majority. When a group of seventy-five prominent New Democrats signalled their unease with the Accord in November,[92] Pawley was unmoved. "I feel that on balance it is worthy of our support."[93]

In late December, however, Pawley briefly pulled back. Piqued by Ottawa's relentless pursuit of free trade with the United States, the Manitoba premier withdrew his public support for the constitutional deal. "Now, I feel my only obligation is to present Meech to the people and listen," he asserted. "I will not promote or push for Meech Lake."[94] Paradoxically, Pawley also indicated to reporters that he "privately" continued to back the Accord.[95] One day later, perhaps in anticipation of being labelled as "uncertain, irresolute and untrustworthy,"[96] Pawley returned to the status quo ante by stressing that he was "still prepared to urge the legislature to approve the accord."[97]

Even so, pressure began to build within the Manitoba NDP's extra-parliamentary wing for the government to insist that the deal be amended to take into account the particular concerns of women, of Aboriginals, and of northerners. While three constituency associations submitted policy resolutions in favour of Meech Lake in advance of the party's March 1988 annual meeting, there were fifteen resolutions to the contrary. Anxious not to embarrass their premier, the convention's policy committee crafted an ingenious composite resolution, which, while complaining that the Accord was still marred by "significant flaws," nonetheless urged the party to endorse the recognition of Quebec, to demand a more open process for future constitutional talks, to call for the entrenchment of Aboriginal rights, to praise Howard Pawley for the improvements he had secured through negotiations, to listen carefully to the views expressed in public hearings, and "to take steps to deal with the flaws in the Accord prior to giving final approval to the Accord in the legislature."[98] Both the nature of these steps (amendments? a parallel accord? an agenda for future discussions?) as well as their requisite level of success were left unspecified. The resulting debate was grotesquely confused, since both defenders and opponents of the Accord spoke vigorously in favour of the resolution. The premier's emotional intervention ("several times, his voice almost broke in mid-sentence")[99] urged delegates to support the deal: "The document on balance deserves the support of Manitobans and deserves the support of New Democrats." The premier agreed to seek amendments if, during public hearings, the "collective wisdom of Manitobans" uncovered any "fundamental flaws"; tellingly, he revealed that nothing he had yet heard fit that description.[100] With the support of both Meechophiles and Meechophobes, the resolution passed easily; back at the legislature, a relieved Pawley informed reporters that the wording did not require him to change course.[101] On the following day, however, his government fell.

The period between 8 March 1988 (when Walding voted against the budget) and 23 June 1990 (when the Meech Lake Accord officially expired) is less relevant to this discussion. The decisive event, as several contemporary observers detected, had already transpired. "I initially thought that the chances (of the Accord's ratification) were a bit more than 50-50, then I thought they were considerably higher than that," observed Peter Leslie of Queen's University in early April 1988; "now I think they're probably less than that."[102] Three weeks later, the startling electoral breakthrough of the Manitoba Liberals punctuated this assessment; Sharon Carstairs's bald summary was that "Meech Lake is dead."[103] Walding's vote had torpedoed both the Manitoba NDP government and the Meech Lake Accord; the death agonies of the latter, however, were rather more drawn out.

In fact, outside Manitoba, the business of ratifying the Accord proceeded apace. In order to overcome objections raised in the Senate, the House of Commons repassed the constitutional amendment (again, by an overwhelming margin), and in early July Newfoundland became the eighth province formally to come onside. While Frank McKenna of New Brunswick continued his delaying strategy, Manitoba's minority Tory government eventually introduced the Accord into the legislature on 16 December 1988. Alas,

Premier Bourassa opted three days later to employ the notwithstanding clause to rescue his province's language law from an adverse Supreme Court decision. Declaring the actions of the Quebec government to be both a "national tragedy" and a violation of the "spirit" of Meech Lake,[104] Filmon withdrew the Accord from legislative consideration and cancelled the proposed hearings on the grounds that they would only elicit "a very negative, anti-Quebec backlash."[105]

The Accord continued to unravel throughout 1989. In April, another of the deal's original signatories lost office, as the Newfoundland electorate turned to Clyde Wells and the Liberal Party. The new premier pledged, if necessary, to rescind his province's previous ratification of the Accord. Public hearings on the package in Manitoba and New Brunswick attracted a wide range of hostile interveners, many of them disturbingly ill-informed; one Winnipeg woman alleged that Premier Bourassa was backed by an "international conspiracy of interests," including the Mafia.[106] Both provinces released the results of their deliberations in October; while the New Brunswick report was relatively conciliatory, Manitoba demanded six major amendments and the effective gutting of the Accord. Heading a shaky minority administration and with both Opposition parties clearly offside, Premier Filmon offered a terse summary: "The simple fact is that the accord, as it now stands, cannot and will not be approved by the Manitoba Legislature."[107] Even so, representatives of both the Quebec and the national government continued to insist that no changes to the package could be contemplated, that, once reopened, the deal could never be stitched back together again. It was, in short, Meech Lake or nothing.

The abyss it would be. A federal-provincial meeting in November 1989 resolved nothing, and the spring of 1990 brought no net progress. True, New Brunswick was soon to pass the Accord, but this was counterbalanced by Newfoundland rescinding its approval. In early June, there was a final attempt to break the impasse. Under intense, emotional, psychological, and, on one occasion, physical pressure from the other nine heads of government, Gary Filmon and Clyde Wells undertook at least to bring the Accord to a vote in their respective legislatures.[108] With less than three weeks to go before the amendment clock would metaphorically strike midnight, this was never going to be a straightforward undertaking. In Manitoba, a single New Democratic MLA, Elijah Harper, skillfully exploited the legislative rules to delay the Accord's introduction until its passage became a practical impossibility.[109] Seeing the outcome in Manitoba, Clyde Wells did not even bother to hold up his end of the bargain. On 23 June 1990, the Meech Lake Accord officially expired.

But it did not have to play out that way. If Howard Pawley's government had simply survived for an additional eight or nine months, there might have been public hearings in Manitoba on Meech Lake in the early summer of 1988, with the Accord receiving legislative ratification later that summer or in the early autumn. Several factors buttress the plausibility of this scenario, not the least of which is the premier's relatively steadfast support of the package. True, Pawley's backing was always conditional on the failure of public hearings to uncover some "fundamental flaw" with the deal. Yet by the outset of 1988, the case against Meech Lake had already been clearly and forcefully articulated; if the Manitoba premier had not yet heard anything that fatally compromised the Accord, he was never likely to do so. Moreover, Pawley's status as a Langevin Block signatory placed on him a duty to see the deal through. "I take it as given that all premiers signed the deal and will have it endorsed by their legislatures," insisted the prime minister. "It's settled, it's done. They gave their word. That's as good as gold to me," he said.[110] Echoed Jake Epp, Manitoba's senior cabinet minister, "Mr. Pawley has his signature on the Meech Lake accord ... He's honored his word on Meech Lake."[111] Nor was Pawley insensitive to this moral obligation. "The commitment to introduce the deal is by the current premiers," he asserted. "It's not binding on a new premier."[112] Since the Manitoba premier was "current," rather than "new," he was manifestly aware that he had made a binding commitment.

Pawley had, in fact, already moved to fulfill his end of the bargain; just prior to the assembly proroguing in 1987, the NDP House leader's attempt to get approval for hearings on the Accord had failed on a technicality. When the House reconvened on 11 February 1988, the new Throne Speech praised Meech Lake: "My Government believes that the Constitutional Accord has much to commend it." The speech contained a specific pledge to introduce a resolution "proposing adoption" of Meech Lake, while also promising "meaningful" public hearings.[113] Had these hearings gone ahead in the spring or early summer, there is every reason to suppose that most of the submissions would have been hostile to the Accord. Opposition to the deal in Manitoba, according to one analysis, could be found among "social democrats; the Charter of Rights coalition; Native and northern citizens; constitutional critics; and the anti-French."[114] The premier would have been particularly solicitous about Aboriginal concerns; he would very likely have demanded (and would probably have received) assurances from Mulroney that the recognition and specification of Aboriginal rights would feature prominently in the first post-Meech round of constitutional discussions.[115]

In contrast, Pawley would have gone some distance not to be on the same side as those whose objections to the Accord seemed principally to be motivated by ill will towards francophones and towards Quebec. Ed Peltz, reeve of the Rural Municipality of Woodlands, spearheaded a movement to get rural municipalities to reject Meech Lake. "We want to be recognized as a province also. We're supposed to be equal in the constitution," said Peltz of Manitoba and Quebec. "They were given some concessions so they would sign the constitution. Nobody gave Manitoba anything to sign. We shouldn't have to buy them in."[116] Since Peltz had also played a key organizing role in the 1983–84 campaign against extending French-language services in the province, the government was unlikely to give his views much credence.

It is worth emphasizing that in the spring and summer of 1988, few Manitobans knew or cared a great deal about Meech Lake.[117] Sharon Carstairs had, almost from the outset, been an implacable foe to the Accord. Yet in the election campaign into which she was thrust after Walding's vote on the budget, Carstairs was obliged to concentrate on other topics. "In a scale of 1 to 10 personally, I put it as a most important issue," she averred. "Unfortunately and regrettably, I do not think it is a major issue for the vast majority of Manitobans."[118] Few pundits disagreed with this assessment, even after her party's breakthrough. "It is doubtful whether many Manitobans had Meech Lake on their minds when they went to the polls,"[119] suggested one editorialist, while another insisted that the Accord was "simply not a big deal in Manitoba," had "nothing to do with Filmon's election," and was "meaningless to the public."[120] The generalized level of antipathy to Meech Lake that developed in the province after Filmon's withdrawal of the package in December 1988 was largely absent in the previous months.[121] Therefore, after listening intently in public hearings (and after extracting a few public reassurances from the prime minister and the Quebec premier about their subsequent willingness to address, in good faith, some of the articulated concerns), the Pawley government would likely have brought the deal to the legislature.

There, it would almost certainly have been ratified. Sharon Carstairs, of course, would have objected vigorously. But it is worth recalling that, as premier, Gary Filmon had hoped to get Meech Lake through a legislative gauntlet containing not just the Liberal leader, but also twenty of her acolytes; Howard Pawley would have easily handled a dissenting Liberal caucus of one. From the NDP premier's perspective, a more significant consideration would have been the disposition towards the Accord of the twenty-six Tory MLAS. With bitter memories of 1983 and 1984 still relatively fresh, Pawley would have wanted to avoid a pitched legislative battle over Meech Lake, and would have sought assurances that the Conservatives would not opportunistically pander to anti-French sentiments in the province. From everything that Gary Filmon said and did between the initial agreement at Meech Lake and the abrupt withdrawal of the Accord from legislative consideration nineteen months later, it seems likely that such sureties would have been forthcoming. When the premier returned to Manitoba in May 1987 with an initial agreement in principle, Filmon's comments were broadly supportive. He claimed not to have any objections to recognizing Quebec as a distinct society. "There is no question there is broad general support for Quebec to come into the constitution," he asserted, "so one wouldn't want to be the only province to refuse consent unless one had substantial reasons."[122] One month later, the eleven heads of government agreed to the legal text; Filmon praised the Accord as "a remarkable achievement,"[123] before observing that "there's been some transfer of power to the provinces and to my view, that's acceptable to most Manitobans."[124] When Pawley's support for the Accord briefly wavered in December 1987, the Opposition leader continued to insist not only that members of his party were "generally in support of the constitutional accord," but also that the Tories were "probably less divided on the accord than Pawley's party."[125] The premier's musings about a free vote in the legislature, complained Filmon, "totally undercuts the Meech Lake accord. He gave his assurance that the government would pass the accord through the legislature."[126]

Since his support for the deal was always predicated on the satisfactory conclusion of public hearings, suspicious New Democrats might have feared that Filmon was merely baiting the trap, that after the government had commenced the ratification process, the Opposition leader would suddenly discover irredeemable flaws with the Accord. Yet Filmon's conduct after the fall of the Pawley administration strongly indicates otherwise. During the election campaign, Filmon explained his backing for Meech Lake: "Why do I support it? Because I believe that most Manitobans support the objective of having Quebec have a signature to the Constitution under terms and conditions that are reasonable."[127] With the party characterizing the deal as an "amazing achievement," election commentators quite sensibly summarized that the Tories were "clearly on record" in support of Meech.[128] Three months later, the new premier reiterated his backing and that of his party for the Accord,[129] and media observers took to characterizing him as "a firm Meech Lake proponent"[130] and as "a staunch supporter" of the Accord.[131] There was even speculation that, in order to ensure the package's ratification, Filmon might hold a snap election to secure a working majority in the legislature.[132] When he finally introduced Meech Lake into the assembly, Filmon spoke at length about its virtues: "The accord does strengthen the Canadian family ... It does provide a stronger voice and stronger protections for smaller provinces like Manitoba ... The real significance of Meech Lake goes to the heart of the idea of co-operative federalism ... Meech Lake marks a new beginning for federalism based on the Pearson/Diefenbaker tradition of co-operation, mutual respect and trust."[133]

Quoting "liberally" from Howard Pawley's speeches on the matter, Filmon urged members on all sides to pass the Accord unamended. This was a party determined to stake out a more centrist position; even the most likely critics in the party were onside. Harry Enns, who five years previously had been in the vanguard of the battle over bilingual services, thought the Accord was attractive "to the small-c conservative rural constituency that believes in less government, especially a less Eastern-controlled government,"[134] while health minister Don Orchard, formerly a vocal agitator for a review of Filmon's leadership, was similarly enthused. "I would have to hear some very, very persuasive arguments against Meech Lake before I would change from a position of supporting it," he claimed.[135] Some rural backbenchers might have grumbled, but the Conservatives would have been unlikely to resist any attempt by a Pawley administration to ratify the Accord.

In fact, had the NDP government lasted long enough to introduce Meech Lake into the legislature, Pawley's most pressing political problem might have been to maintain unity in his own caucus. Canadian social democrats have traditionally supported a strong and active national government; Meech Lake, however, tilted in quite a different direction. The unease of many New Democrats with the Accord's decentralizing thrust would have been heightened by the objections coming from their allies in the Aboriginal and women's movements. In fact, one contemporary observer was hopeful that, after attending to the public hearings, the NDP caucus "could be persuaded to reject the constitutional resolution."[136] What might have kept the doubters onside was the hope of achieving an electoral breakthrough in Quebec. For the previous two decades, NDP strategists had looked covetously at those social democratic Quebec voters who supported the Parti Québécois provincially, but who lacked appropriate representation at the federal level. Ironically, this lacuna in the national party system was to be filled in the spring of 1990 when the imminent demise of the Meech Lake Accord precipitated the formation of the Bloc Québécois. In 1987, however, it was still possible for the NDP to imagine seducing large numbers of these homeless voters. While previous courtships had foundered on the contradictions between the Quebec and Canadian variants of nationalism, the apparent unpopularity in Quebec of both Brian Mulroney's Tories and John Turner's Liberals encouraged the NDP to try a different tack. In March 1987, the party resolved to support Quebec's right to veto any amendments vital to its interests, to opt out of any transfers of power to Ottawa, and to have its particular nature explicitly recognized in the Constitution.[137] As the only New Democratic head of government in the country, Howard Pawley was uniquely situated to put these new commitments into practice. With one poll placing the NDP's Quebec support at a stratospheric 50 percent,[138] national party leader Ed Broadbent was understandably alarmed by the Manitoba premier's public foot-dragging prior to the Langevin negotiations. At the time, Pawley denied being pressured by the party's federal wing,[139] but he has since acknowledged that "Broadbent was very concerned." Added Pawley, "Polling showed at the time, surprisingly, that the NDP was ahead in Quebec. And he phoned me; he knew my uneasiness. He said: 'Howard, if you walk out on this thing, we're dead. You have to assume responsibility that we are dead in Quebec.'"

In fact, Pawley did not walk out, and polls through the rest of 1987 and into 1988 continued to suggest that the NDP was far from dead in Quebec.[140] Broadbent could discipline a member of his caucus, Ian Waddell, for speaking out against the Accord, but he could only cajole those members of the Manitoba NDP who had reservations about the deal. At the party's March 1988 annual meeting, Broadbent pointedly linked the premier's moral obligation to ratify the Accord ("I have a lot of confidence in Howard Pawley and the commitment he has made on the subject") with his own lofty electoral ambitions ("For the first time in history we plan to come out on top").[141]

Of course, four days later, the Pawley government was history, but Broadbent continued to lobby Gary Doer to stay onside.[142] For his part, the new Manitoba NDP leader was content merely to point out some of the Accord's shortcomings without committing his party to vote against it in the absence of remedial amendments. After the federal election of 21 November 1988, however, Doer became markedly less reticent on the subject of Meech Lake. It turned out that the NDP was dead in Quebec, after all; despite pouring in huge resources of time and money, the NDP secured only 14 percent of the province's popular vote and failed to elect a single member of Parliament. The backlash in Manitoba was swift. A scant two days later, Doer announced, "We will not back down from the position that Meech Lake must be improved prior to us voting for it."[143] Queried about whether this represented a shift in the party's position, Doer acknowledged, "It has changed, you're absolutely right."[144] With a haste which "illuminate[d] their opportunism in supporting Meech Lake in the first place,"[145] the New Democratic leaders in Alberta and Saskatchewan soon added their voices to the growing chorus opposing the Accord.

Had the Pawley government survived, however, it could have beaten the deadline of 15 November 1988; in fact, a mid-campaign ratification vote in Manitoba might have been regarded as precisely the tonic necessary to revive the NDP's flagging fortunes in Quebec. Pawley recalled that during the Langevin negotiations he had prophetically warned Mulroney not to leave Meech's ratification "until the last few weeks of the three-year term," and that "this had better be cleaned up lots of time in advance." Back home, Pawley was determined to follow his own advice. "Certainly," he now asserts, "I would have wanted Manitoba to clear up its position before the end of 1988." The party whip, Marty Dolin, has claimed that even on a free vote, there would only have been six or seven dissenters in the NDP caucus. On a whipped division, by contrast, only Elijah Harper (who had, in any case, received a special indulgence on the matter from the premier) and perhaps one or two others would have been likely to vote against Meech Lake. Thus, a ratification vote in the fall of 1988 would likely have passed through the legislature with a substantial majority.

Not that assent by Manitoba would have ensured the Meech Lake Accord's entrenchment in the Canadian Constitution, since New Brunswick would still have been offside. If Howard Pawley's de facto ratification deadline was 15 November 1988, Frank McKenna's was 21 April 1989, when anti-Meech zealot Clyde Wells was elected premier of Newfoundland. Nine months earlier, that province had approved the Accord, but Wells had promised to reverse the decision should he become premier in time. "It would be open to Newfoundland to rescind this resolution, so long as it is done before the proclamation," Wells declared. "I would take steps to see that is done."[146] On election night, it was clear that Wells's position on the Accord had not softened in the interim. "I am not prepared to stand by," he averred, "and see our ability to function as a federal nation destroyed by Meech Lake."[147] The new premier's resolve was only stiffened by ill-considered interventions by federal trade minister John Crosbie (who warned that the province would suffer if it failed to "play ball" on the Accord)[148] and by Quebec Premier Bourassa (who remarked that Newfoundland should consider the economic advantages associated with having "a very cordial relationship with its neighbor").[149] High-handed federal officials "don't give a damn about Newfoundland's concerns,"[150] Wells subsequently complained, while the prime minister's observations were simply "paternalistic tripe."[151] Without dramatic changes to the Accord, Newfoundland was determined to rescind its previous ratification. "We will do it," insisted Wells, "with or without New Brunswick and Manitoba."[152] As long as neither of these two holdout provinces made any move to ratify Meech Lake, Wells had no need to carry out his threat. His hand was forced, however, when McKenna introduced the Accord into the New Brunswick legislature on 21 March 1990; the following day, Wells tabled a motion to rescind his province's approval, and the deed was quickly done.

Clyde Wells, it is important to emphasize, had fundamental objections to almost all aspects of Meech Lake. He opposed recognizing Quebec as a distinct society, hedging the federal spending power, rigidifying the amending formula, and giving provinces a greater say over both immigration and the nomination of Supreme Court justices. Once Clyde Wells joined the club of Canadian provincial premiers, the Accord was all but dead. For Meech Lake to have become part of the Canadian Constitution, therefore, it would need to have been passed by all eleven legislatures and proclaimed prior to 21 April 1989.

If the Pawley government had not been brought down by Jim Walding, such a timeline was certainly possible. With Manitoba moving the ratification process ahead in the summer of 1988, attention would have turned to New Brunswick as the sole remaining holdout. During the last days of the Richard Hatfield regime, Frank McKenna had urged federal parliamentarians not to ratify Meech Lake, and when his Liberals swept all fifty-eight seats in the 13 October 1987 provincial election the new premier understandably claimed that he had received a mandate to renegotiate the Accord. McKenna was, after all, now the premier of Canada's only officially bilingual province. Meech Lake promised to give the government of Quebec the power "to preserve and promote" its distinct society, whereas other governments were enjoined only "to preserve" Canada's linguistic minorities. This seemingly created a status hierarchy among Canada's francophones, with those inside the province of Quebec implicitly recognized as more worthwhile than their confreres elsewhere in the country. "To only preserve a minority," McKenna observed, "is to condemn it to eventual assimilation."[153] Yet Quebec clearly feared that any stronger commitment to Canada's minority language groups in the Accord would gut the distinct-society clause. McKenna's principal objection to Meech Lake was, therefore, a potential deal-breaker.

Nevertheless, there are good reasons to suspect that, had Manitoba proceeded with ratification, New Brunswick would have advanced its public hearings from January and February 1989 and legislative approval would have quickly followed. First, after initially supporting McKenna,[154] some of the leaders of the province's Acadian community soon undercut their premier's central objection to the Accord by announcing their support for Meech Lake. "As French-Canadians," Société Nationale des Acadiens president Réal Gervais subsequently observed, "the possible exclusion of Quebec (from the constitution) does not leave us indifferent."[155] The constitutional ambitions of New Brunswick's Acadian community were essentially external to the Accord; they sought instead the entrenchment of New Brunswick's policy of providing educational and cultural services in both languages, and despite Meech Lake's eventual demise this was achieved in 1993.

Second, McKenna's remaining objections to the Accord did not strike at the heart of the package. Repeatedly, he signalled a preference for improving, rather than destroying, the Accord. After a March 1988 meeting with Howard Pawley, New Brunswick Deputy Premier Aldea Landry emerged to reassure listeners that her boss "even before he was premier (had) said that he whole-heartedly supported Meech Lake but there were areas of concern."[156] Seven weeks later, with Sharon Carstairs proclaiming the death of the Accord, McKenna opted to put a positive spin on her words. "I don't believe the right approach is to call the Accord a non-starter and I don't really think that's what she's getting at," he bravely insisted. "I believe all of us should work together to seek something which is more consensual and really represents an improvement to the document."[157] And when Filmon suddenly removed Meech Lake from the Manitoba assembly's consideration in response to Bourassa's invocation of the notwithstanding clause, McKenna decried this linkage and appealed for everyone to stay calm: "What this debate needs are reasonable, temperate approaches by reasonable, temperate people."[158]

Unlike many of Meech Lake's critics, the New Brunswick premier eventually came to support distinct-society recognition for Quebec.[159] Nor was McKenna a committed Senate reformer; thus, he was not overly concerned that rigidifying the amending formula might forever frustrate changes to the Upper House. McKenna did believe that public hearings should be required for all constitutional amendments. He was also concerned that women's rights might potentially be at risk under the Accord, he wanted Canada's heads of government to reopen talks about the fisheries and about Aboriginal rights, and he thought it unwise to raise too high the constitutional bar for the eventual admission of new provinces and to hedge too broadly the federal government's spending power. Most of these ideas were contained in the parallel accord that the New Brunswick legislature passed along with Meech Lake in the spring of 1990. All could have been accommodated in a subsequent constitutional round. As one senior minister from another province commented, "Here's the guy [McKenna] who essentially caused all the trouble and at the end of the day, his agenda was trivial."[160]

Third, with such a small agenda for change, it would have been very difficult for any province, let alone a dependent hinterland with less than 3 percent of the national population, to stand alone against the Accord. One observer saw the uncertainty of the April 1988 Manitoba election results as critical to McKenna's attempts to remain offside: "It makes it easier for any province not to be identified, or identifiable, as the only one to spoil it."[161] On a deal widely construed as an exercise in national reconciliation, dissent was only likely in numbers. If, rather than being saddled with an uncertain minority government, Manitoba had been moving towards ratification under Howard Pawley, the forces on New Brunswick to complete the consensus would have ramped up considerably. At the time, only a very few members of the Canadian political elite (perhaps Wells, Carstairs, and Trudeau) could have been characterized as anti-Meech fanatics (in the Churchillian sense of "one who can't change his mind and won't change the subject"). Only such an individual might have resisted the pressures towards national conformity, but Frank McKenna, most emphatically, did not fall under this rubric. In fact, even Clyde Wells, judging from his speech of November 1989, would have had a difficult time standing alone against the Accord: "I say no province ... has the right to hold up the rest of the nation. No province can hold up the constitutional development of this country forever."[162] Approval of the Meech Lake Accord by a tenth legislature, therefore, would likely have been followed in good time by ratification in the eleventh.

Finally, the national government, judging by past behaviour, would not have been shy about employing its considerable policy leverage to bring onside the final Meech holdout. During the 1986 Saskatchewan election, Prime Minister Mulroney had rescued embattled ally Grant Devine not only by announcing a $1 billion bailout for grain farmers, but also by delaying until after the vote the news that the CF-18 maintenance contract would go to Montreal rather than Winnipeg.[163] And federal officials had similarly refused to confirm a $3.6 billion frigate contract for the Saint John shipyard until Premier McKenna had indicated his support for free trade with the United States.[164] Thus, when Mulroney emissary Lowell Murray, amid reports that Ottawa was prepared to "pump money into the province,"[165] arrived in Winnipeg in mid-July 1988 for private meetings with Premier Filmon, Sharon Carstairs was understandably suspicious: "This (approval) is very high on the agenda of the federal government and I think they will use whatever possible means to get it."[166] The principals repudiated all talk of a quid pro quo[167] (or as the *Winnipeg Sun* indelicately headlined "Filmon denies dollars-for-Meech deal").[168] Nevertheless, much progress was made at a follow-up meeting between the premier and the prime minister on what were euphemistically characterized as "issues important for the future economic well-being of Manitoba."[169] Later that year, when Filmon abruptly withdrew Meech Lake from legislative consideration, the steel inside the prime minister's velvet glove came into view. In language impossible to misapprehend, Mulroney warned the Manitoba premier that he needed to reflect "very carefully" on his decision.[170]

But what if Howard Pawley had remained in office through 1988 and had orchestrated the Accord's ratification in Manitoba? Under those circumstances, Mulroney's "penchant for back-scratching with federal funds"[171] would have been directed entirely towards New Brunswick. On at least four occasions (and twice within a week in September 1988), Mulroney called McKenna to suggest that he was "very sympathetic" to New Brunswick's case for federal monies to upgrade the Trans-Canada Highway and that he would "try to make a deal."[172] Although McKenna's government subsequently unveiled a $100 million program to begin fixing highway potholes ("a project that they hope will attract federal financing"),[173] provincial officials took eloquent umbrage to suggestions that New Brunswick's vote on the Accord was for sale: "We'll not trade our principles for trinkets."[174] Privately, however, they tried to alert Ottawa to the dangers inherent in the forthcoming Newfoundland election. According to Pierre McGuire, one of McKenna's closest advisors, "We kept on warning them, telling them they had to move quickly. We weren't asking for things that fundamentally challenged what Quebec wanted. Clyde Wells was a very different kettle of fish. In our case, we were saying, 'We can live with what is in there for Quebec, but we have to have our demands met too.' Clyde was fundamentally opposed to the spirit and concept of Meech."[175]

Perhaps, like J.R.R. Tolkien's Sauron, the prime minister's eye was focussed too intently on events in far-off Manitoba. No arrangement was struck between New Brunswick and Ottawa before April 1989. One year hence, the New Brunswick legislature did ratify the Accord, but by then it was much too late. If, by the summer of 1988, however, New Brunswick had been (de facto) the only remaining holdout, Meech Lake would likely have been stitched up some time before Clyde Wells thundered over the electoral horizon.

On 8 March 1988, Jim Walding stood, on shaky legs, and voted with the Opposition members of the Manitoba assembly. To state that there were consequences from this act is hardly profound. All acts by all human agents have some consequences, even if, as in the overwhelming majority of cases, these consequences do not impinge, in a non-trivial fashion, on anyone else. This chapter has made two much stronger claims. First, Walding's act certainly had significant consequences for himself, for his (erstwhile) friends and associates, for his (presumably erstwhile) fellow partisans, and for his (soon to be erstwhile) fellow Manitobans. Assuming that, in liberal democracies, a link exists between constitutional strictures, on the one hand, and dominant social values and institutional practices, on the other, then it is plausible that Walding's act had significant consequences for his fellow Canadians as well. Second, in the absence of Walding's act, few, and arguably none, of these significant consequences would have obtained. Walding would not have had to flee the province in disgrace. He would have retained the respect of most, and the friendship of many, St. Vital New Democrats. The NDP would have governed Manitoba for an additional two years and would have sought re-election under less adverse circumstances. Most contentiously, the Meech Lake Accord might well be part of Canada's Constitution. We shall return to the plausibility of this counterfactual scenario in the concluding chapter.

8

Conclusion

T HE EVENTS DOCUMENTED in the preceding chapters were profoundly affected by the setting in which they played out. Since Confederation, the place of francophones and their language has been contentious in Manitoba and, more particularly, in St. Vital. That Louis Riel's
homeland came to be represented by an ardent anglophile intent on sabotaging a modest extension of French-language rights and services may have been
an historical irony, but it was certainly consistent with the socio-demograph-
ic evolution of the community. St. Vital's location astride Manitoba's political
diagonal was also significant. Jim Walding won five consecutive elections, but
none of these were sure things and, on more than one occasion, he commenced the campaign in second place. Walding came to attribute his skein of
victories to his own endeavours, but before, during, and after Walding's run
as an MLA, St. Vital's status as an electoral bellwether was readily apparent. In
fact, in the thirteen provincial elections between 1953 and 1995 the NDP vote
in St. Vital deviated, on average, less than 3 percent from the party's results
province-wide. As Manitoba went, in other words, so too did St. Vital.

Nominating conventions are a common feature of the Canadian political
landscape. Assuming a four-year electoral cycle, the federal and provincial
branches of the Liberal, Conservative, and New Democratic parties orga-
nize, between them, over six hundred such events per year. Despite this
ubiquity, the nomination meeting has been largely ignored by members of
the academy. Certainly, we know much more about its rare and colourful
cousin—the leadership convention. These gatherings, after all, elevate gen-
erals; although the victors may not realize it at the time, most nominating

conventions conscript foot soldiers. Nevertheless, in politics as in war, the impact of even a humble private can occasionally prove decisive. This book has chronicled one such instance.

The 1986 St. Vital NDP nominating convention was, in fact, an extraordinary event. Any challenge to a sitting legislator is both an unusual and engrossing spectacle. That there were not one, but two would-be usurpers made the event even more atypical. The contest, moreover, was decided by a single vote, the first in a connected sequence of three unlikely occurrences documented in this book. First, Jim Walding won his 1986 nomination by a single ballot. Second, he was returned in the subsequent election as part of a government whose working majority was soon reduced to one vote. Third, he was an MLA in one of the only two provinces that, at the time, represented a significant threat to the Meech Lake Accord. The odds against this particular combination of events transpiring were almost astronomical. If one assumes, for the moment, that all 406 conceivable results for Jim Walding on the second ballot were equally possible (the number of valid votes cast plus one), and if one further assumes that all fifty-eight conceivable results for the NDP in the 1986 election were equally possible (the number of available seats plus one), then the arithmetic is straightforward. The odds of Jim Walding receiving precisely 203 votes at the nominating convention, the NDP winning twenty-nine or thirty seats in the assembly, and Manitoba being one of only two holdout legislatures are exactly one in 64,757.[1] No self-respecting gambler would play such a trifecta.

If some aspects of the struggle for the nomination in St. Vital were extraordinary, others were entirely unremarkable. All students of Canadian nominating conventions would recognize, for example, the pre-contest skirmishing—the rumours, the confidential appeals for support, and the floating of trial balloons. Once the battle had been joined, Jim Walding, Sig Laser, and Gerri Unwin behaved like thousands of others who have aspired to elected office. They either endured or enjoyed the hard slogging of door-to-door campaigning, they spoke little of public policy, they paid particular heed to lapsed partisans, they delayed registering some of their fresh recruits until the last possible moment, and, on the day of decision, they attempted to pull the vote. Those with the capacity to shape the timing, location, and rules of the convention did not hesitate to use their influence to the advantage of a particular candidate. Inevitably, the number of members eligible to vote swelled as the number of those genuinely undecided declined. And from beginning to end, the familiar tension between local autonomy and central control loomed over the enterprise.

Chapter 1 outlined three variations that are peculiar to NDP nominating conventions. Broadly speaking, these were also present in our particular case. Certainly, the NDP's commitment to fielding a more gender-balanced slate of candidates than their Liberal and Conservative counterparts came to the fore. Indeed, considerations of gender were central to Gerri Unwin's candidacy. A cadre of St. Vital women believed that it was essential for one of their own to enter the nomination race and approached Unwin to serve as their standard-bearer. Her husband and Colin Trigwell aside, Unwin's core group of advisers were almost entirely female, and her cause was championed by the party's Status of Women Committee. As the campaign progressed, Unwin grew more vocal on gender-infused topics such as pay equity and domestic violence, and her visible presence as a woman in the contest encouraged some members to find favour with her candidacy. There are echoes of this phenomenon in the two traditional parties, but they are muted and irregular.

The other two differentiating features of NDP nominating conventions are enveloped in Sayers's term of "party democracy." Their contests are typically closed affairs, relatively impermeable to the participation as either candidates or voters of those outside the party. Not for the NDP the nomination of a local notable with little or no pedigree in the party. Likewise not for the NDP the temporary enlistment of large numbers of partisan tourists. The 1986 nomination in St. Vital, however, only partially conformed to Sayers's model of party democracy. Admittedly, all three candidates were party stalwarts of some renown, although Sig Laser was the closest thing to an upstart in the race. But if Laser's presence was, at most, a minor breach in the norm that prospective NDP candidates must have lengthy party credentials, his campaign clearly contradicted the norm that the choice of nominee should be left in the hands of the established membership. Chapter 4 highlighted the strategic imperative that obliged Laser's team to undertake an intensive recruitment drive amongst those residents of St. Vital who had not previously been associated with the New Democratic Party; without a significant expansion of the electorate, Laser was destined to run a distant third in the race. Yet while Laser's disregard for this party norm vaulted him into serious contention for the nomination, it paradoxically also limited his chances for victory. It was the Laser team's recruiting practices that brought Colin Trigwell's professionalism into the race on behalf of Gerri Unwin to siphon off some of the anti-Walding sentiment. It was these same recruiting practices that cemented Unwin's antipathy towards Laser and propelled her core supporters to move to Jim Walding on the decisive ballot. Thus, Sig Laser could not win the nomination without flouting his party's customary recruitment practices, but his disregard for this norm unleashed a backlash just strong enough to deny him the prize.

In fact, although challenges to sitting legislators are decidedly uncommon, the period prior to the nomination was marked by the usual signs of an incumbent in trouble. Family members aside, Jim Walding had managed to place only one, utterly inconsequential, acolyte on the constituency executive. The local association was debt-ridden and lethargic, and even many of those who had vigorously promoted Walding's cause for over a decade were now grumbling. Nor could Walding rely on the customary support of the party brass. Neither the premier nor any member of his staff wished for a Walding renomination, and it is likely that the same unanimity of opinion pervaded the caucus as well.[2] While Walding was not without cards to play, few fifteen-year veterans of the legislature can have held such a weak hand in their quest for renomination.

And yet he won his nomination and then won in the subsequent election. Two years on, he was perfectly situated to exact his revenge when the balance of power suddenly tumbled into his lap and Jim Walding became the poster boy for embattled incumbents everywhere. Admittedly, some of the fallout from Walding's act proved to be ephemeral. Walding briefly hobbled his party as an electoral force both in St. Vital and, more generally, in Manitoba.

Since 1999, however, the NDP has been restored to a position of dominance both in Walding's old constituency and in the province. Similarly, while Manitobans were undoubtedly affected by the abrupt ouster of Howard Pawley's administration, the cautious PC minority government that took office in the 1988 to 1990 interval did not leave behind a substantial policy legacy. And while feelings of animus continue to fester in some individuals, their numbers are thankfully few.[3]

Somewhat surprisingly, the major long-term impact of Walding's act may have been on his fellow Canadians. In the preceding chapter, it was argued that in the absence of Walding's vote the Meech Lake Accord might well have been entrenched in the Constitution.[4] Yet few have even hinted that Jim Walding bore some responsibility for the Accord's failure. One timeline of the rise and fall of Meech Lake itemizes eighty-seven key events between 30 April 1987 and 23 June 1990 (eleven of which occurred in Manitoba), but Jim Walding's decisive vote in the provincial legislature is not among them.[5] As Meech Lake expired, the principal players at the end game were more inclined to point the finger of blame at each other. In Brian Mulroney's mind, the chief culprit was Clyde Wells ("He cancelled the most fundamental and noble dimension of a democracy").[6] The Newfoundland premier, however, preferred to castigate the federal-provincial relations minister Lowell Murray for his last-minute attempt to extend the ratification deadline ("That's the final manipulation. We're not prepared to be manipulated any longer").[7] For his part, Senator Murray was appalled at Gary Filmon's refusal to fast-track consideration of the Accord in the Manitoba legislature ("I find it incredible that one MLA can tie up a legislature in knots indefinitely").[8] Whereupon, the Manitoba premier blithely passed the buck back to the Prime Minister's Office ("They had better accept the fact that they have bungled this and bungled it horribly.... They chose to roll the dice ... and now they're reaping what they sowed").[9] Only spokespersons for Canada's Aboriginal community seemed anxious to accept responsibility for killing Meech. Elijah Harper, the Ojibway-Cree MLA who, on nine separate occasions, said "No, Mr. Speaker" to frustrate the final opportunity for the Accord's ratification in the Manitoba legislature, was jubilant at the outcome.

"We have won," he told supporters. "We have said no to Meech Lake."[10] "We're here to celebrate the rebirth of our people and the death of the accord," echoed Phil Fontaine, leader of the Assembly of Manitoba Chiefs. "We've pulled off a tremendous achievement."[11] Perversely, federal Opposition leader John Turner refused to take these gentlemen at their word. "Let no one put blame on Elijah Harper or on the aboriginal people of this country," he thundered at the beleaguered prime minister.[12]

While not ignoring the contributions of these key players, scholarly interpretations of Meech Lake's demise have typically emphasized more abstract social and institutional forces. What "eventually stymied the Accord," according to Tom Courchene, "was and is the clash of two conflicting views of what federalism and constitutional amendment are all about."[13] As befitting a last-minute compromise, the *Constitution Act, 1982* contained conflicting messages. On the one hand, it gave ordinary Canadians an entrenched catalogue of rights and freedoms. On the other hand, it left the power to alter these rights and freedoms entirely in the hands of governments. The Meech Lake affair cruelly exposed this contradiction. Blind to the emerging potency of the Charter, the eleven first ministers assumed that the traditional practices of executive federalism remained central to the constitutional amending formula and were clearly taken aback by the ensuing firestorm of controversy. It was bad enough that the Meech Lake Accord was crafted in secret and without citizen input by what were disparagingly referred to as "eleven men in suits." It was even worse that the fruit of their labours was presented to the Canadian public for their inspection only, and certainly not for their approval. Worst of all, the eleven First Ministers had come to a deal that seemingly threatened the emerging primacy of Charter rights. According to Alan Cairns, the Meech Lake "failure" was the consequence of "an outdated constitutional theory that had not caught up with post-1982 constitutional realities."[14] Much of the unhappiness in English Canada came to focus on the distinct society provision for "the form of cultural establishmentarianism that the clause represented."[15] The Charter, for obvious reasons, had much shallower roots in Quebec. In the end, the battle of Meech Lake came down, according to one interpretation, to a contest between English Canada's Charter of Rights and Freedoms and Quebec's distinct society. In Pierre Fortin's words, "The Charter won."[16]

Even so, English Canadian critics of the Accord required an avenue into the debate. Simply hammering their fists against the outside of the Meech Lake locomotive as it hurtled towards ratification was obviously insufficient. In the end, it was "a simple feature of the citizens' world—elections, the antithesis of the closed first ministers' meeting" that broke down the governmental consensus and "perhaps determined Meech Lake's fate."[17] Les Pal points, in particular, to the importance of the New Brunswick, Manitoba, and Newfoundland elections between October 1987 and April 1989. As events actually played out, this focus is perfectly appropriate. Yet if one changes the central question from the factual ("What killed Meech Lake?") to the counterfactual ("What might have resulted in the Accord's passage?"), then the action of Jim Walding leaps abruptly into focus. It was his decision to bring down the Pawley government that directly precipitated the second of Pal's three elections. Indeed, without Walding's vote the results of the first election would likely have been neutralized in sufficient time to render the outcome of the third election irrelevant. The Meech Lake Accord could have been stitched up and proclaimed with more than a year to spare.[18]

Counterfactual scenarios are central to many legal proceedings in Canada ("Is it not true, Mr. Boutilier, that if you had not consumed six double scotches with lunch, you would have been unlikely to drive through the showroom's plate-glass window?"). Is the consideration of such counterfactuals a legitimate scholarly enterprise? Many prominent historians believe otherwise. Michael Oakeshott states definitively that the historian "is never called upon to consider what might have happened had circumstances been different,"[19] while E.P. Thompson summarily dismisses counterfactual scenarios as "unhistorical shit."[20] Such assessments typically betray either a philosophical determinism (a belief that events had to turn out precisely as they did) or a methodological conservatism (a belief that there can be no evidence, and thus no knowledge, about events that failed to occur). To the former, there can be no effective rebuttal, although it would be surprising if most determinists did not, on an almost daily basis, seek to improve the effectiveness and appropriateness of their own behaviour through the judicious inspection of counterfactual scenarios. The methodological objections are no less serious, but their force can at least be blunted. Employing a sufficiently demanding bar of plausibility will winnow out all but a few of the infinite number of possible alternative histories of an event. There must, for example, be evidence that an agent actively entertained a different option. There must, as well, be evidence of the likely responses from those agents who would have been most directly affected by such a change in course. Above all, the dividing line between the plausible and the implausible "lies at that point at which the agents in question would cease to recognize or to acknowledge themselves as the agents they were."[21]

Chapter 7 argued that Jim Walding's decision to bring down Howard Pawley's government had implications for the health of Meech Lake, that had the maverick MLA acted otherwise, the Accord might well have been entrenched in the Canadian Constitution. Unpacking this counterfactual claim reveals two distinct components. First, Jim Walding could have voted to sustain the NDP in office on 8 March 1988, and for many months thereafter, and remained recognizable (both to himself and to others) as Jim Walding. Indeed, this seems particularly likely given the widespread shock and confusion occasioned by his actual behaviour. Jim Walding was deeply conflicted over his budgetary vote. We know that he was highly motivated to maximize his legislative pension. We know, as well, that his wife (and closest political confidante) had counselled him a fortnight earlier not to oust the government. And we also know that, however intense his disillusionment with the party establishment, a quarter-century of labours on behalf of the Manitoba New Democratic Party had created a web of affective and psychological attachments. Jim Walding had threatened to bring down the Pawley government over the Throne Speech before ultimately backing away from the abyss. Walding's vote on the budget is explicable, but it hardly strains credulity to claim not only that he could have acted otherwise, but also that he could have done so without changing any of the interconnected antecedents that contributed to his actual decision.

The likely consequences of Jim Walding sustaining the Pawley government constitute the second, and more problematic, component of the unpacked counterfactual claim. Given the inherent "unpredictability of past futures,"[22] it might be tempting not to venture on to such uncertain terrain. The assertion that a different vote by Walding on the budget would have greatly enhanced Meech Lake's chances of ratification implicitly carries the "other things being equal" caveat, though there can obviously be no assurance that other things would have remained even approximately equal. Perhaps if they had still been engaged in regulating the people's business in Winnipeg, rather than out on the electoral hustings, two Manitoba NDP cabinet ministers would have been fatally struck by a bus while crossing Broadway Avenue one fine morning in April 1988, and the Pawley majority would have been lost in any case. Perhaps, but the likelihood of any such event occurring among a small cast of characters over a relatively confined period of time seems hearteningly remote. A "recurrent" weakness with counterfactual analysis is that "the line of inference is often drawn too far into the future."[23] In the case of Jim Walding and the Meech Lake Accord, however, the "line of inference" extends only a matter of months, rather than decades or, in some egregious instances, centuries.[24]

Thus, it seems plausible that Jim Walding's vote had consequences for his fellow Canadians. What is less apparent is whether these consequences were largely baneful or beneficial. Popular assessments of the Meech Lake Accord were often propelled by straightforward considerations of linguistic identity; for some anglophones and francophones, if the deal found favour with "the other" it was to be rejected, and vice versa. Thus, two-thirds of Canadians could hold strong views about the package, even though that same proportion of Canadians also knew little or nothing about its contents. Yet most of the country's social scientists, acutely aware of their primitive understanding of cause and effect, had a more difficult time evaluating the package. Much depended upon the post-Meech behaviour of a range of key actors. Would future national governments be more or less reluctant to employ their spending power? Had meaningful Senate reform become more or less likely? Would Quebec governments of all stripes, armed with the distinct society provision, push more or less vigorously against the limits of Ottawa's jurisdiction? It was impossible to be confident about these sorts of issues, and a contemporary conference of political scientists and legal scholars reflected these uncertainties. One analyst suggested that the provisions on linguistic duality would "limit rights under the Charter, although in what manner and to what degree is not yet clear."[25] A second observed sensibly that "there is room for debate about the interpretation of the amendments, and a final determination of the meaning of the provisions can only be given by the Supreme Court of Canada."[26] Nor was past experience much help. "Canadian constitutional history," noted a third expert, "is replete with examples of apparently straightforward constitutional provisions that have given rise to unexpected developments."[27] There was a broad consensus that a ratified Accord would have some impact on the political identity of Quebecers and, by extension, on future iterations of the Quebec nationalist project. What was less clear was whether Quebecers' appetite for greater autonomy from Canada was likely to be satiated or merely whetted by Meech Lake's constitutional entrenchment. In no small measure owing to the action of Jim Walding, we do not know the answers to these questions and are, accordingly, uncertain whether to cast him as the hero or villain of the piece. If the former, the old verse should be revised to read: "For want of a nail ... the kingdom was saved."

Despite the risks, the temptation to rewind the counterfactual clock to 12 January 1986 cannot be resisted. Even a cursory reading of earlier chapters will have revealed a myriad of ways in which the second-round results could have been reversed. If only Ron Cavaluce had not mistakenly announced that Gerri Unwin was still on the ballot. If only Wayne Farmer had not been called into work and Rita Cayer and Frank Melia had not fallen ill. If only Barb Parkin and Verna Sinclair had been persuaded to stay and cast their second-round ballots before decamping for bingo. If only Jules Legal had realized that his daughter was eligible to become a party member. If only the Laser team had picked up the little old lady from the lobby of the Forester's Haven. If only Sharon Kula had not gone back a third time to convert and deliver the same little old lady to the Walding camp. If only Jay Goldstein had not defected on the decisive ballot. If only Laser's team of "outlaws" had surreptitiously cast the four extra ballots for their champion. If only. If only.

One can, however, push this argument just so far, since there is manifestly a memory bias at work. People are much more likely to perceive and remember those aspects that were critical (rather than those that were redundant) to an event's outcome. Thus, the fact that Hugh and Madeleine McMeel moved out of St. Vital in the year prior to the nominating convention was noticed because they were Laser supporters and their votes could have reversed the outcome. But recall that Walding's backers were drawn disproportionately from the community's senior citizens. It is entirely possible that several of his potential voters not only might have left St. Vital in the preceding year, but also might have shuffled off the mortal coil altogether. For every one hundred Canadians who turned sixty-four in 1985, between two and three did not live to see their next birthday.[28] Because Walding triumphed at the nominating convention, the untimely demise of one or more of his backers in the preceding months was entirely unremarked by contemporary observers. Had the results been reversed, had Laser won by a single vote, we can likewise be certain that the absence of the McMeels from the membership rolls would have occasioned no comment whatsoever.

The presence of this memory bias does not detract from the central argument. This book has not suggested that everything went right with the Walding campaign (although, on a range of matters from pulling the vote to providing babysitter assistance, it is obvious a great deal did)[29] or that everything went wrong with the Laser campaign (although, on those same matters, it is again obvious that a great deal did). The point, therefore, is not that all plausible counterfactual scenarios would have resulted in a Laser victory. Rather, the reader need only be convinced that Jim Walding's triumph was not inevitable, that there were a variety of plausible means by which the outcome could have been reversed.

If it is plausible to suggest that Sig Laser could easily have been the NDP's candidate in the 1986 provincial election, does this mean that the fate of the Meech Lake Accord was perhaps shaped by the outcome of the nominating convention? Despite Unwin's disastrous results in 1988, it seems likely that

Laser would have held St. Vital for the NDP in 1986, when the government started the campaign five points up in the polls, rather than twenty-five points behind. As well, it is worth recalling that Walding won his final election without the benefit of any constituency appearances from his popular leader and with at least some party stalwarts staying aloof from the campaign. Laser, by contrast, would have been hobbled by neither of these constraints, and while he would obviously have lacked the name recognition that goes with being a fifteen-year member of the legislature, it is at least suggestive that in three of the four instances in the 1997 federal election in which an incumbent was denied renomination the challenger was able to hold the riding for his party.[30] Thus, it is probable, although by no means certain, that Laser would have vanquished his Liberal and Conservative opponents and ensured his party's slender majority in the legislature, a majority which the NDP would presumably have maintained until well after a ratification vote on the Meech Lake Accord.

At its close, therefore, this stands as a salutary tale for democrats of all persuasions. We live in an age when a distressingly high proportion of young people have opted out of the electoral process. Perhaps they regard it as a hollow ritual. Perhaps they prefer other avenues of political representation. Yet the actions of those ordinary citizens who gathered over twenty years ago in a high-school auditorium will continue, arguably for the indefinite future, to resonate in the Canadian body politic. Both Sig Laser (who never did achieve elected office) and Denise Mignot (who tenaciously stuck with Jim Walding despite the frantic importuning of her family members) still live in St. Vital. Occasionally, their paths cross, and Laser wryly observes, "We know what one vote can do, don't we, Denise?"

Appendix A: List of Interviewees

All interviews were conducted between May 2005 and April 2008.

Abs, Leonard
Ananichuk, Agnes
Bardy, Jim
Barrett, Becky
Batzel, Brenda and Vic
Besant, Barbara
Boboski, Dennis
Bostrum, Harvey
Boutang, Ivy
Buckley, Bruce
Bourrier, Robert
Buvik, Ronald
Cadigan, Robert (and Margaret)
Cayer, Reg (and Rita)
Chudy, Louise
Dodd, Glen (and Janice)
Dodick, Doreen
Dolin, Marty
Dotremont, Elizabeth
Duffey, Frances
Farmer, Wayne
Frame, Doreen (and Lloyd)
Fyfe, Ivy (and Ian)
Girouard, Monica
Goldstein, Carol and Jay
Halstead, Roy (and Betty)
Haresign, Hank (and Margaret)

Harvey, Betty
Herriot, Paul
Hitchings, Diane
Hudson, Wilf and Louise
Huss, Keith
Kennedy, Daniel
Kula, Sharon and Vic
Laser, Sig and Tannis
Leclerc, Yaroslava
Lecuyer, Gerard
Legal, Jules
Lemoine, Pierre
Leo, Chris
Lewco, Richard
Light, George
Malloway, Jim
McBride, Glen (and Bev)
McLean, Ernie
McMeel, Hugh
McNevin, Jo-anne
Melia, Frank
Mignot, Denise and Gilbert
Mochoruk, Jim
Nicholl, Tom
Nolan, Peter
O' Leary, Brian
Olinyk, Dave
Pagan, Joan (and Bud)

Pagan, William (and Nora)
Parasiuk, Wilson
Pawley, Howard
Penny, Al (and Pearl)
Pitcairn, Lawrence
Portsmouth, Patricia
Prefontaine, Denis
Redpath, Reverend Joseph
Reilly, Nolan
Remnant, Binx
Riel, Al (and Wendy)
Ritchot, Paul (and Debbie)
Rodie, Jack
Rossman, Irene
Rowntree, Ross (and spouse)
Sawka, Aurore and Ed
Schamber, George
Schellenberg, David
Schettler, Dianne and Gordon
Schreyer, Ed
Scotton, Joyce
Small, Catherine and Larry
Smith, Margaret
Sotas, Mike
Stimpson, Michael
Stunden, Nancy
Swain, Altje

Thompson, D.W. (and
  spouse)
Trigwell, Colin
Trudel, Elaine
Tucovic, Peter
Unwin, Gerri and Fred
Uskiw, Sam
Walding, Jim and Valerie
Warren, Peter
Williams, Darlene
  and David
Woodbury, David
Zahari, Shirley (and Ed)
Zastre, Fred

( ) *Signifies indirect data from spouse*

Appendix B: Correspondence

HOWARD PAWLEY TO JIM WALDING, 21 FEBRUARY 1984

February 21st, 1984

The Honourable D. James Walding
Speaker of the House
Room 244 Legislative Building
Winnipeg, Manitoba
R3C 0V8

Dear Mr. Walding:

On February 8, 1984, you stated in your ruling on repeated bell ringing that "the House should not be prevented from deciding whether this (bell ringing) constitutes a breach of privilege."

You had ruled that on the face of the evidence, obstruction by repeated bell ringing was abuse of the rules, a contempt of the House and therefore a breach of its privileges. Your ruling was supported by a vote of the House.

Now, the Official Opposition are using prolonged bell ringing to prevent a decision by the Legislative Assembly to deal with the breach of privilege by providing a two hour limit to bell ringing.

This is an extraordinary and unprecedented situation. There can be no more serious attack upon the House than a deliberate decision to prevent the Members from protecting their right and privilege to duly execute the powers of the Legislative Assembly.

This defiance of the rights of the Assembly also attacks the constitutional principle of responsible government. A fundamental right of the House is that a majority of Members may form a government and assure it of support. The operation of this constitutional principle ensures that the choice of the electorate, expressed at a general election, will be respected.

The Opposition has had an unusually full opportunity to question and debate the matter of privilege. The rights of the minority in the House have thus been respected.

It is unacceptable for the rights of the House and the principle of responsible government to be defied any longer.

With all due respect, and in view of the continuing obstruction, I request that you act now to notify both Whips of a specific time when the two votes will be conducted to decide the question of privilege before the House.

Members of the Government Caucus intend to be in the Chamber at 2:00 p.m. today for these votes.

Because this matter is of such importance to all Members of the House and the people of Manitoba, I will provide a copy of this letter to each Caucus Chairperson and to the Press Gallery.

Sincerely,

Howard Pawley

cc. Gary Filmon, MLA
Leader of the Opposition

Source: Jim Walding Papers, Archives of Manitoba

JIM WALDING TO HOWARD PAWLEY, 21 FEBRUARY 1984

February 21, 1984

The Honourable Howard Pawley, Premier,
Room 204 Legislative Building,
Winnipeg, Manitoba,
R3C 0V8

Dear Premier Pawley:

Thank you for your letter of February 21st containing your request that I intervene and set a definite time for the division now in progress.

The Rules and Procedures of the Legislature are well-known and well-established. They constitute a clear set of procedures which the House expects to be enforced by its Speaker with fairness and impartiality.

It has been made clear to you and your colleagues that the Rules of the House would be observed and that any change in those Rules would come from the House itself.

Since the House is close to effecting a change in its Rules, I am surprised that you would request that I contravene the existing Rules and Procedures at this time. Any unilateral action on my part could only be a betrayal of the impartiality of the Chair and would seriously undermine the integrity of the Speakership.

In view of the foregoing, I cannot accede to your request to contravene our Rules and Procedures.

Yours sincerely,

D. James Walding,

Speaker.

Source: Jim Walding Papers, Archives of Manitoba

JIM WALDING, APPEAL FOR SUPPORT, 4 OCTOBER 1985

Dear Constituent,

As the member of the Manitoba Legislature for St. Vital, I have always believed my first responsibility is to maintain a very close level of contact with all the residents of the St. Vital-Norwood community. To represent you effectively, I must be familiar with your views regarding the important issues facing our province during the remainder of the 1980's.

It has been my practice during the past fifteen years to visit personally in the neighborhood with constituents. This personal contact has served to keep me well in touch and up to date with constituency opinion. I have always valued the straightforward comments and support I have received, comments which I have conveyed on your behalf to the government of Manitoba.

When I first sought election as a new candidate I received 35% of the vote, which I raised steadily in subsequent elections to 52% in the last provincial election. This level of support can be maintained with the continuing assistance of constituents.

I respectfully ask for your support.

With your support I will continue, as your full-time MLA, to fight for government action to meet your needs.

Yours sincerely,

Jim Walding

Source: Jim Walding Papers, Archives of Manitoba

JIM WALDING, APPEAL FOR SUPPORT, 17 OCTOBER 1985

Dear Member,

I have just heard that you have become a current member of the St. Vital NDP Association. Congratulations on taking this important decision to join us.

I hope to call on you personally in the near future to welcome you to our Association.

When I first sought election in this constituency it was considered to be a safe Conservative seat. It took sixteen years of hard work and struggle to raise the level of support, slowly and steadily, from 35% to 52%. I have held the seat for the last four elections with the loyal support and confidence of the people of St. Vital/Norwood.

The battle is a continuing one. We can expect our Tory opponents to commit considerable resources and money in the attempt to win St. Vital and form a government with a working majority.

I hope I can count on your support, at the nomination and the election, to present a united and determined effort to win again in St. Vital.

As your full-time MLA, I can be reached at any time at 237-0053.

Yours sincerely,

Jim Walding

Source: Jim Walding Papers, Archives of Manitoba

GERRI UNWIN, APPEAL FOR SUPPORT, NOVEMBER 1985

Dear Friend:

As New Democrats, we face an important battle in the upcoming provincial election. To build upon the accomplishments of the Pawley Government, we must move forward with new ideas; listening, caring and responding to the changing needs of Manitobans.

As a candidate for the nomination in St. Vital I am dedicated to opening and building our party as a means of achieving these goals.

As a leader in local church and YMCA activities; as the former coordinator of evening programs for the St. Vital school division; and, as a lifelong resident of St. Vital and Norwood, I believe my local community credentials are solid.

As your party president this past year and as a 20 year member of the NDP, my party credentials are local and my views on many issues well known.

As Vice Chair of the Social Services Advisory Committee and a member of the Auto Pac Rates Appeal Board, I have had ample opportunity to learn first hand about important "people" issues.

As a mother and wife, I know the fears and hopes of our young people and the difficult times many families are facing.

To win at election time we must build our party here in St. Vital. We must attract workers, members and supporters. As your party president I was dedicated to that purpose. As your candidate, I believe we can work together to do even more. And, to win in '86!

If you have any questions or concerns, or if you would like to become personally involved in my campaign, please call me.

Sincerely,

Gerri Unwin

Source: Sig Laser, personal papers

JIM WALDING, APPEAL FOR SUPPORT, DECEMBER 1985 (I)

Dear Member:

As you know, a nomination meeting has been set to choose a candidate for the NDP in St. Vital in the coming provincial election.

In speaking to our members, two concerns have been made to me repeatedly.

Firstly, that fighting among ourselves is wasteful, causes bad publicity, and interferes with the real job of fighting the Conservatives.

Secondly, it puts the future of St. Vital as an NDP seat at risk. While we have a proven winner as our MLA, why gamble with a seat critical to the re-election of our present provincial government?

I respectfully ask for your careful consideration of these two important concerns.

Yours sincerely,

Jim Walding

Source: Jim Walding Papers, Archives of Manitoba

JIM WALDING, APPEAL FOR SUPPORT, DECEMBER 1985 (II)

Dear Member:

The nomination meeting for the next provincial election in St. Vital has been confirmed for Sunday, January 12, 1986 at Norberry School. Registration will be from 1:30 p.m. to 2:30 p.m.

To avoid any disputes, personal identification will be required from everyone, such as driver's license, medical insurance card, student card, etc.

Should you need a ride to the meeting or can provide one, and we have not discussed it, please call to let me know.

It is VERY important that you attend the nomination meeting, the future of St. Vital constituency as an NDP seat is at risk.

Many members of the St. Vital New Democratic Party have told me that there is no doubt in their minds that if I am not the party candidate in the next provincial election, the seat will be won by the Conservatives.

Yours sincerely,

Jim Walding

Source: Jim Walding Papers, Archives of Manitoba

SIG LASER, APPEAL FOR SUPPORT, 4 JANUARY 1986

January 4, 1986

Dear Fellow New Democrats:

The Nomination Meeting is soon upon us and January 12th looks to be an interesting day.

All three campaigns have worked hard, but it won't surprise you if I tell you that I feel my campaign has out-performed the others.

I think that the numbers of renewed and new members brought in by the campaigns speak for themselves:

Laser	330
Walding	150
Unwin	150

As well, I'm sure that by now you have seen our orange and black signs.

This indicates that I have a team ready and capable of building the N.D.P. in St. Vital. We must set our sights on the Tories and present a vigorous and committed candidate.

I have previously indicated that if successful I will undertake to open a Constituency Office in St. Vital to provide a visible presence and "close to home" service to the electors in St. Vital. I believe this is long overdue.

Most of all, however, what must happen on January 12th no matter who wins the nomination, is that the party must come out of this contest unified and stronger. On this you have my pledge!

I am looking forward to meeting you on Sunday, if I haven't seen you already, and I hope that you will consider supporting me for a strong new voice for the New Democratic Party in St. Vital.

Yours sincerely,

Sig Laser

Source: Sig Laser, personal papers

JIM WALDING, LETTER OF RESIGNATION FROM SPEAKERSHIP, 16 JANUARY 1986

On Sunday January 12th, I contested a political party nomination in the constituency of St. Vital, an action necessary to facilitate the continuance of my career in provincial politics.

While occupying the position of Speaker, it has always been my responsibility to uphold the high ideals of the Speakership in the parliamentary process and conduct the affairs of the Assembly in a fair and impartial manner.

Since the principle of impartiality is incompatible with my recent partisan actions, I have no other alternative than to give notice that I intend to tender my resignation as Speaker to the Assembly when it next convenes. Until such time, to permit the smooth functioning of the Department of Legislation, I intend to perform only duties of an administrative nature.

May I take this opportunity to express my gratitude for being given the honour of serving all members of the House and being entrusted with the traditions of the parliamentary system in Manitoba.

Yours sincerely,

D. James Walding

Speaker

Source: Jim Walding Papers, Archives of Manitoba

JIM WALDING TO ST. VITAL NEW DEMOCRATS, [JANUARY?] 1986

Dear New Democrat:

Thank you for attending the recent NDP nominating meeting in St. Vital. Your active support for the democratic system demonstrates an expression of confidence in our movement in St. Vital and is an encouraging indication of continuing electoral success.

This is clearly the time to put aside any differences there might have been and to close ranks in the unity of common purpose. We can best pursue the cause of fighting the next election by combining our efforts and resources to conduct another effective and successful campaign.

For your information and interest I enclose,

1) A copy of the bell-ringing rule changes requested recently by a constituent,

2) A copy of my letter of intent to resign the Speakership, sent to all MLA's.

Your constituency executive met last Sunday to assess our readiness for the shortly-expected election campaign. An Election Planning Committee is almost complete, an active search is underway for an election headquarters and a first pamphlet is being prepared. We are in good shape to fight the election whenever the writs are issued.

There will always be problems to overcome however, and your help will be needed once again to supply the necessary effort and finances needed to fight a successful campaign.

We have the talent and determination to win again in St. Vital.

With your help we will win!

Yours sincerely,

Jim Walding

Source: Sig Laser, personal papers

JIM WALDING TO HOWARD PAWLEY, 3 APRIL 1986

April 3, 1986

PERSONAL & CONFIDENTIAL

Honourable H. Pawley
Premier
Room 204
Legislative Bldg.
Winnipeg, Manitoba
R3C 0V8

Dear Premier Pawley:

Further to our discussion of April 1st, I have given the matter considerable thought and discussed it with my political advisors and constituency officials.

While not losing sight of the realities of the present situation and the possible consequences of precipitate action, I would ask you to bear in mind the following points.

1. My work and research while in opposition in '77 – '81 undoubtedly contributed to the defeat of the Lyon Government in 1981.

2. When I first ran in 1969, I received 35.5% of the vote, I increased this to 37% in 1971, 39% in 1973, 41.5% in 1977, when the NDP vote plunged and we lost several seats, and a further increase to 45% in 1986. This steady build-up of voter support has not been won without a great deal of hard work and constituency service.

3. The instances of Caucus Chairman, Chairman of Family Law Committee, Chairman of Public Accounts Committee, Education and Crown Corporations critic, Chairman of Estimates Committee, and Speakership, all demonstrate a loyalty to the Manitoba New Democratic Party and a willingness to assume any duties assigned to me.

4. Having been continuously elected since 1971, I have far more seniority than any of your back-benchers and more seniority than 3/4's of your cabinet. Of the four members of the NDP caucus who have more seniority than me, 3 have a mere 18 months' seniority each more than me.

5. Members of your government have admitted to me, that had your French Language Services Resolution passed in 1984, the NDP would have been soundly crushed at the last election. It was only my actions in standing firm on the application of the Rules, despite considerable pressure to do otherwise, that enable you to occupy the position you do today.

6. I am already receiving constituency requests from Riel. The loss of a seat in South East Winnipeg indicates a need to maintain a presence in this area of the city and begin the work needed to win Riel in the next election.

7. At every election, expectations are raised among New Democrats in St. Vital that at last they will have representation in the provincial cabinet, yet those expectations are consistently dashed. What other constituency has been denied for so long? It would be an insult to St. Vital to be passed over in favour of more junior and less experienced members.

8. The recent nomination battle in St. Vital was widely perceived by the people of St. Vital to be an unwarranted and unfair attack on their Member. When canvassing, they told me in no uncertain terms that it was not appreciated and rallied to my support in a solid and convincing demonstration of support.

In view of the points enumerated above, I am unable to accept any responsibility less than a cabinet portfolio.

In order to enhance the position of the New Democratic Party in a depleted South East Winnipeg and permit me to perform in a position within my capabilities, it would seem that the portfolios of Consumer and Corporate Affairs, Cultural Affairs or Urban Affairs would be seen as most beneficial to this part of the province.

I trust that this brief overview will be of assistance to you and look forward to receiving an early reply.

Yours sincerely,

Jim Walding

M.L.A. for St. Vital

Source: Jim Walding Papers, Archives of Manitoba

JIM WALDING TO FRANCES RUSSELL, 21 APRIL 1986

April 21, 1986

Mrs. Frances Russell
Free Press
300 Carlton Street
Winnipeg, Manitoba

Dear Mrs. Russell:

This letter refers to an article in the Winnipeg Free Press of April 16th, 1986 under your name.

The article attributes actions to me which are described as "blackmail and extortion", both of which are Criminal Code offences.

I view these accusations as highly defamatory, injurious to my reputation, and are a source of considerable mental pain and anguish to me. While your profession as a journalist entitles you to express your opinion in print, I do not believe it gives you a licence to destroy the reputation of an other.

Even if you were able to read into my letter any imputation of blackmail and extortion, (although none was intended), surely responsible journalistic integrity would have required a simple telephone call to me to obtain my side of the story.

Given this deplorable breach of journalistic ethics, I must request an apology and a full retraction to be printed in the newspaper.

Without prejudice, I should inform you that I was informed by legal counsel that an action for libel may exist in this matter, but I assure you that this information should not be construed as a threat, blackmail, or extortion.

Yours sincerely,

Jim Walding

c.c. Mr. M. Burt.

Source: Jim Walding Papers, Archives of Manitoba

MARTY DOLIN TO MEMBERS OF ST. VITAL EXECUTIVE OF THE NDP, 28 APRIL 1987

April 28, 1987

Valerie Walding,
26 Hemlock Pl.,
Winnipeg, MB.
R2H 1L7

Dear Valerie:

I am, with considerable regret, requesting that your executive take steps to try to convince your member, Jim Walding, to take on his responsibilities as the elected representative of the St. Vital constituency. Mr. Walding has been negligent in attending caucus meetings, committees of the Legislature and the Legislative sessions. He is, by his non-attendance at caucus (or just "dropping in" for the last ten minutes of the meetings when he comes at all – see attendance record attached) unable to participate in the debate on the policies and legislation of the government and, thereby, unable to represent the wishes or concerns of his constituents. Mr. Walding does attend the televised question period, but has been negligent in attending estimates review, debates on most legislation and leaves the Legislative Building when he pleases without informing me, in my position as government whip, or his colleagues.

As you are aware, cooperation is required from all our elected members to ensure that our programs, policies and legislation are passed in the house. Mr. Walding has not been cooperative and appears not to be willing to take on the responsibilities borne by the other 29 elected New Democrats.

The precipitating situation which prompts this correspondence took place on Thursday, April 23, 1987. The opposition had called a vote on a Bill presented by them which would have replaced the President of the University of Manitoba with the President of the Union of Manitoba Municipalities on the Electoral Boundaries Commission. For various reasons your government believes this is not in the best interests of Manitobans and wished to defeat the proposal. The vote was called at 5:15 P.M. (sitting hours are 1:30 – 6:00 P.M.). The Premier was out of town on important business and not paired. All members gathered, but Jim Walding was not in the building. I called his home (at about 5:20 P.M.) and found him there. I explained the situation and requested he attend at the Legislature as soon as possible. He stated he would. All government members waited in the caucus room (the bells are allowed to ring for one hour before the Speaker calls the vote). At about 5:40 P.M. I requested the secretary to call to see if Jim Walding had left home yet. She reported back that she had spoken to Jim and he "had changed his mind" and would not be returning to the Legislature. I then called him myself and was told by another person (male) that Mr. Walding was "eating his supper and would not come to the phone" and he would call after he finished his supper. He did not. Luckily none of our other elected members reneged on their responsibilities and the Tories did not have their full complement in the House (and Ms. Carstairs was not present) so we won the vote 27-18. If, in the future, on an important issue, all the Tories and Ms. Carstairs attended and we had just one other member either sick or otherwise unavailable we could face serious consequences.

I have reminded Mr. Walding, on numerous occasions, of his responsibilities and have warned him that, although I have limited power as whip, I would have to take some action if he persisted. He told me he would make a greater effort, but obviously does not feel obliged to do so. Mr. Walding, has been inconsiderate of his fellow elected members and has not been taking his responsibilities in the Legislature as an elected member even to the point of non-attendance when the House is in session.

My authority as whip is dependent on the sincerity and willingness of our members to voluntarily take their responsibilities and to act in a disciplined and cohesive manner. If one or more members refuses to cooperate I can impose minor sanctions, such as withdrawal of legislative services, changing seating arrangements in the House, etc. I can recommend disciplinary action to Caucus, which I will do if there are no other alternatives apparent.

Jim Walding has been an elected member for 16 years. He knows his responsibilities to his caucus colleagues, his constituents and to the Party that elected him. I urge you to meet with Mr. Walding to prevail upon him to, once again, be a cooperative member of the government caucus. If the situation does not improve I will have to consult with my colleagues and the Premier to see what action shall be taken.

I appreciate your anticipated cooperation and any action you may take which will rectify the situation and am

Sincerely,

Marty Dolin

Caucus Whip

c.c. *Jim Walding*
Hon. Howard Pawley
N.D.P. Provincial Office
Encl.

SECOND SESSION – THIRTY THIRD LEGISLATURE

1987

February 27	Absent	March 9, noon	Absent
March 2, noon	Absent	March 9, dinner meeting	Absent
March 2, dinner meeting	Absent	March 10	Absent
March 3	Absent	March 11	Absent
March 4	Absent	March 12	Absent
March 5	Absent	March 16, noon	Absent
March 6	Absent	March 16, dinner meeting	Absent

March 17	Absent	April 10	Absent
March 18	Absent	April 13, noon	Absent
March 19	Absent	April 13, dinner meeting	Absent
March 20	Absent	April 14	Absent
March 23, noon	Late	April 15	Late
March 23, dinner meeting	Late	April 16	Absent
March 24	Absent	April 21, noon	Absent
March 25	Absent	April 21, dinner meeting	Absent
March 26	Late	April 22	Present
March 27	Absent	April 23	Absent
April 6, noon	Absent	April 24	Absent
April 6, dinner meeting	Late	April 27, noon	Absent
April 7	Late	April 27, dinner meeting	Absent
April 8	Absent	April 28	Absent
April 9	Absent		

Source: Jim Walding Papers, Archives of Manitoba

JIM WALDING TO MARTY DOLIN, 4 MAY 1987

Mr. M. Dolin,

Room 234,
Legislative Building,
Winnipeg.
Man.

Dear Mr. Dolin,

I acknowledge receipt of your letter of April 28th which I find to be inaccurate, offensive and lacking a sense of good judgment.

It is highly presumptuous of you to lecture me on my responsibilities as an elected representative, conduct which has been approved by my constituents in five consecutive elections with a steadily increasing share of the vote. Should I need advice, you may rest assured that I would seek if from someone with sufficient legislative experience to give it.

You should be aware that I receive legislative services from the Legislature as an elected Member; such services are not yours to bestow or withhold. Even if you had the power to change seating arrangements in the House, it would be seen as an act of petulant childishness to do so.

The attempts at intimidation contained in your letter are obviously unacceptable, and vaguely worded threats are more likely to achieve exactly the opposite affect from what you intend. Your caucus colleagues will decide whether you acted with good political judgment or whether you exceeded the bounds of your responsibilities.

Your decision to write to the members of my constituency executive is an intolerable intrusion into the internal affairs of a constituency association. It interferes with the cohesiveness of the association in St. Vital and makes my job as the Member more difficult. The timing could not be worse, occurring just before our constituency Family Dinner, our major fund-raising event of the year. I would not dream of intruding into the internal affairs of Kildonan constituency and I would have expected the same courtesy to be extended to my constituency.

Who is the next caucus member to be subjected to your harassment?

Your actions leave me no other alternative than to demand a written apology, which will reassure me that I am still welcome to attend caucus meetings.

I am sending a copy of this letter and a copy of your letter to all members of our caucus so that each may judge individually whether your actions have enhanced or detracted from the security of tenure of the Government.

Yours sincerely,

D. James Walding

Source: Jim Walding Papers, Archives of Manitoba

SIG LASER TO MARTY DOLIN, 7 MAY 1987

Marty Dolin

234 Legislative Building
Winnipeg, Manitoba

Dear Marty:

At our meeting of May 6, 1987 the executive of the St. Vital Constituency Association requested that I write in response to your letter of April 28, 1987.

We thank you for the information provided and appreciate that cooperation is required from all our elected members. The record of Mr. Walding's caucus attendance which you have provided causes us concern. We have in the past on numerous occasions tried to persuade Mr. Walding to take a more active role.

St. Vital elected a New Democrat and it is our sincere hope that our M.L.A. will in the future represent the people who put their trust in him by attending seriously to his duties as M.L.A. for St. Vital.

For our part at the constituency level we feel that we have expended every reasonable effort to encourage Mr. Walding to be a team player. With respect to your responsibilities as caucus whip, we can only defer to your sense of the situation as it may develop.

We trust that in consultation with your colleagues and the Premier you will take whatever action you deem necessary.

Sincerely,

Sig Laser

President, St. Vital
NDP Association

c.c. Jim Walding
Hon. Howard Pawley
Provincial Office

Source: Sig Laser, personal papers

JAY COWAN TO HOWARD PAWLEY, 2 MARCH 1988 (EXCERPT)

STRATEGY FOR THE WALDING PROPOSAL:

1) You and I should meet with Jim today to discuss his proposal. I would be involved because any changes in the present system, were they to occur, would be managed by the House Leader.

   You should start the meeting by indicating we want to seriously consider his proposal and wish to gain a better understanding of exactly what it is he is proposing.

I would then ask a series of questions regarding:

(a) his specific proposal, and

(b) the process he would contemplate as being required to effect any major change in the role of the Speaker.

(c) the role he would want to play in both the process of change. ~~and any resultant changes which might be approved.~~

(d) I would arrange for continuing meetings with him.

2) We should inform both Caucuses and Cabinet of this latest development so they are not taken by surprise by any public announcement of it. We do not want them responding to the Press. Only you and I should respond to the Press on this.

3) We should expect a public announcement on this at any time.

4) We should be prepared for a question in the House either from Jim or the Opposition. The question will probably be directed to you. You may want to pass if off to me by indicating that matters such as this are traditionally dealt with by House Leaders.

5) I would recommend the following general response to either Opposition or press questions:

a) Mr. Walding has long promoted this concept. There is nothing new, extraordinary or of undue significance in his continuing to advance this suggestion.

b) As a matter of fact, the concept of a permanent Speaker has been advanced by many CCF-NDP leaders in the past. (M.J. Coldwell, Stanley Knowles, David Lewis, Donald C. MacDonald) and some prominent Conservatives (Stanfield).

c) Given Jim's tenure in the House and his experience as a Speaker, we want to hear him and others out very carefully on this issue.

d) The House Leader has been asked to work with Jim to further review his proposal.

e) We think major change such as has been suggested will require thorough review and as much consensus as possible. Mechanisms for review could include general research, special reviews, and/or committees, including Committees of the House.

f) Therefore, we would like to hear from members opposite as to how they feel about the suggestion.

g) There are a number of options as to how to proceed and we do not want to prejudge any of them without full consideration. All options are open.

h) We do not see any significance in his request for an early reply. We receive similar requests for early responses all the time. (It would be nice to have a letter from Gary Filmon and Sharon Carstairs calling for early responses).

i) We believe Jim wrote to Gary Filmon in the finest parliamentary tradition of dealing with items such as this in a non-partisan way.

LONGER TERM STRATEGY

1) Seek agreement with Jim that this matter be either: a) referred to the Rules Committee; or, b) referred to a Special Committee which would be empowered to review this matter and report back to the House at the next Session. Either course of action will require a motion of referral which would have to be approved (voted upon) by the House. We would need full support of our Caucus and the Whip would have to be on for this vote.

2) Offer Jim the Chairperson of the Committee.

3) The Committee would be empowered to visit other jurisdictions where this matter has been dealt with and/or resolved.

4) We should indicate that our first preference (but not our bottom line) should be that there should be an all party consensus for any major changes. (Please note that any major changes would require amendments to existing Acts.)

5) We should not initiate any discussion as to who would be a permanent Speaker if we chose to go that route. If Jim asks the question, we should be flexible and non-committal in our response.

6) We should not commit to any specific changes until we see the Report of the Committee, but we can indicate general support of any action which would enable the Speaker to better serve the Legislature.

Thanks.

Source: Howard Pawley, personal papers

GARY FILMON TO JIM WALDING, 7 MARCH 1988

March 7, 1988

Mr. D. James Walding, M.L.A.
Room 234, Legislative Bldg
Winnipeg, Manitoba
R3C 0V8

Dear Mr. Walding;

Thank you for your letter of March 1, 1988. At this point, my opinion on a continuing Speakership has not changed since our last conversation on this matter. However, I would be willing to further discuss this issue with you if you are interested in pursuing such a proposal at this time.

Yours sincerely,

Gary Filmon

Source: Jim Walding Papers, Archives of Manitoba

Notes

Chapter 1: Introduction

1 Geoffrey Hawthorn, *Plausible Worlds: Possibility and Understanding in History and the Social Sciences* (Cambridge: Cambridge University Press, 1991).

2 Niall Ferguson, ed., *Virtual History: Alternatives and Counterfactuals* (New York: Basic Books, 1999).

3 Hawthorn, *Plausible Worlds*, 166.

4 Ferguson, *Virtual History*, 86-87.

5 Since I was not undertaking a quantitative analysis, the interviews were relatively unstructured with open-ended questions about such subjects as the respondent's relationship with, and recollections of, Jim Walding, as well as their roles in, and recollections of, the 1986 race for the NDP nomination in St. Vital. For a helpful overview of this methodology, see Beth L. Leach, "Asking Questions: Techniques for Semistructured Interviews," *Political Science* 35 (2002): 665-668, and, in particular, Jeffrey M. Berry, "Validity and Reliability Issues in Elite Interviewing," *Political Science* 35 (2002): 679-682.

6 Eugene J. Webb, Donald T. Campbell, Richard D. Schwartz, Lee Sechrest, and Janet Belew Grove, *Nonreactive Measures in the Social Sciences*, 2nd ed. (Boston: Houghton Mifflin, 1981), 196.

7 The voices of interviewees take a significant role in this book. To avoid additional metatextual clutter, quotes from the interviews I conducted are identified in the text as recollections from individual interviewees, but are not cited in endnotes. A full list of interviewees can be found in Appendix A.

8 John Meisel, *The Canadian General Election of 1957* (Toronto: University of Toronto Press, 1962), 120.

9 Howard A. Scarrow, "Three Dimensions of a Local Political Party," in John Meisel, ed., *Papers on the 1962 Election* (Toronto: University of Toronto Press, 1964), 53.

10 Robert J. Williams, "Candidate Selection," in Howard R. Penniman, ed., *Canada at the Polls: 1979 and 1980* (Washington: American Enterprise Institute, 1981), 87 and 91. Williams was the first scholar to undertake an extensive analysis of Canadian nomination practices.

11 R.K. Carty and Lynda Erickson, "Candidate Nomination in Canada's National Political Parties," in Herman Bakvis, ed., *Canadian Political Parties: Leaders, Candidates and Organization* (Toronto: Dundurn, 1996), 98-105.

12 Carty and Erickson, "Candidate Nomination," 153-157. As well, it is worth noting that Canadian nomination practices differ from those of other liberal democracies. See Joseph Wearing, *Strained Relations: Canada's Voters and Parties* (Toronto: McClelland and Stewart, 1988), 192. See also Michael Gallagher and Michael Marsh, eds., *Candidate Selection in Comparative Perspective* (London: Sage, 1988).

13 Carty and Erickson, "Candidate Nomination," 136.

14 Carty and Erickson, "Candidate Nomination," 106.

15 Lynda Erickson and R.K. Carty, "Parties and Candidate Selection in the 1988 Canadian General Election," *Canadian Journal of Political Science* 24 (1991): 337.

16 Williams, "Candidate Selection," 89.

17 R.K. Carty, "Party Organization and Activity on the Ground," in A. Brian Tanguay and Alain-G. Gagnon, eds., *Canadian Parties in Transition: Discourse, Organization and Representation*, 2nd ed. (Scarborough: Nelson, 1996), 192-193.

18 R.K. Carty, *Canadian Political Parties in the Constituencies* (Toronto: Dundurn, 1991), 112.

19 Anthony M. Sayers, *Parties, Candidates and Constituency Campaigns in Canadian Elections* (Vancouver: University of British Columbia Press, 1999), 36.

20 William Cross, "Grassroots Participation in Candidate Nomination," in Joanna Everitt and Brenda O'Neill, eds., *Citizen Politics: Research and Theory in Canadian Political Behaviour* (Don Mills: Oxford University Press, 2002), 377.

21 Keith Archer and Alan Whitehorn, *Political Activists: The NDP in Convention* (Toronto: Oxford University Press, 1997), 92.

22 Carty, *Canadian Political Parties*, 109-110.

23 Lisa Young and Elaine Campbell, "Women and Political Representation," in Hugh G. Thorburn and Alan Whitehorn, eds., *Party Politics in Canada*, 8th ed. (Toronto: Prentice-Hall, 2001), 68.

24 Sayers, *Parties, Candidates*, 56.

25 Since the national NDP is simply a federation of its provincial branches, there is, in one sense, no question of membership stability varying across levels. On the other hand, it is certainly possible that membership stability could be higher or lower in Manitoba than the average figure for the other provincial branches.

26 Rand Dyck, "Relations Between Federal and Provincial Parties," in A. Brian Tanguay and Alain-G. Gagnon, eds., *Canadian Parties in Transition: Discourse, Organization and Representation*, 2nd ed. (Scarborough: Nelson, 1996), 171 and 175.

27 Carty, *Canadian Political Parties*, 106.

28 Meisel, *Canadian General Election*, 124.

29 Erickson and Carty, "Parties and Candidate Selection," 342.

30 Lynda Erickson, letter to the author, 9 June 2006. These figures exclude the Liberal Party, which in 1993 protected all incumbent MPs from nomination challenges.

31 Carty and Erickson, "Candidate Nomination," 171.

32 Since the merger of the Canadian Alliance and Progressive Conservative parties, similar observations can be made about federal politics in Alberta. As one Conservative candidate in the 2006 national election noted: "For me the nomination is the election ... Once I'm nominated, the election is over." William Cross, "Candidate Nomination in Canada's Political Parties," in Jon H. Pammett and Christopher Dornan, eds., *The Canadian Federal Election of 2006* (Toronto: Dundurn Press), 173.

33 Williams, "Candidate Selection," 100.

34 F.C. Engelmann and M.A. Schwartz, *Political Parties and the Canadian Social Structure* (Scarborough: Prentice-Hall, 1967), 142 and 166.

35 William Cross, *Political Parties* (Vancouver: University of British Columbia Press, 2004), 59-60.

36 Dick Spencer, *Trumpets and Drums: John Diefenbaker on the Campaign Trail* (Vancouver: Douglas and McIntyre), 151.

37 J. Murray Beck, *Pendulum of Power: Canada's Federal Elections* (Scarborough: Prentice-Hall, 1968), 402.

38 Carty and Erickson, "Candidate Nomination," 158. The data from 1993, however, do not display any particular regional pattern.

39 Cross, *Political Parties*, 61.

40 Carty and Erickson, "Candidate Nomination," 132.

41 Ibid.

Chapter 2: The Setting

1 T. Peterson, "Manitoba: Ethnic and Class Politics in Manitoba," in Martin Robin, ed., *Canadian Provincial Politics* (Scarborough: Prentice-Hall, 1972), 70.

2 Doug Smith, *As Many Liars: The Story of the 1995 Manitoba Vote-Splitting Scandal* (Winnipeg: Arbeiter Ring, 2003), 45.

3 Kenneth McNaught, *A Prophet in Politics: A Biography of J.S. Woodsworth* (Toronto: University of Toronto Press, 1959).

4 Nelson Wiseman, *Social Democracy in Manitoba: A History of the CCF-NDP* (Winnipeg: University of Manitoba Press, 1983), 15. Wiseman's book is indispensable to a full understanding of the evolution of the Manitoba CCF-NDP, and his analysis informs the first half of this chapter.

5 Peterson, "Manitoba," 79-82.

6 Their coalition partners were not always respectful of the CCF. In 1941, one Liberal-Progressive pamphlet urged voters: "Think! Can you support the C.C.F. candidate? A stranger in our midst who has no interest in you or your community." Wiseman, *Social Democracy*, 33.

7 Wiseman, *Social Democracy*, 36.

8 Wiseman, *Social Democracy*, 66.

9 Wiseman, *Social Democracy*, 65 and 67.

10 Lloyd Stinson, *Political Warriors: Recollections of a Social Democrat* (Winnipeg: Queenston House, 1975), 119.

11 Ian Stewart, "Of Customs and Coalitions: The Formation of Canadian Federal Parliamentary Alliances," *Canadian Journal of Political Science* 13 (1980): 459-460.

12   W.L. Morton, *Manitoba: A History* (Toronto: University of Toronto Press, 1967), 481. Ironically, proportional representation was eliminated in Winnipeg just one year after the secretary of the Proportional Representation Society of Britain "certified that he was completely satisfied" with the Manitoba system. M.S. Donnelly, *The Government of Manitoba* (Toronto: University of Toronto Press, 1963), 78.

13   Stinson, *Political Warriors*, 210.

14   Alex Netherton, "Paradigm and Shift: A Sketch of Manitoba Politics," in Keith Brownsey and Michael Howlett, eds., *The Provincial State in Canada: Politics in the Provinces and Territories* (Peterborough: Broadview, 2001), 216.

15   Wiseman, *Social Democracy*, 88-105.

16   Wiseman, *Social Democracy*, 91.

17   Gad Horowitz, *Canadian Labour in Politics* (Toronto: University of Toronto Press), 222.

18   Wiseman, *Social Democracy*, 108.

19   Wiseman, *Social Democracy*, 106.

20   Stinson, *Political Warriors*, 197.

21   Wiseman, *Social Democracy*, 121-124.

22   Stinson, *Political Warriors*, 188.

23   *St. Vital Lance*, 23 October 1958, p. 3.

24   *St. Vital Lance*, 6 November 1958, p. 3.

25   James A. Jackson, *The Centennial History of Manitoba* (Toronto: McClelland and Stewart, 1970), 87.

26   *St. Vital Lance*, 13 November 1958, p. 9.

27   St. Vital Historical Society, "St. Vital: Past, Present and Future," undated paper, 1-3.

28   Richard Wilson, "St. Vital—1912," *The Dominion*, December 1912.

29   *St. Vital Lance*, 28 November 1963, p. 3.

30   David Williams, interview with the author, 4 May 2005.

31   Victor Turek, *Poles in Manitoba* (Toronto: Polish Alliance Press, 1967), 101.

32   *Winnipeg Free Press*, 18 February 1964, p. 1, and *Winnipeg Tribune*, 18 February 1964, p. 1.

33   Elections Manitoba, Statement of Votes/Historical Summaries, 228-255. http://www.electionsmanitoba.ca/pdf/2003_statvotes_history.pdf (accessed 9 June 2006).

34   St. Vital Historical Society, "Depression," undated paper, 2.

35   *Winnipeg Tribune*, 9 June 1962, p. 5.

36   St. Vital Historical Society, "St. Vital: Past, Present and Future," undated paper, 7.

37   Elections Manitoba, Statement of Votes/Historical Summaries, 228-255. http://www.electionsmanitoba.ca/pdf/2003_statvotes_history.pdf (accessed 9 June 2006).

38   Leaving aside the thirty-one hospital ballots and the 126 advance votes.

39   Original map scanned by Elections Manitoba staff and electronically received on 31 August 2006.

40   Elections Manitoba, *Statement of Votes for the 28th Provincial General Election*, 23 June 1966, unpaginated copy.

Chapter 3: The Incumbent

1   Jim Walding died on 23 April 2007 after a brief battle with cancer. I am grateful to Mr. Walding for agreeing to be interviewed in May 2005, and for his helpful correspondence over the subsequent months.

2   Walding noticed a Canadian optician's advertisement in a trade magazine and applied for the position. Only after he had been accepted did he discover the job was in Winnipeg.

3   Sayers, *Parties, Candidates*, 6. Of course, the prohibition against "carpet-baggers" is not absolute. Lester Pearson, for one, secured Algoma East on eight occasions despite having no residence there, nor "any earlier connection with it." Lester B. Pearson, *Mike: The Memoirs of the Right Honourable Lester B. Pearson, Volume 2* (Toronto: University of Toronto Press, 1973), 7. Moreover, the Newfoundland Liberal Party under Joey Smallwood was renowned for nominating candidates who had "only the most tenuous connections with the constituencies they represent[ed]. For most outport electors, it [had] been enough to know that their Liberal candidate, even if he happened to be yet another St. John's lawyer who had never seen their district before, [had] been sent to them as 'Joey's man.'" S.J.R. Noel, *Politics in Newfoundland* (Toronto: University of Toronto Press, 1971), 284. Yet these examples are very much exceptions to the norm.

4   *St. Vital Lance*, 12 June 1969, p. 7.

5   James A. McAllister, *The Government of Edward Schreyer* (Kingston: McGill-Queens University Press, 1984), 144-154.

6   McAllister, *Edward Schreyer*, 148.

7   *St. Vital Lance*, 21 October 1969, p. 8.

8   *St. Vital Lance*, 21 October 1969, p. 8.

9   *Winnipeg Free Press*, 21 November 1970, p. 3.

10   *St. Vital Lance*, 26 November 1970, p. 1.

11   *Winnipeg Tribune*, 12 February 1971, p. 3.

12   *St. Vital Lance*, 4 March 1971, p. 1.

13   *St. Vital Lance*, 4 March 1971, p. 16.

14   *St. Vital Lance*, 11 March 1971, p. 1.

15   Most candidates who seek elected office after having lost in a previous general election are, in fact, successful at the nomination stage. In the 1988 federal election, for example, 79 percent of candidates in this circumstance won their nomination contests. Data provided by Ken Carty, letter to the author, 26 October 2006.

16   *St. Vital Lance*, 18 March 1971, p. 1.

17   *St. Vital Lance*, 25 March 1971, p. 1.

18   *St. Vital Lance*, 18 March 1971, p. 1.

19   *St. Vital Lance*, 1 April 1971, p. 20.

20   *St. Vital Lance*, 1 April 1971, p. 6.

21   *St. Vital Lance*, 18 March 1971, p. 1.

22   *Winnipeg Free Press*, 1 April 1971, p. 8.

23   *Winnipeg Tribune*, 6 April 1971, p. 1.

24   *St. Vital Lance*, 8 April 1971, p. 1.

25   *Winnipeg Tribune*, 6 April 1971, p. 1.

26   *Winnipeg Tribune*, 6 April 1971, p. 1.

27   Legislation making Unicity a reality was finally passed later in the summer of 1971.

28 *St. Vital Lance*, 22 April 1971, p. 1.

29 *St. Vital Lance*, 6 May 1971, p. 3.

30 *St. Vital Lance*, 16 May 1973, p. 1.

31 *St. Vital Lance*, 6 June 1973, p. 1.

32 Nelson Wiseman's assessment is that without Schreyer, "it was doubtful that the NDP would have been elected in 1969 or re-elected in 1973." Wiseman, *Social Democracy*, 127.

33 *St. Vital Lance*, 7 March 1973, p. 7.

34 *St. Vital Lance*, 6 June 1973, p. 1.

35 Hugh McMeel, letter to the author, 2 August 2006. Kennedy's appointment provided some confirmation for the old saw that "the electoral fortunes of the Manitoba Liberal Party would improve dramatically if judges were allowed the vote." *Globe and Mail*, 14 October 1982, p. 7. All *Globe and Mail* references are from the Atlantic edition.

36 Manitoba NDP, "Report of the Polling Sub-Committee," 2, P3665-3668, Archives of Manitoba (hereafter cited as Jim Walding Papers).

37 Manitoba NDP, "Report of the Polling Sub-Committee," 4, Jim Walding Papers.

38 "Manitoba New Democratic Party Election '77," media release, 27 September 1977, Jim Walding Papers.

39 *South East Lance*, 5 October 1977, p. 18.

40 Eddie Coutu Election Committee, election pamphlet, 1977, Jim Walding Papers.

41 Eddie Coutu Election Committee, election pamphlet, 1977, Jim Walding Papers.

42 Thanksgiving fell just before election day in 1977; only in St. Vital, according to the provincial party president, was there no lull in campaign activities.

43 According to Sterling Lyon, the Conservatives were determined to "throw out the socialists who follow alien doctrines laid down in Europe in the nineteenth century." Wiseman, *Social Democracy*, 128.

44 CBC TV, 15 March 1980, Jim Walding Papers.

45 CBC Radio, 8 April 1981, Jim Walding Papers.

46 CBC Radio, 13 January 1979, Jim Walding Papers.

47 Sidney Green, *Rise and Fall of a Political Animal: A Memoir* (Winnipeg: Great Plains, 2003), 168-9.

48 The final tally was 10 votes for Howard Pawley, 8 for Sid Green, and 3 for Saul Cherniak.

49 Russell Doern, *Wednesdays are Cabinet Days* (Winnipeg: Queenston House, 1981), 186.

50 Jim Walding, letter to Jan D'Arcy, 14 June 1979, Jim Walding Papers.

51 Manitoba NDP Organization Committee Meeting Minutes, 30 March 1981, 4. New Democratic Party of Manitoba, Box 1-Box 15, Archives of Manitoba (hereafter cited as NDPM).

52 *Winnipeg Free Press*, 14 October 1981, p. 1.

53 *Winnipeg Free Press*, 7 October 1981, p. 5.

54 *Winnipeg Free Press*, 21 November 1981, p. 7. Nor did the city's public relations community learn from this mistake. Eight years later, Tourism Winnipeg devised the slogan: "Nowhere else in the world, no taste like the great taste of Winnipeg." Alas, this soon became known as the "Nowhere, no taste" campaign. *Vancouver Sun*, 2 June 1990, p. B1.

55 *Winnipeg Free Press*, 11 September 1981, p. 8.

56 Original map scanned by Elections Manitoba staff and electronically received on 18 March 2005.

57 Jim Walding Papers.

58 John Robertson campaign pamphlet, 1981, Jim Walding Papers.

59 *Winnipeg Free Press*, 13 October 1981, p. 7.

60 *Winnipeg Free Press*, 7 October 1981, p. 5.

61 *Winnipeg Free Press*, 13 October 1981, p. 7.

62 Elections Manitoba, *Statement of Votes for the 30th Provincial General Election*, 28 June 1973, 31; Elections Manitoba, *Statement of Votes for the 31st Provincial General Election*, 11 October 1977, 22; Elections Manitoba, *Statement of Votes for the 32nd Provincial General Election*, 17 November 1981, 19.

63 *Winnipeg Free Press*, 23 October, 1981, p. 4.

64 Walding's campaign team organized an office pool on which canvasser would secure the largest number of sign commitments for their candidate.

65 Walding was, for example, imported to chair the contested 1981 NDP nomination meeting in the constituency of Seven Oaks (won by Eugene Kostyra).

66 According to one Walding confidante, Pawley had previously claimed confusion as to why Walding had never been included in a Schreyer cabinet. His jilting by Pawley now led Walding dryly to observe: "I guess he must have found out why."

67 Appointing such a small initial cabinet was a piece of election-night advice from Saskatchewan premier Allan Blakeney.

68 Al Mackling did join the cabinet shortly thereafter on 12 February 1982.

69 *Winnipeg Free Press*, 23 October 1981, p. 1.

70 Jim Walding, letter to the author, 28 May 2006.

71 *Winnipeg Free Press*, 22 April 1986, p. 7.

72 Jim Walding, letter to Howard Pawley, 17 December 1981, Jim Walding Papers.

73 *Winnipeg Sun*, 5 February 1984, p. 5.

74 *Act to Amend the Legislative Assembly Act*, draft bill, 21 April 1982.

75 Howard Pawley, letter to Jim Walding, 1 June 1982, Jim Walding Papers.

76 Jim Walding, letter to Howard Pawley, 3 June 1982, Jim Walding Papers.

77 *Winnipeg Free Press*, 16 June 1983, p. 4.

78 *Winnipeg Free Press*, 15 March 1983, p. 7.

79 Pawley subsequently acknowledged that there may have been more to the supper visit than simply obtaining a copy of Hansard. "I was very upset about something," he recalled, but "actually Walding didn't require pressure on that (matter); he had already made his mind up on that."

80 *Globe and Mail*, 18 December 1982, p. 4.

81 *Winnipeg Free Press*, 8 March 1983, p. 7.

82 *Winnipeg Free Press*, 6 March 1983, p. 8.

83 *Winnipeg Free Press*, 15 March 1983, p. 7.

84 *Winnipeg Sun*, 8 March 1983, p. 7.

85 *Winnipeg Free Press*, 6 March 1983, p. 2. The Tories kept up their attack even after Walding released data that indicated that he had given them "overwhelming preference" during question period. Since the start of the session, he had allowed 390 PC questions, as opposed to sixteen from the NDP and three from the lone independent. *Winnipeg Free Press*, 10 March 1983, p. 6.

86 *Winnipeg Free Press*, 8 March 1983, p. 6.

87 *Winnipeg Sun*, 10 March 1983, p. 6.

88 *Winnipeg Free Press*, 8 March 1983, p. 10.

89 Andy Anstett and Paul G. Thomas, "Manitoba: The Role of the Legislature in a Polarized Political System," in Gary Levy and Graham White, eds., *Provincial and Territorial Legislatures in Canada* (Toronto: University of Toronto Press, 1989), 90.

90 See, in particular, Frances Russell, *The Canadian Crucible: Manitoba's Role in Canada's Great Divide* (Winnipeg: Heartland Associates, 2003), and Raymond M. Hébert, *Manitoba's French-Language Crisis: A Cautionary Tale* (Montreal: McGill-Queens, 2004).

91 A. Kerr Twaddle, legal opinion, 14 April 1982, Jim Walding Papers.

92 Dale Gibson, legal opinion, 10 May 1982, Jim Walding Papers.

93 Would this deal have greatly strengthened Manitoba's francophone community? Nelson Wiseman, for one, has subsequently argued that "constitutional guarantees for francophones and the laws abridging and expanding those rights have been to date largely irrelevant to the linguistic and political welfare of Franco-Manitobans." Nelson Wiseman, "The Questionable Relevance of the Constitution in Advancing Minority Cultural Rights in Manitoba," *Canadian Journal of Political Science* 25 (1991): 699.

94 *Winnipeg Free Press*, 21 May 1983, p. 6.

95 Hébert, *Manitoba's French*, 99-101.

96 Hébert, *Manitoba's French*, 78-82.

97 *Winnipeg Free Press*, 9 July 1983, p. 7.

98 Bill Hutton, letter to members of the NDP caucus, 16 June 1983, Jim Walding Papers.

99 Sterling Lyon, French Language Services, 4 September 1981, Jim Walding Papers.

100 *Winnipeg Free Press*, 25 May 1983, p. 7.

101 *Winnipeg Sun*, 22 July 1983, p. 6.

102 *Winnipeg Free Press*, 22 July 1983, p. 3. See also *Winnipeg Sun*, 26 August 1983, p. 5.

103 *Winnipeg Free Press*, 6 August 1983, p. 9.

104 Manitoba Department of Attorney General, *Constitutionally Speaking*, July 1983, Jim Walding Papers.

105 *Winnipeg Sun*, 20 July 1983, p. 10.

106 Hébert, *Manitoba's French*, 140-146. See also *Winnipeg Sun*, 27 October 1983, p. 6. Riel MLA Doreen Dodick endured many crank calls over the issue; frequently, she would answer the phone to be greeted by the roar of a vacuum cleaner.

107 Russell, *Canadian Crucible*, 317.

108 *Winnipeg Free Press*, 5 October 1983, p. 7. Racist attacks on Manitoba's francophone community were regular occurrences even before the Pawley government's constitutional initiative. See *Globe and Mail*, 10 February 1983, p. 9.

109 *Winnipeg Free Press*, 4 August 1983, p. 11. Lyon's understated comment: "You'll hear the bells for quite a long time, you bloody reds." Hebert, *Manitoba's French*, 114.

110 *Winnipeg Free Press*, 3 August 1983, p. 2.

111 *Winnipeg Free Press*, 18 August 1983, p. 7.

112 *Winnipeg Free Press*, 11 August 1983, p. 13.

113 Although Anstett was widely seen as having better relations than Penner with the Tories, Pawley dismissed as "crap" suggestions that the move was a sign of non-confidence in Penner. *Globe and Mail*, 5 November 1983, p. 11.

114 *Winnipeg Free Press*, 7 January 1984, p. 4.

115 *Winnipeg Sun*, 5 February 1984, p. 2. See also *Globe and Mail*, 1 February 1984, p. 3.

116 *Winnipeg Sun*, 27 January 1984, p. 3. The overheated rhetoric around this issue extended to the House of Commons. Conservative MP Charles Mayer criticized Prime Minister Trudeau's intervention in the debate thus: "People that would stoop to those levels would almost kidnap little children, that's the level they have degenerated to." *Globe and Mail*, 29 February 1984, p. 6.

117 *Winnipeg Sun*, 3 February 1984, p. 3. See also *Globe and Mail*, 25 February 1984, p. 5.

118 *Globe and Mail*, 20 February 1984, p. 3.

119 Hébert, *Manitoba's French*, 167.

120 *Winnipeg Sun*, 27 January 1984, p. 2.

121 *Winnipeg Sun*, 3 February 1984, p. 6.

122 *Winnipeg Free Press*, 3 February 1984, p. 4.

123 *Winnipeg Free Press*, 4 February 1984, p. 4.

124 *Winnipeg Free Press*, 7 February 1984, p. 4.

125 Howard Pawley, letter to Jim Walding, 21 February 1984, Jim Walding Papers.

126 Jim Walding, letter to Howard Pawley, 21 February 1984, Jim Walding Papers.

127 *Winnipeg Sun*, 22 February 1984, p. 7.

128 *Winnipeg Free Press*, 5 March 1984, p. 7.

129 According to Roland Penner, Anstett had already cited "innumerable precedents" that would have permitted Walding to end the bell-ringing. See Roland Penner, *A Glowing Dream: A Memoir* (Winnipeg: J. Gordon Shillingford Publishing, 2007), 189.

130 In fact, the Manitoba legislature has buzzers, not bells; by this point, Walding had instructed that all buzzers be disconnected except for the one outside the Tory caucus room.

131 Tom McMahon, "Bell-ringing Revisited: A Lack of Leadership from the Speaker," *The Table* 55 (1987): 53–56.

132 In 1983, neither house leader had seen any need to change the rules on bell-ringing. "Before you move on," cautioned the legislative clerk to no avail, "you need to understand that if there is prolonged bell-ringing, there will be nothing the chair can do about it."

133 Hébert, *Manitoba's French*, 170.

134 McMahon, "Bell-ringing," 77.

135 Jim Walding, letter to Howard Pawley, 21 February 1984, Jim Walding Papers.

136 *Globe and Mail*, 22 February 1984, p. 4.

137 McMahon, "Bell-ringing," 71.

138 *Winnipeg Free Press*, 20 February 1984, p. 16.

139 Russell Doern, *The Battle Over Bilingualism: The Manitoba Language Question, 1983–1985* (Winnipeg: Cambridge Publishers, 1985), 36–37.

140 Russell, *Canadian Crucible*, 428. Val Walding, as we shall subsequently see, denounced this allegation as untrue in June 1984.

141 *Winnipeg Sun*, 22 February 1984, p. 7.

142 Russell, *Canadian Crucible*, 428.

143 *Winnipeg Sun*, 1 June 1984, p. 8.

144 *Winnipeg Sun*, 31 May 1984, p. 3.

145 *Winnipeg Free Press*, 1 June 1984, p. 3.

146 *Winnipeg Sun*, 3 June 1984, p. 3.

147 *Winnipeg Free Press*, 12 July 1984, p. 2.

148 Howard Pawley, letter to Jim Walding, 10 August 1984, Jim Walding Papers.

149 Jim Walding, letter to Howard Pawley, 25 September 1984, Jim Walding Papers.

150 *Winnipeg Sun*, 18 December 1984, p. 8.

151 John Walsh, letter to Howard Pawley, 14 July 1981, Jim Walding Papers.

152 Howard Pawley, letter to Jim Walding, 10 August 1984, Jim Walding Papers.

153 Jim Walding, letter to Shirley Lord, 19 October 1984, Jim Walding Papers.

154 Shirley Lord, letter to Jim Walding, 15 November 1984, Jim Walding Papers.

155 Jim Walding, letter to Shirley Lord, 30 January 1985, Jim Walding Papers.

156 Manitoba NDP, Membership and Finance, 1981, NDPM.

157 Jim Walding, letter to Jim Smith, 2 April 1982, Jim Walding Papers.

158 Manitoba New Democratic Party, Accounts Receivable: Provincial Constituency Assessments, 13 June 1984, NDPM.

159 Manitoba New Democratic Party, Accounts Receivable: Provincial Constituency Assessments, 31 August 1985, NDPM.

160 *Winnipeg Sun*, 5 February 1984, p. 5.

161 *Winnipeg Sun*, 1 May 1985, p. 14.

162 *Winnipeg Sun*, 4 April 1985, p. 4.

163 W.H. Remnant, letter to Jim Walding, 20 November 1984, Jim Walding Papers.

164 D.W. Moylan, letter to Jim Walding, 15 March 1985, Jim Walding Papers.

165 Jim Walding, letter to all members of the legislative assembly, 25 March 1985, Jim Walding Papers.

166 *Winnipeg Free Press*, 4 April 1985, p. 3.

167 *Winnipeg Sun*, 4 April 1985, p. 4.

168 Jim Walding, statement to the legislature, 30 April 1985, Jim Walding Papers.

169 Duff Roblin, letter to Jim Walding, 10 May 1985, Jim Walding Papers.

170 Gerard Amerongen, letter to Jim Walding, 4 September 1985, Jim Walding Papers. For another perspective on this matter, see Philip Laundy, "The Future of the Canadian Speakership," *The Parliamentarian* 53 (1979): 113-117.

171 *Winnipeg Free Press*, 2 May 1985, p. 2.

172 *Winnipeg Free Press*, 1 May 1985, p. 2.

173 *Winnipeg Sun*, 1 May 1985, p. 12.

174 *Winnipeg Free Press*, 2 May 1985, p. 6.

175 *Winnipeg Free Press*, 14 May 1985, p. 7.

176 Tom Brook, *Getting Elected in Canada* (Stratford: Mercury, 1991), 26.

Chapter 4: The Campaign

1 In fact, one long-time executive member baldly asserted: "George and Hugh made Jim."

2 *Winnipeg Sun*, 29 August 1985, p. 4. All other quotes in this paragraph come from the same source.

3   Report of the Status of Women Committee to Provincial Council, September 1985, NDPM.

4   Manitoba New Democratic Party Provincial Council Minutes, 21 and 22 September 1985, 6, NDPM.

5   *Winnipeg Free Press*, 24 September 1985, p. 3.

6   *Winnipeg Free Press*, 24 September 1985, p. 3.

7   Carty and Erickson, "Candidate Nomination," 120.

8   *Winnipeg Sun*, 12 December 1985, p. 10. Norma Buchan telephoned Doreen Dodick to give her advance warning of the nomination challenge; it was only some time after she hung up that Dodick realized Buchan had signalled her intention to seek the nomination in Riel, rather than St. Vital. Dodick, in fact, blames her subsequent defeat in the 1986 election on having to divert resources to beat back Buchan's nomination challenge.

9   *Winnipeg Free Press*, 18 October 1985, p. 12.

10   *St. Vital Lance*, 23 October 1985, p. 7.

11   *Winnipeg Sun*, 18 October 1985, p. 8.

12   *Winnipeg Free Press*, 10 September 1985, p. 30. This is not to imply that Laser would not have entered the race in the absence of this astrological morsel.

13   *Winnipeg Free Press*, 20 August 1984, p. 3.

14   *Winnipeg Free Press*, 29 March 1985, p. 3.

15   Cross, *Political Parties*, 63.

16   Brook, *Getting Elected*, 34.

17   Carty and Erickson, "Candidate Nomination," 121.

18   Doern, *Battle Over Bilingualism*, 185.

19   Sig Laser, meeting notes. Intriguingly, the notes also indicate not only that Walding was prepared to "think about" some unspecified proposal, but also that Laser got the "feeling that, yes perhaps (Walding's) hearing all this for the first time."

20   *Winnipeg Sun*, 23 February 1984, p. 6.

21   Laser's appeal to supporters of separate schools provides a modest exception to the claim that this was not an issue-based campaign.

22   *Winnipeg Free Press*, 24 September 1985, p. 3.

23   See, for example, Paul Beaulieu, "The Transfer of Electoral Allegiance in Ethnic Politics: A Study of the Voting Behaviour of Franco-Manitobans, 1969–1974," unpublished paper, Winnipeg, 1976.

24   Gerri Unwin, nomination pamphlet, 1986.

25   *St. Vital Lance*, 23 October 1985, p. 7.

26   Richard Starr, *Richard Hatfield: The Seventeen Year Saga* (Halifax: Formac, 1987), 15.

27   *Thompson Citizen*, 23 October 1975, p. 1.

28   *Winnipeg Free Press*, 27 October 1983, p. 19.

29   Election – October 26, 1983: Results of the Voting for Mayor and Councillors, City of Winnipeg Archives.

30   *Winnipeg Sun*, 18 October 1985, p. 8.

31   *New Democrat*, November 1985, p. 9.

32   *Winnipeg Sun*, 12 January 1986, p. 17.

33   Beck, *Pendulum of Power*, 401.

34 Donald Johnston, *Up the Hill* (Montreal: Optimum, 1986), 32.

35 R. Kenneth Carty, William Cross, and Lisa Young, *Rebuilding Canadian Party Politics* (Vancouver: University of British Columbia Press, 2000), 164.

36 Erickson and Carty, "Parties and Candidate Selection," 345.

37 Brook, *Getting Elected*, 32. It is perhaps noteworthy that, eight years later, the NDP actually triumphed in this particular constituency.

38 Of course, even if the Laser team knew that some of their recruits would never show up on nomination day, they also realized that their rivals would waste valuable resources investigating these new members.

39 David Street, letter to the Manitoba NDP Executive, 22 August 1986. On that same day, Street gave an interview in which he suggested that misrepresenting the employment status of new recruits to make them eligible for lower membership fees was a "minor" trick which occurred in every constituency. "We're not lily white," Street declared. "If we were we'd be organizing for a religious group." *Winnipeg Free Press*, 22 August 1986, p. 3.

40 *Winnipeg Sun*, 6 November 1986, p. 14.

41 Sig Laser, appeal for support, 4 January 1986, Sig Laser, personal papers.

42 Erickson and Carty, "Parties and Candidate Selection," 345.

43 Carty, *Canadian Political Parties*, 117.

44 Unwin's expenditures were closer than Laser's to the NDP norm. Even as recently as the 2004 federal election, only 11 percent of New Democratic candidates for nominations spent more than $1000. See Munroe Eagles, Harold Jansen, Anthony Sayers, and Lisa Young, "Financing Federal Nomination Contests in Canada – An Overview of the 2004 Experience," paper presented to the Annual Meeting of the Canadian Political Science Association, London, Ontario, 2005, 5.

45 This figure is derived from tracking data compiled by the Sig Laser campaign. Five days before the convention, the Laser camp identified 128 confirmed Unwin backers.

46 Jim Walding must be left out of this comparison as his home street was much shorter.

47 Derived from data in Sig Laser's personal papers.

48 In the end, Ivy Boutang did not attend the nomination meeting.

49 V.O. Key coined the term "friends and neighbours" in attempting to characterize the support patterns of politicians in the US South. In Key's terminology, "neighbours" were those with a common regional bond, while "friends" were of the same race. In the present context, the term is being employed literally, rather than metaphorically. See V.O. Key, *Southern Politics in State and Nation* (New York: Alfred A. Knopf, 1949).

50 Carty, Cross, and Young, *Rebuilding Canadian,* 160. See also David C. Docherty, *Mr. Smith Goes to Ottawa: Life in the House of Commons* (Vancouver: University of British Columbia Press, 1997), 61, and Wearing, *Strained Relations*, 243.

51 See, for example, Réjean Pelletier, "The Structures of Canadian Political Parties: How They Operate," in Herman Bakvis, ed., *Canadian Political Parties: Leaders, Candidates and Organization* (Toronto: Dundurn, 1996), 242-243.

52 Erickson and Carty, "Parties and Candidate Selection," 334.

53 See, for example, R. MacGregor Dawson, *The Government of Canada*, 5th ed. (Toronto: University of Toronto Press, 1970), 446. See also Stephen Clarkson, "The Liberal Threepeat: The Multi-System Party in the Multi-Party System," in Jon H. Pammett and Christopher Dornan, eds., *The Canadian General Election of 2000* (Toronto: Dundurn, 2000), 27.

54   Jo Surich, "Purists and Pragmatists: Canadian Democratic Socialism at the Cross-roads," in Howard Penniman, ed., *Canada at the Polls: The General Election of 1974* (Washington: American Enterprise Institute for Public Policy Research, 1975), 141.

55   Williams, "Candidate Selection," 103.

56   Sayers, *Parties, Candidates*, 9.

57   Joey Smallwood, *I Chose Canada: The Memoirs of the Hon. Joseph R. 'Joey' Smallwood* (Toronto: Macmillan, 1973), 504. See also George Perlin, "St. Johns West," in John Meisel, ed., *Papers on the 1962 Election* (Toronto: University of Toronto Press, 1964), 7. The book includes fifteen papers on the Canadian general election of 1962. William Aberhart practised a modified version of the Smallwood system as leader of Alberta Social Credit. See Williams, "Candidate Selection," 92.

58   Michael B. Stein, "Social Credit Party in the Canadian General Election of 1974," in Howard R. Penniman, ed., *Canada at the Polls: The General Election of 1974* (Washington: American Enterprise Institute, 1975), 169-172.

59   Cross, *Political Parties*, 54. For some historical perspective on this matter, see Engelmann and Schwartz, 163-164, and Reginald Whitaker, *The Government Party: Organizing and Financing the Liberal Party of Canada, 1930-58* (Toronto: University of Toronto Press, 1977), 413.

60   Cross, "Candidate Nomination," 177.

61   Denis Smith, "The Campaign in Eglington," in John Meisel, ed., *Papers on the 1962 Election* (Toronto: University of Toronto Press, 1964), 73.

62   John Wood, "A Visible Minority Votes: East Indian Electoral Behaviour in the Vancouver South Provincial and Federal Elections of 1979," in Jorgen Dahlie and Tissa Fernando, eds., *Ethnicity, Power and Politics in Canada* (Agincourt: Methuen, 1981), 187-188.

63   *Winnipeg Sun*, 18 October 1985, p. 8.

64   *Winnipeg Sun*, 20 October 1985, p. 18.

65   *Winnipeg Sun*, 22 October, 1985.

66   *Winnipeg Free Press*, 18 October 1985, p. 12.

67   Pawley was committed to building up the party's membership base; according to the premier, however, Walding disparaged such efforts as "rushing around to sell tickets."

68   Jim Walding, letter to Art Davis, 29 September 1982. Jim Walding Papers.

69   Jim Walding, letter to the author, 5 October 2006. Anthony Sayers was certainly correct to assert that incumbents "may try to ensure that supporters hold important positions in the association." Sayers, *Parties, Candidates*, 38. Jim Walding, however, was spectacularly unsuccessful in this endeavour.

70   *Winnipeg Free Press*, 29 August 1985, p. 4.

71   *Winnipeg Sun*, 3 December 1985, p. 4.

72   Manitoba New Democratic Party, *MLA Indemnities and Future Fund Quotas* 13 (December 1985).

73   Carty and Erickson, "Candidate Nomination," 119.

74   Had the rule existed in 1973, the NDP constituency association in Rupertsland would have exceeded their quota many times over. At that time, membership totaled 48 percent of the party's winning tally in the previous provincial election. Wiseman, *Social Democracy*, 133.

75 "Nominations Calendar," 2 August 1985, NDPM.

76 Tannis Laser, letter to Ron Cavaluce, 19 November 1985, NDPM.

77 *Winnipeg Sun*, 12 January 1986, p. 17.

78 *Winnipeg Sun*, 20 October 1985, p. 18.

79 *Winnipeg Free Press*, 24 September 1985, p. 3.

80 *Winnipeg Sun*, 18 October 1985, p. 8.

81 Jim Walding, appeals for support, 4 October 1985; 17 October 1985; December 1985 (I); December 1985 (II), Jim Walding Papers.

82 *Winnipeg Free Press*, 13 January 1986, p. 3.

83 Jim Walding, letter to Pierre Jeanniot, 18 June 1985, Jim Walding Papers.

84 Jim Walding, letter to Canadian Imperial Bank of Commerce, 31 October 1985, Jim Walding Papers.

85 A tactic favoured by Val Walding to drum up support was to hold teas in senior citizens' residences.

86 Brook, *Getting Elected*, 25.

87 Carty and Erickson, "Candidate Nomination," 138.

88 *Winnipeg Sun*, 10 December 1985, p. 5.

89 *Winnipeg Free Press*, 9 December 1985, p. 1.

90 Sig Laser, personal papers.

91 Brook, *Getting Elected*, 29.

92 *New Democrat*, December 1985, p. 2.

93 Claire Hoy, *Bill Davis: A Biography*, (Toronto: Methuen, 1985), 74. Similarly, at the 1984 British Columbia NDP convention, the second- and third-place candidates (Bob Skelly and Bill King) followed through on "a secret pact to support each other against (frontrunner David) Vickers should the need arise." Terry Morley, "Leadership Change in the CCF/NDP," in R. Kenneth Carty, Lynda Erickson, and Donald E. Blake, eds., *Leaders and Parties in the Canadian Provinces: Experiences of the Provinces* (Toronto: Harcourt Brace Jonavitch, 1992), 142. And it is worth recalling that even Jean Chrétien's entry into the 1984 Liberal leadership race was apparently the trigger to such an arrangement. Concerned about the prospects of a John Turner coronation, the five weaker candidates urged an apparently coy Chrétien to jump into the fray. In reply, Chrétien declared: "Okay, if I run and I have a chance of winning, you'll have to remember that I ran on your advice and you'll owe me something." Jean Chrétien, *Straight From the Heart* (Toronto: McClelland and Stewart, 1985), 195.

94 Rae Murphy, Robert Chodos, and Nick Auf der Maur, *Brian Mulroney: The Boy From Baie Comeau* (Toronto: James Lorimer, 1984), 187.

95 Paul Hellyer, *Damn the Torpedos: My Fight to Unify Canada's Armed Forces* (Toronto: McClelland and Stewart, 1990), 275.

96 Greg Weston, *Reign of Error: The Inside Story of John Turner's Troubled Leadership* (Toronto: McGraw-Hill, Ryerson, 1988), 61.

97 The Telegram News Staff, *Balloons and Ballots: The Inside Story of Robert Stanfield's Victory* (Toronto: The Telegram, 1967), 110 and 116.

98 *Globe and Mail*, 28 June 1984, p. 5.

99 *Winnipeg Sun*, 12 January, 1986, p. 17.

Chapter 5: The Vote

1 Manitoba NDP, *Constituency Association Manual*, 6. This booklet also advised constituency executives that it was "always wise to book a hall or a room that will hold fewer people than you expect. This will create a crowded, exciting atmosphere, and the media will be more inclined to report a 'high turnout' instead of 'a sparse crowd' (6-7).

2 Admittedly, such considerations are not always decisive. Eugene Whelan's first nomination victory came despite taking place in his opponent's bailiwick during a severe electrical storm. Eugene Whelan, *Whelan: The Man in the Green Stetson* (Toronto: Irwin, 1986), 60.

3 Cross, "Grassroots Participation," 383. Occasionally, these mobilization efforts have had tragic consequences. In 1935, a truck taking unemployed workers from a relief camp to the Liberal nominating meeting in Fort William, Ontario, was struck by a train; twenty men were killed or maimed. Robert Bothwell and William Kilbourn, *C.D. Howe: A Biography* (Toronto: McClleland and Stewart, 1979), 58.

4 A member of the party brass was similarly distressed to see the extent of the Walding team's organizational capability. This contest, he realized, would not be the anticipated "cakewalk" for one of the challengers.

5 The Laser team was successful at pulling some of their fresh recruits to the meeting. One long-time party member who was backing Laser that afternoon looked around at some of his newfound allies and wondered, "Who dredged these guys up?"

6 André Pratte, *Charest: His Life and Politics*, (Toronto: Stoddart, 1998), 60. Laser's failure to adopt Charest's beer-bash strategy might suggest that the old English rhyme should more appropriately be entitled "For Want of an Ale" (with thanks to Steve Slipp).

7 Likewise, Frank Melia, who would have voted Unwin on the first ballot and Laser on the second, was ill with the flu and unable to attend.

8 Cross, "Grassroots Participation," 378-379, and Carty and Erickson, "Candidate Nomination," 114-115.

9 Carty, Cross, and Young, *Rebuilding Canadian*, 165.

10 Such low turnout levels are curious. One study discovered that for 45 percent of party activists, the opportunity to participate in a nominating convention was a "very important" factor in the decision to take out party membership (with an additional 27 percent rating it as "somewhat important"). See Lisa Young and William Cross, "Incentives to Membership in Canadian Political Parties," *Political Research Quarterly* 55 (2002): 557.

11 *Winnipeg Sun*, 29 August 1985, p. 4. In fact, Lewco had been approached by Peter Buchan (Norma's husband) to provide information on the logistics of securing a nomination. Peter Buchan had been Lewco's band instructor in junior high school, at which time their mutual interest in the Manitoba NDP had become apparent.

12 Such caution is quite common. Judy LaMarsh's initial nomination triumph came at the expense of six male contestants. Party leader Lester Pearson had been scheduled to attend the meeting, but fearing a donnybrook, had opted to stay away, a decision the outspoken LaMarsh decried as "gutless." Judy LaMarsh, *Memoirs of a Bird in a Gilded Cage* (Toronto: McClelland and Stewart, 1988), 5-6.

13 Richard Lewco of the party's election planning committee had also assumed that Walding would not win the nomination. Indeed, the expectation among the party brass had been that either Laser or Unwin would be ahead on the first ballot.

14 At the very least, Pawley now acknowledges that he could have sent his able organizer John Walsh into the fray to work against Walding.

15 The practice of delivering speeches at Canadian nominating conventions of almost Castroesque proportions has mercifully ended. John Diefenbaker's 1953 address, for example, consumed a tidy two hours. Spencer, *Trumpets and Drums*, 10.

16 Brian Land, *Eglington* (Toronto: Peter Martin Associates, 1965), 23.

17 Dawson, *Government of Canada*, 445.

18 *Winnipeg Free Press*, 7 February 1984, p. 4.

19 Winnipeg History professor Vic Batzel had been one of the few undecided members walking into the meeting, although by the time he had taken his coat off, he had decided to back Walding. Batzel was well-disposed towards Laser (one of his former students), but did not like "to see people being jerked around, and believed so strongly that Walding had been jerked around, that, damn it, the party had to take its lumps."

20 Ian Stewart and David Stewart, *Conventional Choices: Maritime Leadership Politics* (Vancouver: UBC Press, 2007).

21 That Walding did seem to receive the lion's share of the undecided vote should not be taken as advice to aspiring politicos about the wisdom of making a hash of the nomination speech.

22 The text of speeches by Jules Legal, Heather Hunter, and Sig Laser presented at the 12 January 1986 meeting were provided by Sig Laser.

23 In fact, Unwin wore a yellow rose corsage in honour of her grandmother.

24 The three speeches may have been respectful in tone, but at least they were not as diffident as those given by Pierre Trudeau and prominent pediatrician Victor Gold-bloom in their contest for the 1965 federal Liberal nomination in Mount Royal. "It was the most awkward convention I have ever seen," recalled Jean Marchand, "with Goldbloom saying that Trudeau was the best candidate and Trudeau saying Goldbloom was the best candidate." George Radwanski, *Trudeau* (Toronto: Macmillan, 1978), 90.

25 M. Lewis, *Campaign Worker Evaluation: Gil Mignot*, June 1977, Jim Walding Papers.

26 Patrick Brown, Robert Chodos, and Rae Murphy, *Winners, Losers: The 1976 Tory Leadership Convention* (Toronto: James Lorimer, 1976), 125.

27 John C. Courtney, *The Selection of National Party Leaders in Canada* (Toronto: Macmillan, 1973), 206.

28 Norman Snider, *The Changing of the Guard: How the Liberals Fell From Grace and the Tories Rose to Power* (Toronto: Lester and Orphan Dennys, 1985), 113.

29 The Telegram News Staff, *The Inside Story*, 115.

30 L. Ian MacDonald, *Mulroney: The Making of the Prime Minister* (Toronto: McClelland and Stewart, 1984), 7.

31 James Johnston, *The Party's Over* (Don Mills: Longman, 1971), 192.

32 Ron Graham, *One-Eyed Kings: Promise and Illusion in Canadian Politics* (Toronto: Totem Books, 1986), 180. One final example of this visual chicanery will suffice. Bert Lawrence was eliminated on the first ballot of the 1971 Ontario PC leadership convention and refused to endorse any other candidate. Allan Lawrence, on the other hand, was still very much alive and was able to take full advantage of the fact that his section of the hall was adjacent to that of his namesake. Instead of "using persuasion, Allan Lawrence supporters simply mixed with those of the resigned candidate and waved their signs. To everyone in the arena it looked as though Bert Lawrence's people had thrown their support to Allan Lawrence." Jonathan Manthorpe, *The Power and the Tories: Ontario Politics, 1943 to the Present* (Toronto: Macmillan, 1974), 121.

33 Stewart and Stewart. *Conventional Choices.*

34 David L. Humphreys, *Joe Clark: A Portrait* (Ottawa: Deneau and Greenberg, 1978), 218.

35 After the third ballot at the 1971 national NDP convention, John Harney "sat grimly alone with his shattered ambition," while his supporters fled to the David Lewis camp. Desmond Morton, *The New Democrats, 1961-1986* (Toronto: Copp Clark Pitman, 1986), 128. Eighteen years later, Simon De Jong was briefly paralyzed by indecision. CBC microphones picked up his plaintive appeal to his mother: "Mommy, what should I do?" Eventually, De Jong did endorse Audrey Mclaughlin. See http://www/friends.ca/print/News/Friends_News/archives/articles03270402.asp (accessed 15 August 2003).

36 John Turner, for example, was able to resist all entreaties that he drop out and declare for Robert Winters on the fourth ballot of the 1968 national Liberal leadership convention. First, Turner's position in the party was secure irrespective of the outcome; noted Jerry Grafstein, "You can't promise him anything but a cabinet job, and he's got to be included anyway. Martin Sullivan, *Mandate '68: The Year of Pierre Elliot Trudeau* (Toronto: Doubleday Canada, 1968), 302. Second, Turner was unsure if he could deliver his supporters en bloc to Winters; many of his younger backers, in particular, would have opted for Trudeau over Winters on the final ballot. Hellyer, *Damn the Torpedoes*, 280.

37 They either wish to avoid "ganging up" on a particular candidate or their commitment to the democratic ideal causes them to balk at the prospect of strategic alliances. At the 1971 Ontario PC leadership convention, for example, Bob Welch had campaigned for a more open party. After being eliminated from the contest, Welch concluded that "he would be going against all that he talked about if he attempted to throw his support to anyone." Manthorpe, *Power and the Tories*, 122.

38 Claire Hoy, *Friends In High Places* (Toronto: Key Porter, 1987), 47.

39 Murphy, Chodos, and Auf der Maur, *Brian Mulroney*, 109.

40 Humphreys, *Joe Clark*, 222.

41 Brown, Chodos and Murphy, *Winners, Losers*, 131.

42 Such misinformation abounds at national leadership conventions; in 1967 Diefenbaker was reported to be declaring for Roblin (The Telegram News Staff, *Balloons and Ballots*, 118); in 1976 rumours circulated of a Flora Macdonald-Claude Wagner alliance (!) (Brown, Chodos and Murphy, *Winners, Losers*, 39); and in 1983 Crosbie was purportedly moving over to the Clark camp (MacDonald, *Mulroney*, 18). Indeed, this latter rumour was apparently started by Mulroney's people on the penultimate ballot in order to shore up the mortally wounded Clark.

43 *Winnipeg Free Press*, 12 December 1985, p. 2. Such a discrepancy is uncommon, but hardly unprecedented. In 1949, future British Columbia premier W.A.C. Bennett lost a federal nomination for the Progressive Conservatives after a first count had been overturned in which there had been "18 more ballots than accredited delegates." Paddy Sherman, *Bennett* (Toronto: McClelland and Stewart, 1966), 62.

44 Sig Laser, personal papers.

45 Brook, *Getting Elected*, 38.

46 Ibid.

47 At around four hours, this particular meeting must have struck many of the participants as interminable, but its length was hardly unprecedented. The 1968 PC nomination in Vegreville, Alberta, for example, commenced on one evening and did not conclude until 5:15 the following morning! Beck, *Pendulum of Power*, 401.

48   *Winnipeg Free Press*, 13 January 1986, p. 3.

49   In response to a query about whether she was "happy" with the second ballot result, Unwin acknowledged: "In my heart of hearts, probably."

50   Brook, *Getting Elected*, 39.

51   *Winnipeg Free Press*, 13 January 1986, p. 3.

52   Ibid.

53   *Winnipeg Sun*, 13 January 1986, p. 3.

54   *St. Vital Lance*, 22 January 1986, p. 1.

Chapter 6: The Aftermath

1   The Laser camp also made some strategic miscalculations in pulling the vote. One member, Nolan Reilly, had never cared for Walding, but had bridled at being repeatedly called by Laser campaigners. Fearing that their actions were pushing Reilly towards Unwin, the Laser team inserted a final notation on Reilly's tracking sheet: "Let come on own—do not pull." As it turned out, Reilly did not "come on his own," and another certain second-ballot supporter was lost.

2   In fact, the following month the Manitoba NDP rejected, at its annual conference, a motion to raise from fourteen to eighteen the age for participation at nomination meetings. *Winnipeg Free Press*, 11 February 1986, p. 15.

3   Although approximately one-fifth of the electorate was interviewed for this study, Jay Goldstein's move from Laser to Walding was the only such instance uncovered.

4   One of the few exceptions was Louise Hudson who moved from supporting Unwin on the first round to Laser on the second. Her husband, Wilf, another member of the St. Vital executive, was unable to participate, however, as he was in Ottawa for a meeting of the Canadian Labour Congress executive that day.

5   Jim Walding, letter of resignation from speakership, 16 January 1986, Jim Walding Papers. One long-time executive member recalled urging Walding to retain the speakership: "Jesus, you're not going in the cabinet. You've got a good position as Speaker. If I was you, I would try to keep that."

6   *Winnipeg Free Press*, 5 January 1986, p. 7.

7   *Winnipeg Free Press*, 24 January 1986, p. 6.

8   Jim Walding, press release, 22 January 1986, Jim Walding Papers.

9   *Globe and Mail*, 23 January 1986, p. A7. As party leader, in fact, Schreyer had actively discouraged a group of "Young Turks" who had been anxious to dispossess Russell Doern of the NDP nomination in Elmwood.

10   *Winnipeg Free Press*, 24 January 1986, p. 6.

11   *Winnipeg Free Press*, 23 January 1986, p. 4.

12   *Halifax Chronicle-Herald*, 23 January 1986, p. 4.

13   *Winnipeg Free Press*, 23 January 1986, p. 1.

14   Howard Pawley, letter to Jim Walding, 4 February 1986, Jim Walding Papers. In contrast, Muriel Smith, the deputy premier, sent Walding a far more effusive note in which she not only complimented him on having "admirably" fulfilled his role as Speaker, but also expressed the wish that they would work together for another four years. Muriel Smith, letter to Jim Walding, 3 February 1986, Jim Walding Papers.

15   Howard Pawley, letter to Jim Walding, 7 February 1986, Jim Walding Papers.

16　In fact, Pawley now believes that he should have employed his prerogative not to accept Walding's nomination: "I should not have signed his papers with all the tension and the friction and the uncertainty." From Walding's perspective, however, this was never under active consideration.

17　Ron Cavaluce, letter to Glen McRuer, 20 May 1986, Jim Walding Papers. As party president Brian O'Leary wryly observed: "We never budgeted on getting all of Walding's constituency indemnities."

18　David J. Mitchell, *W.A.C. Bennett and the Rise of British Columbia* (Vancouver: Douglas and McIntyre, 1983), 55.

19　Whelan, *Green Stetson*, 52.

20　David V.J. Bell and Catherine M. Bolen, "The Mass Media and Federal Election Campaigning at the Local Level: A Case Study of Two Ontario Constituencies," in David V. J. Bell and Frederick J. Fletcher, eds., *Reaching the Voter: Constituency Campaigning in Canada* (Toronto: Dundurn Press, 1991), 80.

21　Jim Walding, letter to St. Vital New Democrats, 1986, Sig Laser, personal papers.

22　*Winnipeg Free Press*, 15 March 1986, p. 6.

23　*Winnipeg Free Press*, 26 February 1986, p. 7.

24　*Winnipeg Free Press*, 27 February 1986, p. 7.

25　*Winnipeg Free Press*, 11 March 1986, p. 8.

26　*Winnipeg Free Press*, 4 March 1986, p. 13.

27　*Winnipeg Free Press*, 18 March 1986, p. 1.

28　*Winnipeg Free Press*, 4 March 1986, p. 13.

29　*Winnipeg Free Press*, 17 February 1986, p. 7.

30　*Winnipeg Free Press*, 13 March 1986, 7.

31　*Winnipeg Free Press*, 10 March 1986, p. 6.

32　*Winnipeg Free Press*, 13 February 1986, p. 7.

33　*Globe and Mail*, 8 March 1986, p. 1.

34　*Winnipeg Free Press*, 15 March 1986, p. 12.

35　*Winnipeg Free Press*, 27 December 1985, p. 2.

36　*Winnipeg Sun*, 14 March 1986, p. 21.

37　*Winnipeg Free Press*, 13 March 1986, pp. 1 and 4.

38　*Winnipeg Free Press*, 13 February 1986, p. 7.

39　*Winnipeg Free Press*, 17 March 1986, p. 1, and 18 March 1986, p. 7.

40　*Winnipeg Free Press*, 21 April 1987, p. 2.

41　See http://archives.cbc.ca/400d.asp?id=1-73-2354-13649 (accessed 10 October 2006).

42　Ross Rowntree, for example, considered Jim Walding to be much too "conservative," and had voted for Sig Laser on both ballots. Nevertheless, at Laser's urging, he canvassed actively for Walding in the 1986 campaign.

43　*Winnipeg Free Press*, 12 March 1986, p. 2.

44　Sayers, *Parties, Candidates*, 77. Subsequent research has confirmed that the "party insiders" who typically triumph in the closed and impermeable contests that are characteristic of competitive NDP associations generally play, in attracting workers and finances, a "subsidiary" role in the subsequent campaign. See R. Kenneth Carty, D. Munroe Eagles, and Anthony Sayers, "Candidates and Local Campaigns: Are There Just Four Canadian Types?" *Party Politics* 9 (2003): 619-636.

45 *Winnipeg Free Press*, 21 March 1986, p. 7.

46 *Winnipeg Sun*, 23 March 1986, p. 21.

47 When Portsmouth told a British Columbia friend that she was heading back to St. Vital in 1986, the caustic reply was: "Oh crumbs, what have you done that got you sent back there again?"

48 "Door-knockers" are election day reminders left behind by those workers charged with pulling the vote.

49 R.M. Colwell, "'Order Please….' The Speakership in Manitoba," unpublished paper, 1986, 37.

50 Historical precedents, however, did not favour Walding. Only about 20 percent of previous Manitoba Speakers were subsequently appointed to the cabinet. Anstett and Thomas, "Manitoba," 99.

51 *Winnipeg Free Press*, 27 March 1986, p. 7.

52 *Winnipeg Free Press*, 2 April 1986, p. 7.

53 Jim Walding, letter to Howard Pawley, 3 April 1986, Jim Walding Papers.

54 *Winnipeg Sun*, 8 April 1986, p. 5.

55 Howard Pawley insists that, throughout his term as premier, he had little difficulty with unauthorized leaks from his office.

56 *Business In the Information Age*, November 1987, p. 9.

57 *Winnipeg Free Press*, 16 April 1986, p. 7.

58 *Winnipeg Sun*, 15 April 1986, p. 4. Only a week previously, a press report had tipped Walding as a potential minister of urban affairs. *Winnipeg Free Press*, 8 April 1986, p. 5.

59 *Winnipeg Sun*, 15 April 1986, p. 4.

60 *Winnipeg Free Press*, 16 April 1986, p. 7.

61 *Winnipeg Free Press*, 18 April 1986, p. 5.

62 *Winnipeg Free Press*, 16 April 1986, p. 7.

63 *Winnipeg Sun*, 15 April 1986, p. 4.

64 *Winnipeg Sun*, 16 April 1986, p. 6.

65 *Winnipeg Sun*, 15 April 1986, p. 4.

66 *Winnipeg Sun*, 16 April 1986, p. 6.

67 *Vancouver Sun*, 18 April 1986, p. C6.

68 *Winnipeg Sun*, 17 April 1986, p. 9.

69 *Winnipeg Free Press*, 16 April 1986, p. 7.

70 *Vancouver Sun*, 18 April 1986, p. C6. One *Winnipeg Free Press* reporter also detected an unrelenting undertone to Pawley's decision. Walding's exclusion was "a reminder that the premier has a much longer memory than the people who elected him. Having failed to deny Walding the party nomination, the premier has at last shown him who is boss." *Winnipeg Free Press*, 21 April 1986, p. 7.

71 *Winnipeg Sun*, 16 April 1986, p. 6.

72 *Globe and Mail*, 30 April 1986, p. A4.

73 Jim Walding, letter to Frances Russell, 21 April 1986, Jim Walding Papers.

74 *Winnipeg Free Press*, 10 May 1986, p. 12.

75 *Winnipeg Sun*, 29 April 1986, p. 5.

76 *Winnipeg Free Press*, 30 April 1986, p. 3.

77 *Winnipeg Free Press*, 30 April 1986, p. 6.

78 *Winnipeg Free Press*, 1 May 1986, p. 7.

79 *Winnipeg Free Press*, 30 April 1986, p. 3. While he was mulling his options, Walding received a wide range of communications from members of the public. Some blamed Pawley's "spite" for Walding's "disgraceful" exclusion from the cabinet and encouraged him to bolt the party, while others compassionately counselled that, if he jumped ship, Walding risked losing "everything—respect, loyalty, a comradeship with New Democrats." One particularly irate correspondent berated Walding for "behaving like a spoiled child" and warned him not to "get any fancy ideas of switching sides." See J.L. Ayre, letter to Jim Walding, 27 April 1986; Howard and Eva Nixon, letter to Jim Walding, 20 April 1986; and Evelyn Hajavitch, letter to Jim Walding, 15 April 1986, Jim Walding Papers.

80 Jim Walding Papers.

81 *Winnipeg Free Press*, 30 April 1986, p. 3.

82 *Winnipeg Sun*, 13 June 1986, p. 4.

83 *Winnipeg Free Press*, 13 June 1986, p. 1.

84 *Winnipeg Sun*, 16 June 1986, p. 8.

85 Russell Doern, "Inside the Legislature," 18 June 1986, 2, Jim Walding Papers. As it turned out, these pungent commentaries would soon cease. After a failed bid to become Winnipeg's mayor, Russell Doern committed suicide on 19 February 1987.

86 Sharon Carstairs, *Not One of the Boys* (Toronto: Macmillan, 1993), 100.

87 Carstairs, *Not One*, 102.

88 Jim Walding, "Report from the Legislature," January 1987, Jim Walding Papers.

89 Jim Walding, letter to Howard Pawley, 18 February 1987, Jim Walding Papers.

90 Howard Pawley, letter to Jim Walding, 20 February 1987, Jim Walding Papers.

91 Jim Walding, letter to Howard Pawley, 5 March 1987, Jim Walding Papers.

92 Howard Pawley, letter to Jim Walding, 5 May 1987, Jim Walding Papers.

93 *Winnipeg Free Press*, 24 March 1987, p. 7.

94 *Winnipeg Sun*, 13 March 1987, p. 5.

95 Ibid.

96 *Winnipeg Free Press*, 12 March 1987, p. 1.

97 *Winnipeg Free Press*, 12 March 1987, pp. 1 and 4.

98 *Winnipeg Sun*, 15 March 1987, p. 20. Although urban affairs minister Gary Doer characterized Walding as "the only man in Winnipeg who does now want the legislation passed quickly" (*Winnipeg Free Press*, 12 March 1987, p. 1), Walding did receive several letters of support for his stand, including one from Sharon Carstairs stating: "You did what you thought was right and we need more politicians with conscience. Should you need it or want it you have my support." Sharon Carstairs, letter to Jim Walding, 12 March 1987, Jim Walding Papers.

99 *Winnipeg Sun*, 13 March 1987, p. 5.

100 *Winnipeg Free Press*, 13 March 1987, p. 3.

101 Ibid.

102 Ibid.

103 *Winnipeg Sun*, 12 March 1987, p. 4.

104 Marty Dolin, letter to members of St. Vital NDP executive, 28 April 1987, Jim Walding Papers.

105 *Winnipeg Sun*, 13 March 1987.
106 Jim Walding, letter to Marty Dolin, 4 May 1987, Jim Walding Papers.
107 *Winnipeg Sun*, 4 May 1987, p. 8.
108 *Winnipeg Sun*, 5 May 1987, p. 3.
109 *Winnipeg Sun*, 9 May 1987, p. 3.
110 Ibid.
111 Sig Laser, letter to Marty Dolin, 7 May 1987, Sig Laser, personal papers.
112 *Winnipeg Sun*, 9 May 1987, p. 3.
113 Jim Walding, "Report from the Legislature," November 1987, Jim Walding Papers.
114 *Winnipeg Sun*, 18 September 1987, p. 4.
115 Ironically, Dolin used to smoke the occasional illicit cigarette in Walding's office.
116 *Winnipeg Sun*, 18 April 1986, p. 7.
117 *Winnipeg Free Press*, 20 October 1987, p. 7. Not everyone agrees that Phillips was a partisan Speaker. Binx Remnant, legislative clerk under five different Speakers, could find no fault with Phillips's conduct in the chair.
118 *Winnipeg Free Press*, 18 August 1987, p. 7.
119 *Winnipeg Free Press*, 14 October 1987, p. 6.
120 *Winnipeg Free Press*, 11 October 1987, p. 4.
121 *Winnipeg Free Press*, 24 May 1988, p. 7.
122 St. Vital NDP Constituency Association, Annual Meeting Minutes, 17 November 1987.
123 Jim Walding, "Report from the Legislature," November 1987, Jim Walding Papers.
124 *Winnipeg Free Press*, 20 November 1987, p. 2.
125 Desjardins was briefly out of the House in the mid-1970s after losing an exceedingly tight race in 1973. When that result was thrown out by the court, Desjardins triumphed in the subsequent by-election.
126 A contemporary claims that one of the factors motivating Desjardins was that "he could no longer abide the constant harping of party feminists for abortion-on-demand." Herb Schulz, *A View from the Ledge: An Insider's Look at the Schreyer Years* (Winnipeg: Heartland Associates, 2005), 508.
127 Carstairs, *Not One*, 115.
128 *Winnipeg Sun*, 18 November 1987, p. 16.
129 *Winnipeg Free Press*, 17 November 1987, p. 6.
130 *Globe and Mail*, 5 September 1988, p. A7.
131 *Winnipeg Free Press*, 19 November 1987, p. 6.
132 *Toronto Star*, 22 February 1988, p. A3.
133 *Toronto Star*, 23 February 1988, p. A2.
134 *Winnipeg Free Press*, 23 February 1988, p. 1.
135 *Toronto Star*, 23 February 1988, p. A2.
136 *Vancouver Sun*, 23 February 1988, p. B7.
137 *Winnipeg Free Press*, 23 February 1988, p. 1.
138 *Winnipeg Free Press*, 23 February 1988, p. 4.

NOTES

139 *Winnipeg Free Press*, 23 February 1988, p. 1. Among others, Walding had consulted his loyal foot-soldier Peter Nolan, who had advised him: "You can't cross the floor; you can't take sides with the Conservatives."

140 *Vancouver Sun*, 23 February 1988, p. B7.

141 *Toronto Star*, 23 February 1988, p. A2.

142 *Winnipeg Free Press*, 7 March 1988, p. 2.

143 *Globe and Mail*, 7 March 1988, p. A1. "I suppose it's ironical," said Walding of his party's sudden appreciation of his views. *Globe and Mail*, 7 March, p. A4.

144 *Globe and Mail*, 9 March 1988, p. A4.

145 Another Walding confidante, Sam Uskiw, was less sanguine about the government's prospects. After his own lunch date with the unhappy MLA, Uskiw was certain that Walding would soon pull the plug.

146 Carstairs, *Not One*, 116.

147 *Winnipeg Free Press*, 15 March 1988, p. 7.

148 The text of the Opposition motion was: "In presenting its budget, the government has: ignored the long-term effects of uncontrolled spending by once more increasing its expenditures at twice the rate of inflation; and dipped into the pockets of ordinary Manitobans for an enormous tax haul of $185 million more in personal income taxes; and absorbed the largest increase in the province's history while applying less than 15% of it to deficit reduction; and because of its continued policies of foreign borrowing and deficit financing, has brought about an increase in interest costs of almost 20% in this year's budget; and thereby lost the confidence of this House and the people of Manitoba."

149 *Western Report*, 21 March 1988, p. 5.

150 In mid-February, government House leader Jay Cowan had subdivided the twenty-eight-member caucus into nine teams of "buddies," who were charged with the responsibility of ensuring that at least one member of each team was present in the House at all times. Not surprisingly, Walding was placed in the only four-member buddy team (with Don Scott, Conrad Santos, and Steve Ashton). Jay Cowan, letter to Jim Walding, 17 February 1988, Jim Walding Papers. Yet as Marty Dolin sardonically observed, "Jim wouldn't be 'buddies' with anyone."

151 *Toronto Star*, 10 March 1988, p. A20.

152 Beverley Bosiak, "By One Vote: The Defeat of the Manitoba Government," *Canadian Parliamentary Review* 12, 1 (1989): 15.

153 Carstairs, *Not One*, 117.

154 *Globe and Mail*, 9 March 1988, p. A4.

155 In fact, Walding left the chamber even before the vote on the main motion as amended. Had NDP House leader Jay Cowan been quicker on his feet to call for a recorded vote, and had he been able to communicate the desirability of a "no" vote to the other New Democrats, the result would have been a 27-27 tie, which Speaker Phillips would have presumably broken on behalf of the government. Whether the defeat of the main budgetary motion as amended by the Opposition would have given Pawley's government any room to manoeuver is not entirely clear.

156 See http://archives.cbc.ca/400d.asp?id=1-73-2354-13650 (accessed 10 October 2006). This site contains a video clip of events in the Manitoba legislature on 8 March 1988, including Walding sitting down while his fellow New Democrats stand up in support of the budget.

157 *Globe and Mail*, 9 March 1988, p. A4.

158 *Vancouver Sun*, 9 March 1988, p. A1.

159 *Winnipeg Sun*, 10 March 1988, p. 5. The government had apparently sought, in vain, for parliamentary precedents which might permit them to avoid an election.

160 *Winnipeg Free Press*, 11 March 1988, p. 2.

161 *Western Report*, 21 March 1988, p. 6.

162 *Vancouver Sun*, 12 March 1988, p. A6. While in hiding, Walding's home and office had been inundated with a wide range of messages; Doug Moore, the former New Brunswick Conservative MLA who had been part of an unsuccessful putsch against leader Richard Hatfield, sent Walding a telegram which offered congratulations from a "fellow rebel." Doug Moore, telegram to Jim Walding, 9 March 1988, Jim Walding Papers.

163 *Globe and Mail*, 12 March 1988, p. A1.

164 *Winnipeg Free Press*, 15 March 1988, p. 7.

165 Ibid.

166 *Winnipeg Sun*, 13 March 1988, p. 4.

167 *Winnipeg Free Press*, 15 March 1988, p. 7.

168 *Winnipeg Free Press*, 27 May, 2005, p. A12.

169 "Commercial and Residential Real Estate Sales," *Digest Business and Law Journal— Weekly Publication*, p. 25.

170 Walding's 13 March 1987 statement of assets and interests (necessary under Manitoba's *Legislative Assembly and Executive Council Conflict of Interest Act*) reveals, for example, that he possessed an investment fund of unspecified value.

171 *Winnipeg Free Press*, 15 March 1988, p. 7.

172 Ibid.

173 *Winnipeg Free Press*, 10 January 1999, p. A4.

174 *Winnipeg Free Press*, 12 March 1988, p. 4. At approximately the same time, Gary Filmon was dismissing rumours that the federal PCs had offered Walding a patronage appointment in return for his vote on a non-confidence motion. *Winnipeg Free Press*, 23 February 1988, p. 4.

175 *Winnipeg Free Press*, 10 March 1988, p. 10. One St. Vital New Democrat claimed to have been "shocked, but not surprised" by Walding's vote.

176 Carstairs, *Not One*, 117–118.

177 Jim Walding, letter to A.P.D. Westhead, 17 October 1984, Jim Walding Papers.

178 *Winnipeg Sun*, April 17, 1986, p. 9.

179 Jim Walding, letter to A.W. Pressey, 3 March 1988, Jim Walding Papers.

180 Jay Cowan, letter to Howard Pawley, 2 March 1988, Howard Pawley, personal papers.

181 Gary Filmon, letter to Jim Walding, 7 March 1988, Jim Walding Papers.

182 *Winnipeg Sun*, 13 March 1988, p. 4.

183 Bosiak, "By One Vote," 15–16.

184 *Winnipeg Free Press*, 10 January 1998, p. A4. Walding did subsequently acknowledge that he had only been actively considering the defeat of the government for a matter of weeks, rather than months.

185 *Winnipeg Free Press*, 12 March 1988, p. 4.

186 *Winnipeg Sun*, 10 March 1988, p. 5.

187 *Winnipeg Sun*, 13 March 1988, p. 4.

188 Ibid.

189 *Winnipeg Free Press*, 10 March 1988, p. 10.

190 *Vancouver Sun*, 12 March 1988, p. A6.

191 *Winnipeg Free Press*, 12 March 1988, p. 1.

192 *Winnipeg Free Press*, 11 March 1988, p. 2.

193 *St. Vital Lance*, 16 March 1988, p. 3.

194 *Winnipeg Free Press*, 27 April 1988, p. 22.

195 *Toronto Star*, 23 February 1988, p. A2.

196 Michael Stimpson, letter to the author, 15 December 2006. While Stimpson's heated public intervention was unusual behaviour for a member of the constituency executive ("Not my finest moment. But then again, I'm certainly not ashamed of it"), his sentiments were hardly idiosyncratic. According to Peter Warren, the host of the radio show: "Most of the callers expressed displeasure (and I am being 'kind' using that word!) because I believe they thought he was playing a personal game." Peter Warren, letter to the author, 15 December 2006.

197 *Toronto Star*, 23 February 1988, p. A2. Marty Dolin now acknowledges that his comments may have exacerbated the situation.

198 *Globe and Mail*, 12 March 1988, p. A2.

199 *Winnipeg Free Press*, 27 April 1988, p. 29.

200 *Winnipeg Sun*, 13 March 1988, p. 4.

201 As Marty Dolin recalled, amid the tumult that accompanied Walding's decisive vote, he turned to fellow backbencher Jerry Storie and said, "This is an historic moment. Isn't it great to be part of this?"

Chapter 7: The Fallout

1 *Globe and Mail*, 16 March 1988, p. A4.

2 *Vancouver Sun*, 16 March 1988, p. A2.

3 *Globe and Mail*, 16 March 1988, p. A4.

4 *Vancouver Sun*, 2 April 1988, p. A7. In response to the NDP's election slogan, Sid Green quipped that this was the first time an incumbent government had based their campaign on "It's time for a change." Green, *Rise and Fall*, 183.

5 *Vancouver Sun*, 9 April 1988, p. A7.

6 *Vancouver Sun*, 25 April 1988, p. A5.

7 *Vancouver Sun*, 9 January 1988, p. B2.

8 *Winnipeg Free Press*, 12 March 1988, p. 7.

9 *Vancouver Sun*, 22 April 1988, p. B1.

10 *Winnipeg Free Press*, 27 April 1988, p. 18.

11 Ibid.

12 *Winnipeg Free Press*, 27 April 1988, p. 29.

13 *St. Vital Lance*, 16 March 1988, p. 3.

14 *Winnipeg Free Press*, 27 April 1988, p. 29.

15 *Winnipeg Free Press*, 27 April 1988, p. 22.

16 *Winnipeg Free Press*, 27 April 1988, p. 29.

17 Admittedly, long-time St. Boniface MLA Larry Desjardins was unfazed by his part in the affair. True, some NDP MLAs might have blamed the government's defeat on his eleventh-hour resignation. "But that's their problem," said Desjardins dismissively. "I am to this day happy with my decision to leave politics." *Winnipeg Free Press*, 10 March 1988, p. 18.

18 *Winnipeg Free Press*, 30 May 1988, p. 1.

19 *Winnipeg Sun*, 10 March 1988, p. 5.

20 *Winnipeg Sun*, 27 April 1988, p. 4. Pawley also refused to second-guess his decision not to include Walding in his ministry. "Clearly he demonstrated his lack of credibility," Pawley insisted. "He clearly demonstrated that he was not the quality of person that a New Democratic Party government would want in its cabinet." *Winnipeg Free Press*, 27 April 1988, p. 20.

21 *Winnipeg Free Press*, 27 May 2005, p. A12.

22 Ed and Lily Schreyer did likewise.

23 Not all the phone calls to the Walding house were hostile. Walding had recruited Glen and Bev McBride by going to their house with this pitch: "You guys are ordinary folks; I am down to earth. You can come to me with any problems and I will work for you." When Walding brought the government down, Glen McBride thought that was "awesome," but phoned Walding to commiserate that he had lost his seat. Walding replied, "I just did what was right, what you people would have wanted me to do." McBride said, "That's right."

24 *Winnipeg Sun*, 9 October 1988, p. 3.

25 *Winnipeg Free Press*, 8 March 1989, p. 1.

26 *Winnipeg Free Press*, 28 July 1992, 2.

27 Val Walding explained the return to Winnipeg thus: "I hated BC. It was boring. We were in Victoria and I was homesick for Manitoba. Jim tried every angle to get me to stay out there, but the children were all here, and then we were going to get our first grandchild and that settled it. The flowers in Victoria were pretty, but that's all you can say. If we went to Vancouver, we had to go on the ferry, and that's expensive."

28 "Where Are They Now—Jim Walding," audio CD, University of Manitoba Archives and Special Collections.

29 *Winnipeg Free Press*, 5 December 1990, p. 5.

30 Ibid.

31 *Winnipeg Sun*, 5 December 1990, p. 4.

32 Denise Mignot, however, refused to attend the ceremony: "I didn't want to go. I was still so angry."

33 *Winnipeg Free Press*, 6 December 1990, p. 6.

34 *Winnipeg Free Press*, 27 April 1988, p. 22.

35 *Winnipeg Free Press*, 5 December 1990, p. 5.

36 See, for example, *Winnipeg Free Press*, 10 January 1999, p. A2.

37 *Winnipeg Free Press*, 10 January 1999, p. A2.

38 *Winnipeg Free Press*, 10 March 1988, p. 10.

39 *Winnipeg Free Press*, 5 April 1988, p. 7.

40 *Winnipeg Free Press*, 15 March 1988, p. 10.

41 Long-time members Al and Pearl Penny had been very impressed with Laser in the 1986 nomination campaign. Ironically, they had decided then to give Jim Walding one more chance in the belief that Laser would be a terrific candidate the next time around.

42 *Winnipeg Sun*, 21 March 1988, p. 3.

43 *Winnipeg Free Press*, 21 March 1988, p. 8.

44 *Winnipeg Free Press*, 24 April 1988, p. 7.

45 *Winnipeg Free Press*, 29 March 1988, p. 19.

46 Elections Manitoba, *Statement of Votes for the 33rd Provincial General Election*, 18 March 1986, 173-175, and Elections Manitoba, *Statement of Votes for the 34th Provincial General Election*, 26 April 1988, 183-185.

47 *Vancouver Sun*, 15 March 1988, p. B3.

48 *Globe and Mail*, 20 July 1988, p. A9.

49 *Winnipeg Free Press*, 30 June 1989, p. 7.

50 *Winnipeg Sun*, 4 February 1990, p. 4.

51 *Winnipeg Free Press*, 30 June 1989, p. 19. In 1993, the Conservatives abolished the Manitoba Intercultural Council altogether.

52 *Globe and Mail*, 9 August 1988, pp. A1 and A4.

53 *Globe and Mail*, 6 June 1989, p. A10.

54 *Globe and Mail*, 8 June 1989, p. A14.

55 *Globe and Mail*, 6 December 1988, p. A10.

56 *Globe and Mail*, 3 February 1989, p. A4.

57 *Globe and Mail*, 6 November 1989, p. A2.

58 Wiseman, *Social Democracy*, 130.

59 *Winnipeg Sun*, 15 February 1990, p. 16.

60 *Globe and Mail*, 6 December 1988, p. A10.

61 *Globe and Mail*, 31 August 1990, p. A1.

62 *Winnipeg Free Press*, 17 March 1990, p. 17.

63 *Winnipeg Sun*, 23 March 1990, p. 3.

64 *Globe and Mail*, 26 July 1990, p. A15.

65 *Winnipeg Free Press*, 8 May 1990, p. 7.

66 *Globe and Mail*, 20 July 1988, p. A9.

67 *Winnipeg Free Press*, 30 June 1989, pp. 19 and 23.

68 *Winnipeg Free Press*, 10 March 1988, p. 1.

69 *Western Report*, 21 March 1988, p. 5.

70 During the 1984 election, Mulroney promised to make it possible for Quebec to sign the *Constitution Act, 1982* "with honor and enthusiasm." *Globe and Mail*, 2 October 1986, p. A9.

71 Admittedly, the federal government must have been alarmed when delegates to the annual conference of the Alberta Progressive Conservatives "whistled and applauded" when Premier Getty declared that Alberta would not agree "to special status for Quebec as a tradeoff for bringing that province into the Constitution." *Globe and Mail*, 6 April 1987, p. A9.

72 *Winnipeg Sun*, 30 April 1987, p. 8.

73   *Winnipeg Sun*, 23 April 1987, p. 5. Echoed another provincial spokesman, "We are very troubled by these proposals. They tend to hobble the federal government." *Winnipeg Free Press*, 29 April 1987, p. 7.

74   *Winnipeg Free Press*, 23 April 1987, p. 1.

75   *Winnipeg Free Press*, 1 May 1987, p. 4.

76   *Winnipeg Free Press*, 1 May 1987, p. 1.

77   *Winnipeg Free Press*, 2 May 1987, p. 1.

78   Ibid.

79   *Winnipeg Free Press*, 1 May 1987, p. 1.

80   *Winnipeg Free Press*, 5 May 1987, p. 1.

81   *Winnipeg Sun*, 6 May 1987, p. 4.

82   *Winnipeg Free Press*, 29 May 1987, p. 10.

83   *Winnipeg Free Press*, 1 June 1987, p. 4.

84   *Winnipeg Free Press*, 2 June 1987, p. 1.

85   *Winnipeg Free Press*, 1 June 1987, p. 1.

86   Prior to the meeting, Peterson had been under increasing pressure from within his party not to support the Accord. See *Toronto Star*, 1 June 1987, p. A1.

87   *Winnipeg Free Press*, 3 June 1987, p. 1. The Quebec delegation considered the wording change of the spending-power provision to be inconsequential. See *Toronto Star*, 8 June 1987, p. A13.

88   *Winnipeg Sun*, 5 June 1987, p. 3.

89   *Winnipeg Free Press*, 4 June 1987, p. 4.

90   *Winnipeg Free Press*, 5 June 1987, p. 10. Pawley confidante Roland Penner now acknowledges that it might have been wiser for the government to have commenced the ratification process "immediately." Penner, *A Glowing Dream*, 204.

91   *Winnipeg Sun*, 22 September 1987, p. 5.

92   *Winnipeg Free Press*, 20 November 1987, p. 1.

93   *Winnipeg Free Press*, 24 November 1987, p. 3.

94   *Winnipeg Free Press*, 18 December 1987, p. 1.

95   *Winnipeg Free Press*, 18 December 1987, p. 4.

96   *Winnipeg Free Press*, 19 December 1987, p. 6.

97   *Winnipeg Free Press*, 19 December 1987, p. 3.

98   Composite Resolution, *Meech Lake Accord – 88-200-01 to 88-200-13*, Manitoba NDP Annual Meeting, 1988.

99   *Winnipeg Free Press*, 7 March 1988, p. 7.

100 *Winnipeg Sun*, 6 March 1988, p. 5.

101 *Winnipeg Free Press*, 8 March 1988, p. 4.

102 *Vancouver Sun*, 5 April 1988, p. B6.

103 *Winnipeg Free Press*, 29 April 1988, p. 1. In the vernacular of the day, Carstairs also labelled the Accord as "the pits." *Vancouver Sun*, 27 April 1987, p. 2. Several media commentators soon echoed Carstairs's assessment. One observed, "Meech Lake, as we know it, is all but dead"; another editorialized, "Meech Lake really is dead." *Winnipeg Free Press*, 29 April 1988, p. 7; 1 May 1988, p. 6.

104 *Winnipeg Free Press*, 20 December 1988, p. 1.

105 *Winnipeg Sun*, 20 December 1988, p. 1.

106 *Winnipeg Free Press*, 3 May 1989, p. 5.

107 *Globe and Mail*, 24 October 1989, p. A1.

108 *Halifax Chronicle-Herald*, 14 June 1990, p. A1.

109 See Ian Stewart, "Scaling the Matterhorn: Parliamentary Leadership in Canada," in Maureen Mancuso, Richard G. Price and Ronald Wagenberg, eds., *Leaders and Leadership in Canada* (Don Mills: Oxford University Press, 1994), 167–169.

110 *Winnipeg Free Press*, 8 March 1988, p. 1.

111 *Winnipeg Sun*, 22 November 1987, p. 12. This sentiment was supported by members of the local media. One columnist observed that, when a premier signs such a document, "it can mean only one thing: he is committing his government to support that agreement in his legislature." *Winnipeg Sun*, 20 December 1987, p. 21. Likewise, a local editorial opined that the ten premiers "who signed the accord cannot be expected to raise any strong objections to something they have been a part of." *Winnipeg Free Press*, 28 August 1987, p. 6.

112 *Winnipeg Free Press*, 5 June 1987, p. 10.

113 *Manitoba Speech from the Throne*, 11 February 1988, p. 14.

114 Gerald Friesen, *River Road: Essays on Manitoba and Prairie History* (Winnipeg: University of Manitoba Press, 1996), 33.

115 For some insight into the anti-Meech feelings of Manitoba's Aboriginals, see *Winnipeg Free Press*, 17 February 1988, p. 2.

116 *Winnipeg Sun*, 24 January 1988, p. 4. See also *Winnipeg Free Press*, 16 January 1988, p. 2.

117 This pervasive ignorance about the actual contents of Meech Lake was not confined to Manitoba. As late as October 1989, one poll discovered that two-thirds of Canadians knew little or nothing about the Accord. *Globe and Mail*, 26 October 1989, p. A6.

118 *Winnipeg Free Press*, 23 April 1988, p. 59.

119 *Winnipeg Free Press*, 28 April 1988, p. 6.

120 *Winnipeg Sun*, 1 May 1988, p. 62. One poll discovered that only 20 percent of Manitobans agreed that developing a provincial position on Meech Lake was important. See Paul G. Thomas, "Manitoba: Stuck in the Middle," in Ronald L. Watts and Douglas M. Brown, eds., *Canada: The State of the Federation, 1989* (Kingston: Queen's University Institute of Intergovernmental Relations, 1989), 86.

121 This analysis contrasts markedly with that of Patrick Monahan who claims that, even before the fall of the Pawley government, "it was clear that the sentiment against Meech Lake ran very deep in Manitoba." Patrick J. Monahan, *Meech Lake: The Inside Story* (Toronto: University of Toronto Press, 1991), 151.

122 *Winnipeg Free Press*, 9 May 1987, p. 7.

123 *Winnipeg Free Press*, 4 June 1987, p. 1.

124 *Winnipeg Free Press*, 4 June 1987, p. 4.

125 *Winnipeg Free Press*, 18 December 1987, p. 4.

126 *Winnipeg Sun*, 20 December 1987, p. 5.

127 *Winnipeg Free Press*, 23 April 1988, 59.

128 *Winnipeg Free Press*, 23 April 1988, p. 7.

129 *Winnipeg Sun*, 28 July 1988, p. 6.

130 *Winnipeg Free Press*, 20 August 1988, p. 8.

131 *Winnipeg Free Press*, 1 November 1988, p. 4.

132 *Winnipeg Free Press*, 13 December 1988, p. 16.

133 *Winnipeg Free Press*, 1 November 1989, p. 7.

134 *Winnipeg Sun*, 22 December 1988, p. 5.

135 *Winnipeg Free Press*, 25 July 1988, p. 5.

136 Gerald Friesen, "Manitoba and the Meech Lake Accord," in Roger Gibbins, ed., *Meech Lake and Canada: Perspectives from the West* (Edmonton: Academic Printing and Publishing, 1988), 54.

137 *Winnipeg Free Press*, 19 March 1987, p. 6.

138 *Globe and Mail*, 30 May 1987, p. A5.

139 *Winnipeg Free Press*, 2 June 1987, p. 4.

140 See, for example, *Vancouver Sun*, 15 October 1987, p. A9, and *Winnipeg Free Press*, 12 November 1987, p. A1.

141 *Winnipeg Free Press*, 5 March 1988, p. 4.

142 *Winnipeg Free Press*, 26 July 1988, p. 10.

143 *Winnipeg Free Press*, 24 November 1988, p. 1.

144 *Winnipeg Sun*, 25 November 1988, p. 4.

145 *Globe and Mail*, 8 December 1988, p. A6.

146 *Winnipeg Free Press*, 8 July 1988, p. 11.

147 *Globe and Mail*, 22 April 1989, p. A1.

148 Ibid.

149 *Globe and Mail*, 22 April 1989, p. A3.

150 *Globe and Mail*, 26 September 1989, p. A7.

151 *Globe and Mail*, 5 October 1989, p. A8.

152 Ibid. See also *Globe and Mail*, 31 October 1989, p. A5.

153 Phillip Lee, *Frank: The Life and Politics of Frank McKenna* (Fredericton: Goose Lane, 2001), 145.

154 Michael Behiels, "The Dilemma of the Linguistic Minorities: Introduction," in Michael Behiels, ed., *The Meech Lake Primer* (Ottawa: University of Ottawa Press, 1989), 214-215.

155 *Globe and Mail*, 21 October 1989, p. A3. On the other hand, the Fédération des francophones hors Québec did not put aside their objections to the Accord until February 1990. See *Globe and Mail*, 19 February 1990, p. A5.

156 *Vancouver Sun*, 8 March 1988, p. A7.

157 *Winnipeg Sun*, 29 April 1988, p. 5.

158 *Globe and Mail*, 21 December 1988, p. A6.

159 *Globe and Mail*, 13 October 1989, p. A3.

160 Andrew Coyne, *A Deal Undone: The Making and Breaking of the Meech Lake Accord* (Vancouver: Douglas and McIntyre, 1990), 237.

161 Queen's University professor Peter Leslie quoted in *Vancouver Sun*, 5 April 1988, p. B6.

162 *Globe and Mail*, 21 March 1990. p. A3.

163 *Vancouver Sun*, 15 October 1987, p. A8.

164 *Winnipeg Free Press*, 23 December 1987, p. 7.

165 *Winnipeg Sun*, 17 July 1988, p. 4.

166 *Winnipeg Free Press*, 21 July 1988, p. 4.
167 *Winnipeg Free Press*, 19 July 1988, p. 3.
168 *Winnipeg Sun*, 19 July 1988, p. 3.
169 *Winnipeg Sun*, 28 July 1988, p. 6.
170 *Winnipeg Sun*, 22 December 1988, p. 4.
171 *Winnipeg Free Press*, 21 July 1988, p. 4.
172 Lee, *Frank*, 149-154.
173 *Globe and Mail*, 14 March 1990, p. A9.
174 *Vancouver Sun*, 9 April 1988, p. B3.
175 Lee, *Frank*, 151.

Chapter 8: Conclusion

1   These odds are determined by calculating 1/406 x 2/58 x 2/11. In reality, the odds were significantly lower. Two of the possible outcomes of the nominating convention's second ballot, for example, required either Sig Laser to vote for Jim Walding or vice versa. Extremely one-sided nominating conventions have certainly occurred in Canada (Jean Chrétien recalled his initial nomination thus: "I got about 500 votes and my opponent got about ten", but such an outcome was obviously far less likely on a second ballot. See Jean Chrétien, *Straight From the Heart* (Toronto: McClelland and Stewart, 1985), 10. There were, in fact, only about 120 plausible results for the second round of voting. Similarly, Manitoba's vaunted political diagonal meant that some of the fifty-eight possible results for the NDP in the 1986 election were effectively not possible. True, electoral sweeps have occurred in Canada. In 1935, the Liberals secured all thirty seats in the Prince Edward Island legislature, and in 1987 they repeated the trick in New Brunswick's fifty-eight constituencies. But in 1986, there was essentially no chance that the Manitoba New Democratic Party would either lose in some of their strongholds in North Winnipeg or triumph in some of the Tory redoubts in the province's rural southwest. There were, therefore, only around thirty-five plausible outcomes for the Manitoba NDP in the 1986 election. Assuming that all of the plausible results of the nominating convention and of the provincial election were equally possible, there was still only one chance in 11,540 that events would play out in the decisive combination chronicled in this book.
    Walding himself recognized at least part of the freakish combination of circumstances which thrust him into a position of power. "It's purely by accident that I'm in this position," he observed. "I certainly didn't engineer the results of the last election. And I didn't have anything to do with the resignation of Laurent Desjardins." *Globe and Mail*, 7 March, 1988, p. A4.

2   Doreen Dodick, MLA for the neighbouring constituency of Riel, provided a partial exception to this generalization. Dodick preferred Walding to Laser on the decisive ballot.

3   Admittedly, some Manitoba New Democrats continue to be haunted by the fall of the Pawley government. After declaring his suspicion that Walding "went down for thirty pieces of silver," Winnipeg MP Pat Martin quizzed German lobbyist Karlheinz Schreiber about the matter at a 2007 hearing of the House of Commons ethics committee. Schreiber denied any involvement in the affair. *Winnipeg Free Press*, 28 November 2007, p. A4.

4   In the long run, of course, the failure of the Meech Lake Accord may seem less significant, especially if the goals of Quebec nationalists are achieved via extra-constitutional means. An act of the Chrétien government effectively loaned their constitutional veto to the province of Quebec, and in the fall of 2006 Ottawa passed a resolution recognizing that Quebec constitutes a nation within a united Canada.

5   Robert M. Campbell and Leslie A. Pal, *The Real Worlds of Canadian Politics: Cases in Process and Policy* (Peterborough: Broadview Press, 1991), 147-152.

6   *Globe and Mail*, 30 June 1990, p. A4.

7   *Globe and Mail*, 23 June 1990, p. A6.

8   *Globe and Mail*, 19 June 1990, p. A1.

9   *Globe and Mail*, 20 June 1990, p. A4.

10 *Globe and Mail*, 23 June 1990, p. A6.

11 *Globe and Mail*, 25 June 1990, p. A4.

12 Campbell and Pal, *Real Worlds*, 133.

13 Thomas J. Courchene, "Forever Amber," in David E. Smith, Peter MacKinnon, and John C. Courtney, eds., *After Meech Lake: Lessons for the Future* (Saskatoon: Fifth House, 1991), 49.

14 Alan C. Cairns, *Reconfigurations: Canadian Citizenship and Constitutional Change*, edited by Douglas C. Williams (Toronto: McClelland and Stewart, 1995), 268.

15 John Whyte, "The Future of Canada's Constitutional Reform Process," in David E. Smith, Peter MacKinnon, and John C. Courtney, eds., *After Meech Lake: Lessons for the Future* (Saskatoon: Fifth House, 1991), 244.

16 Cairns, *Reconfigurations*, 195.

17 Campbell and Pal, *Real Worlds*, 140.

18 Such a circumstance is not without precedent. One analysis of Irish Home Rule claims that it could have been achieved in the spring of 1912, but that the opportunity had been lost by 1914. See Ferguson, *Virtual History*, 194.

19 Ferguson, *Virtual History*, 7.

20 Ferguson, *Virtual History*, 5.

21 Hawthorn, *Plausible Worlds*, 166.

22 Ged Martin, *Past Futures: The Impossible Necessity of History* (Toronto: University of Toronto Press, 2004), 192.

23 Sidney Hook, *The Hero in History: A Study in Limitation and Possibility* (Boston: Beacon Press, 1955), 131.

24 Hawthorn, *Plausible Worlds*, 39-80.

25 A. Wayne MacKay, "Linguistic Duality and the Distinct Society in Quebec: Declarations of Sociological Fact or Legal Limits on Constitutional Interpretation?" in K.E. Swinton and C.J. Rogerson, eds., *Competing Constitutional Visions: The Meech Lake Accord* (Toronto: Carswell, 1988), 78.

26 Katherine Swinton, "Competing Visions of Constitutionalism: Of Federalism and Rights," in K.E. Swinton and C.J. Rogerson, eds., *Competing Constitutional Visions: The Meech Lake Accord* (Toronto: Carswell, 1988), 285.

27 Ivan Bernier, "Meech Lake and Constitutional Visions," in K.E. Swinton and C.J. Rogerson, eds., *Competing Constitutional Visions: The Meech Lake Accord* (Toronto: Carswell, 1988), 239.

28 Human Mortality Database. University of California, Berkeley, CA, and Max Planck Institute for Demographic Research, Germany, http://www.mortality.org and http://www.humanmortality.de (accessed 28 February 2007)

29 This is not to claim that the Walding camp pulled every possible supporter. Dennis Boboski, for one, would have voted for the incumbent, but was missed in the pre-meeting sweep, and opted not to attend.

30 Carty, Cross and Young, *Rebuilding Canadian*, 165. Richard Lewco, a member of the party's election planning committee, is convinced that the NDP would have held St. Vital in 1986 with either Sig Laser or Gerri Unwin as the party's candidate, irrespective of whether Jim Walding had opted to run as an independent. Echoed party president Brian O'Leary, "No matter who the candidate was, we were not concerned about retaining St. Vital in 1986."

Bibliography

Primary Sources

Archives of Manitoba
P3665-3668. Jim Walding Papers.
New Democratic Party of Manitoba. Boxes 1-15.

City of Winnipeg Archives
Election—October 26, 1983: Results of the Voting for the Mayor and Councillors.

Sig Laser, personal papers.

Howard Pawley, personal papers.

St. Vital Historical Society
Assorted documents.

University of Manitoba Archives and Special Collections
Where Are They Now—Jim Walding, audio CD.

Gerri Unwin, personal papers.

Secondary Sources

Anstett, Andy, and Paul G. Thomas. "Manitoba: The Role of the Legislature in a Polarized Political System." In Gary Levy and Graham White, eds., *Provincial and Territorial Legislatures in Canada.* Toronto: University of Toronto Press, 1989.

Archer, Keith, and Alan Whitehorn. *Political Activists: the NDP in Convention.* Toronto: Oxford University Press, 1997.

Beaulieu, Paul. "The Transfer of Electoral Allegiance in Ethnic Politics: A Study of the Voting Behaviour of Franco-Manitobans, 1969-1974." Winnipeg: unpublished paper, 1976.

Beck, J. Murray. *Pendulum of Power: Canada's Federal Elections*. Scarborough: Prentice-Hall, 1968.

Behiels, Michael. "The Dilemma of the Linguistic Minorities: Introduction." In Michael Behiels, ed., *The Meech Lake Primer: Conflicting Views of the 1987 Accord*. Ottawa: University of Ottawa Press, 1989.

Bell, David V.J., and Catherine M. Bolen. "The Mass Media and Federal Election Campaigning at the Local Level: A Case Study of Two Ontario Constituencies." In David V.J. Bell and Frederick J. Fletcher, eds., *Reaching the Voter: Constituency Campaigning in Canada*. Toronto: Dundurn Press, 1991.

Bernier, Ivan. "Meech Lake and Constitutional Visions." In K.E. Swinton and C.J. Rogerson, eds., *Competing Constitutional Visions: The Meech Lake Accord*. Toronto: Carswell, 1988.

Berry, Jeffrey M. "Validity and Reliability Issues in Elite Interviewing." *Political Science* 35 (2002): 679–682.

Bosiak, Beverley. "By One Vote: The Defeat of the Manitoba Government." *Canadian Parliamentary Review* 12, 1 (1989): 15–16.

Bothwell, Robert, and William Kilbourn. *C.D. Howe: A Biography*. Toronto: McClleland and Stewart, 1979.

Brook, Tom. *Getting Elected in Canada*. Stratford: Mercury, 1991.

Brown, Patrick, Robert Chodos, and Rae Murphy. *Winners, Losers: The 1976 Tory Leadership Convention*. Toronto: James Lorimer, 1976.

Cairns, Alan C. *Reconfigurations: Canadian Citizenship and Constitutional Change*. Edited by Douglas C. Williams. Toronto: McClelland and Stewart, 1995.

Campbell, Robert M., and Leslie A. Pal. *The Real Worlds of Canadian Politics: Cases in Process and Policy*. Peterborough: Broadview Press, 1991.

Carstairs, Sharon. *Not One of the Boys*. Toronto: Macmillan, 1993.

Carty, R.K. *Canadian Political Parties in the Constituencies*. Toronto: Dundurn, 1991.

_____. "Party Organization and Activity on the Ground." In A. Brian Tanguay and Alain-G. Gagnon, eds., *Canadian Parties in Transition: Discourse, Organization and Representation*. *2nd ed.* Scarborough: Nelson, 1996.

Carty, R.K., and Lynda Erickson. "Candidate Nomination in Canada's National Political Parties." In Herman Bakvis, ed., *Canadian Political Parties: Leaders, Candidates and Organization*. Toronto: Dundurn, 1996.

Carty, R.K., William Cross, and Lisa Young. *Rebuilding Canadian Party Politics*. Vancouver: University of British Columbia Press, 2000.

Carty, R.K., D. Munroe Eagles and Anthony Sayers. "Candidates and Local Campaigns: Are There Just Four Canadian Types?" *Party Politics* 9 (2003): 619–636.

Chrétien, Jean. *Straight From the Heart*. Toronto: McClelland and Stewart, 1985.

Clarkson, Stephen. "The Liberal Threepeat: The Multi-System Party in the Multi-Party System." In Jon H. Pammett and Christopher Dornan, eds., *The Canadian General Election of 2000*. Toronto: Dundurn, 2000.

Colwell, R.M. "'Order Please....' The Speakership in Manitoba." N.p.: unpublished paper, 1986.

Courchene, Thomas J. "Forever Amber." In David E. Smith, Peter MacKinnon, and John C. Courtney, eds., *After Meech Lake: Lessons for the Future*. Saskatoon: Fifth House, 1991.

Courtney, John C. *The Selection of National Party Leaders in Canada*. Toronto: Macmillan, 1973.

Coyne, Andrew. *A Deal Undone: The Making and Breaking of the Meech Lake Accord.* Vancouver: Douglas and McIntyre, 1990.

Cross, William. "Grassroots Participation in Candidate Nomination." In Joanna Everitt and Brenda O'Neill, eds., *Citizen Politics: Research and Theory in Canadian Political Behaviour.* Don Mills: Oxford University Press, 2002.

_____. *Political Parties.* Vancouver: University of British Columbia Press, 2004.

_____. "Candidate Nomination in Canada's Political Parties." In Jon H. Pammett and Christopher Dornan, eds., *The Canadian Federal Election of 2006.* Toronto: Dundurn Press, 2006.

Dawson, R. MacGregor. *The Government of Canada.* 5th ed. Toronto: University of Toronto Press, 1970.

Docherty, David C. *Mr. Smith Goes to Ottawa: Life in the House of Commons.* Vancouver: University of British Columbia Press, 1997.

Doern, Russell. *Wednesdays are Cabinet Days: A Personal Account of the Schreyer Administration.* Winnipeg: Queenston House, 1981.

_____. *The Battle Over Bilingualism: The Manitoba Language Question, 1983-1985.* Winnipeg: Cambridge Publishers, 1985.

Donnelly, M.S. *The Government of Manitoba.* Toronto: University of Toronto Press, 1963.

Dyck, Rand. "Relations Between Federal and Provincial Parties." In A. Brian Tanguay and Alain-G. Gagnon, eds. *Canadian Parties in Transition: Discourse, Organization and Representation. 2nd ed.* Scarborough: Nelson, 1996.

Eagles, Munroe, Harold Jansen, Anthony Sayers, and Lisa Young. "Financing Federal Nomination Contests in Canada—An Overview of the 2004 Experience." Paper presented at the Annual Meeting of the Canadian Political Science Association, London, Ontario, 2005.

Engelmann, F.C. and M.A. Schwartz. *Political Parties and the Canadian Social Structure.* Scarborough: Prentice-Hall, 1967.

Erickson, Lynda, and R.K. Carty. "Parties and Candidate Selection in the 1988 Canadian General Election." *Canadian Journal of Political Science* 24 (1991): 331-350.

Ferguson, Niall, ed. *Virtual History: Alternatives and Counterfactuals.* New York: Basic Books, 1999.

Friesen, Gerald. "Manitoba and the Meech Lake Accord." In Roger Gibbins, ed., *Meech Lake and Canada: Perspectives from the West.* Edmonton: Academic Printing and Publishing, 1988.

_____. *River Road: Essays on Manitoba and Prairie History.* Winnipeg: University of Manitoba Press, 1996.

Gallagher, Michael, and Michael Marsh, eds. *Candidate Selection in Comparative Perspective.* London: Sage, 1988.

Graham, Ron. *One-Eyed Kings: Promise and Illusion in Canadian Politics.* Toronto: Totem Books, 1986.

Green, Sidney. *Rise and Fall of a Political Animal: A Memoir.* Winnipeg: Great Plains, 2003.

Hawthorn, Geoffrey. *Plausible Worlds: Possibility and Understanding in History and the Social Sciences.* Cambridge: Cambridge University Press, 1991.

Hébert, Raymond M. *Manitoba's French-Language Crisis: A Cautionary Tale.* Montreal: McGill-Queens University Press, 2004.

Hellyer, Paul. *Damn the Torpedoes: My Fight to Unify Canada's Armed Forces.* Toronto: McClelland and Stewart, 1990.

Hook, Sidney. *The Hero in History: A Study in Limitation and Possibility.* Boston: Beacon Press, 1955.

Horner, Jack. *My Own Brand.* Edmonton: Hurtig, 1980.

Horowitz, Gad. *Canadian Labour in Politics.* Toronto: University of Toronto Press, 1968.

Hoy, Claire. *Bill Davis: A Biography.* Toronto: Methuen, 1985.

_____. *Friends In High Places.* Toronto: Key Porter, 1987.

Humphreys, David L. *Joe Clark: A Portrait.* Ottawa: Deneau and Greenberg, 1978.

Jackson, James A. *The Centennial History of Manitoba.* Toronto: McClelland and Stewart, 1970.

Johnston, Donald. *Up the Hill.* Montreal: Optimum, 1986.

Johnston, James. *The Party's Over.* Don Mills: Longman, 1971.

Key, V.O. *Southern Politics in State and Nation.* New York: Alfred A. Knopf, 1949.

LaMarsh, Judy. *Memoirs of a Bird in a Gilded Cage.* Toronto: McClelland and Stewart, 1988.

Land, Brian. *Eglington.* Toronto: Peter Martin Associates, 1965.

Laundy, Philip. "The Future of the Canadian Speakership." *The Parliamentarian* 53 (1979): 113-117.

Lee, Philip. *Frank: The Life and Politics of Frank McKenna.* Fredericton: Goose Lane, 2001.

Leech, Beth L. "Asking Questions: Techniques for Semistructured Interviews." *Political Science* 35 (2002): 665-668.

MacDonald, L. Ian. *Mulroney: The Making of the Prime Minister.* Toronto: McClelland and Stewart, 1984.

MacKay, A. Wayne. "Linguistic Duality and the Distinct Society in Quebec: Declarations of Sociological Fact or Legal Limits on Constitutional Interpretation?" In K.E. Swinton and C.J. Rogerson, eds., *Competing Constitutional Visions: The Meech Lake Accord.* Toronto: Carswell, 1988.

Manthorpe, Jonathan. *The Power and the Tories: Ontario Politics, 1943 to the Present.* Toronto: Macmillan, 1974.

Martin, Ged. *Past Futures: The Impossible Necessity of History.* Toronto: University of Toronto Press, 2004.

McAllister, James A. *The Government of Edward Schreyer.* Montreal: McGill-Queens University Press, 1984.

McMahon, Tom. "Bell-ringing Revisited: A Lack of Leadership from the Speaker." *The Table* 55 (1987): 51-85.

McNaught, Kenneth. *A Prophet in Politics: A Biography of J.S. Woodsworth.* Toronto: University of Toronto Press, 1959.

Meisel, John. *The Canadian General Election of 1957.* Toronto: University of Toronto Press, 1962.

Mitchell, David J. *W.A.C. Bennett and the Rise of British Columbia.* Vancouver: Douglas and McIntyre, 1983.

Monahan, Patrick J. *Meech Lake: The Inside Story.* Toronto: University of Toronto Press, 1991.

Morley, Terry. "Leadership Change in the CCF/NDP." In R. Kenneth Carty, Lynda Erickson, and Donald E. Blake, eds., *Leaders and Parties in the Canadian Provinces: Experiences of the Provinces.* Toronto: Harcourt Brace Jonavitch, 1992.

Morton, Desmond. *The New Democrats, 1961-1986.* Toronto: Copp Clark Pitman, 1986.

Morton, W.L. *Manitoba: A History.* Toronto: University of Toronto Press, 1967.

Murphy, Rae, Robert Chodos, and Nick Auf der Maur. *Brian Mulroney: The Boy from Baie Comeau.* Toronto: James Lorimer, 1984.

Netherton, Alex. "Paradigm and Shift: A Sketch of Manitoba Politics." In Keith Brownsey and Michael Howlett, eds., *The Provincial State in Canada: Politics in the Provinces and Territories.* Peterborough: Broadview, 2001.

Noel, S.J.R. *Politics in Newfoundland.* Toronto: University of Toronto Press, 1971.

Pearson, Lester B. *Mike: The Memoirs of the Right Honourable Lester B. Pearson Volume 2.* Toronto: University of Toronto Press, 1973.

Pelletier, Réjean. "The Structures of Canadian Political Parties: How They Operate." In Herman Bakvis, ed., *Canadian Political Parties: Leaders, Candidates and Organization.* Toronto: Dundurn, 1996.

Penner, Roland. *A Glowing Dream: A Memoir.* Winnipeg: J. Gordon Shillingford Publishing, 2007.

Perlin, George. "St. Johns West." In John Meisel, ed., *Papers on the 1962 Election.* Toronto: University of Toronto Press, 1964.

Peterson, T. "Manitoba: Ethnic and Class Politics in Manitoba." In Martin Robin, ed., *Canadian Provincial Politics.* Scarborough: Prentice-Hall, 1972.

Pratte, André. *Charest: His Life and Politics.* Toronto: Stoddart, 1998.

Radwanski, George. *Trudeau.* Toronto: Macmillan, 1978.

Russell, Frances. *The Canadian Crucible: Manitoba's Role in Canada's Great Divide.* Winnipeg: Heartland Associates, 2003.

Sayers, Anthony M. *Parties, Candidates and Constituency Campaigns in Canadian Elections.* Vancouver: University of British Columbia Press, 1999.

Scarrow, Howard A. "Three Dimensions of a Local Political Party." In John Meisel, ed., *Papers on the 1962 Election.* Toronto: University of Toronto Press, 1964.

Schulz, Herb. *A View from the Ledge: An Insider's Look at the Schreyer Years.* Winnipeg: Heartland Associates, 2005.

Sherman, Paddy. *Bennett.* Toronto: McClelland and Stewart, 1966.

Smallwood, Joey. *I Chose Canada: The Memoirs of the Hon. Joseph R. 'Joey' Smallwood.* Toronto: Macmillan, 1973.

Smith, Denis. "The Campaign in Eglington." In John Meisel, ed., *Papers on the 1962 Election.* Toronto: University of Toronto Press, 1964.

Smith, Doug. *As Many Liars: The Story of the 1995 Manitoba Vote-Splitting Scandal.* Winnipeg: Arbeiter Ring Publishing, 2003.

Snider, Norman. *The Changing of the Guard: How the Liberals Fell From Grace and the Tories Rose to Power.* Toronto: Lester and Orphan Dennys, 1985.

Spencer, Dick. *Trumpets and Drums: John Diefenbaker on the Campaign Trail.* Toronto: Douglas and McIntyre, 1994.

Starr, Richard. *Richard Hatfield: The Seventeen Year Saga.* Halifax: Formac, 1987.

Stein, Michael B. "Social Credit Party in the Canadian General Election of 1974." In Howard R. Penniman, ed., *Canada at the Polls: The General Election of 1974.* Washington: American Enterprise Institute, 1975.

Stewart, Ian. "Of Customs and Coalitions: The Formation of Canadian Federal Parliamentary Alliances." *Canadian Journal of Political Science* 13 (1980): 451-479.

_____. "Scaling the Matterhorn: Parliamentary Leadership in Canada." In R.H. Wagenberg, M. Mancuso, and R. Price, eds., *Leaders and Leadership in Canadian Politics.* Toronto: Oxford University Press, 1994.

Stewart, Ian, and David Stewart. *Conventional Choices: Maritime Leadership Politics.* Vancouver: University of British Columbia Press, 2007.

Stinson, Lloyd. *Political Warriors: Recollections of a Social Democrat.* Winnipeg: Queenston House, 1975.

Sullivan, Martin. *Mandate '68: The Year of Pierre Elliot Trudeau.* Toronto: Doubleday Canada, 1968.

Surich, Jo. "Purists and Pragmatists: Canadian Democratic Socialism at the Crossroads." In Howard R. Penniman, ed., *Canada at the Polls: The General Election of 1974.* Washington: American Enterprise Institute for Public Policy Research, 1975.

Swinton, Katherine. "Competing Visions of Constitutionalism: Of Federalism and Rights." In K.E. Swinton and C.J. Rogerson, eds., *Competing Constitutional Visions: The Meech Lake Accord.* Toronto: Carswell, 1988.

Telegram News Staff. *Balloons and Ballots: The Inside Story of Robert Stanfield's Victory.* Toronto: The Telegram, 1967.

Thomas, Paul G. "Manitoba: Stuck in the Middle." In Ronald L. Watts and Douglas M. Brown, eds., *Canada: The State of the Federation, 1989.* Kingston: Queen's University Institute of Intergovernmental Relations, 1989.

Turek, Victor. *Poles in Manitoba.* Toronto: Polish Alliance Press, 1967.

Wearing, Joseph. *Strained Relations: Canada's Voters and Parties.* Toronto: McClelland and Stewart, 1988.

Webb, Eugene J., Donald T. Campbell, Richard D. Schwartz, Lee Sechrest, and Janet Belew Grove. *Nonreactive Measures in the Social Sciences.* 2nd ed. Boston: Houghton Mifflin, 1981.

Weston, Greg. *Reign of Error: The Inside Story of John Turner's Troubled Leadership.* Toronto: McGraw-Hill, Ryerson, 1988.

Whelan, Eugene. *Whelan: The Man in the Green Stetson.* Toronto: Irwin, 1986.

Whitaker, Reginald. *The Government Party: Organizing and Financing the Liberal Party of Canada, 1930-58.* Toronto: University of Toronto Press, 1977.

Whyte, John. "The Future of Canada's Constitutional Reform Process." In David E. Smith, Peter MacKinnon, and John C. Courtney, eds., *After Meech Lake: Lessons for the Future.* Saskatoon: Fifth House, 1991.

Williams, Robert J. "Candidate Selection." In Howard R. Penniman, ed., *Canada at the Polls: 1979 and 1980.* Washington: American Enterprise Institute, 1981.

Wiseman, Nelson. *Social Democracy in Manitoba: A History of the CCF-NDP.* Winnipeg: University of Manitoba Press, 1983.

_____. "The Questionable Relevance of the Constitution in Advancing Minority Cultural Rights in Manitoba." *Canadian Journal of Political Science* 25 (1992): 697-721.

Wood, John. "A Visible Minority Votes: East Indian Electoral Behaviour in the Vancouver South Provincial and Federal Elections of 1979." In Jorgen Dahlie and Tissa Fernando, eds., *Ethnicity, Power and Politics in Canada.* Agincourt, ON: Methuen, 1981.

Young, Lisa, and Elaine Campbell. "Women and Political Representation." In Hugh G. Thorburn and Alan Whitehorn, eds., *Party Politics in Canada.* 8th ed. Toronto: Prentice-Hall, 2001.

Young, Lisa, and William Cross. "Incentives to Membership in Canadian Political Parties." *Political Research Quarterly* 55 (2002): 547-569.

Index

Harper, Stephen, 83
Hatfield, Richard, 72, 192
Hawthorne, Geoffrey, 2
Hébert, Raymond, 56
Hellyer, Paul, 95
Hemphill, Maureen, 45, 75
Herriot, Paul, 131-133, 171
Hitchings, Diane, 75, 110, 114
Huband, Charles, 37, 39
Hudson, Wilf, 73
Hunter, Heather, 105
Huss, Keith, 30-31
Hutton, Bill, 23, 30

I

Independent Labor Party (Manitoba), 13, 21, 23
Inkster (Manitoba constituency), 92, 155, 170

J

Johannson, Wally, 39
Johnson, Lyndon, 134
Johnston, Donald, 76

K

Kennedy, Dan, 31, 33, 35, 38
Knowles, Stanley, 16, 62-64
Kostyra, Eugene, 45, 132, 138, 151, 159
Kula, Sharon, 90, 100, 120, 208
Kula, Victor, 100

L

Labour Progressive Party (Manitoba), 15
Landry, Aldea, 193
LaSalle, Roch, 112
Laser, Sig, 1, 3, 10, 128, 131-132, 137, 141, 145, 156, 162, 169-170, 173, 200-202, 208-210; and 1986 St. Vital NDP nomination contest, 67-126
Laser, Tannis, 75, 79, 97, 116, 124
Lawrence, Harold, 21-22
Lecuyer, Gerard, 52, 152
Legal, Jules, 75, 97, 99, 104, 120, 123, 131, 156, 208
Legal, Paula, 123
Leo, Chris, 100

Leslie, Peter, 183
Lewco, Richard, 102
Lewis, David, 14
Liberal Party (Canada), 5-6, 76, 83, 199
Liberal Party (Manitoba), 17, 28, 30-35, 37-39, 42-44, 59, 72, 129, 132, 139, 147, 164-165, 168, 171-172, 174, 176, 183, 187, 210
Liberal-Progressive Party (Manitoba), 15-16
Lisgar (federal constituency), 95
Lord, Shirley, 60-61
Lyon, Sterling, 37-39, 41, 45, 49-50, 52-54, 57, 129-130, 146, 173, 176

M

MacDonald, Flora, 107
Mackling, Al, 16, 45
Maclean, W.F., 7
Malinowksi, Donald, 88-89
Malloway, Jim, 78
Manitoba Centennial Corporation, 30
Manitoba Federation of Labour, 74
Manitoba Health Organizations, 148
Manitoba Hydro, 39-40, 137, 174
Manitoba Intercultural Council, 174
Manitoba Labor Party, 13
Manitoba Labour Education Centre, 176
Manitoba Legislative Assembly Management Committee, 48, 59
Manitoba Lotteries Commission, 148
Manitoba Métis Federation, 176
Manitoba provincial elections,
of 1910, 13; of 1920, 13; of 1936, 13; of 1941, 14; of 1945, 15, 21; of 1949, 15, 21; of 1953, 15, 21; of 1958, 15, 21; of 1959, 16; of 1962, 17; of 1966, 17, 23; of 1969, 17, 25, 27-28; of 1973, 33-35; of 1977, 37-39; of 1981, 41-44; of 1986, 129-132; of 1988, 163-172; of 1990, 172; of 1995, 173; of 1999, 173
Manitoba Public Insurance Corporation, 176
Manitoba Telephone System, 36, 164
Manitoba's "Quiet Revolution," 16
Manness, Clayton, 174-175

R

Radisson (Manitoba constituency), 27, 30, 34, 39

Red River Rebellion, 11, 18

Reid, Angus, 163

Remnant, Binx, 56

Riel (Manitoba constituency), 34, 73, 92, 108

Riel, Al, 90

Riel, Joseph, 18

Riel, Louis, 18-19, 199

Ritchot, Paul, 81

Robertson, John, 43-44

Roblin, Duff, 16-17, 64, 95

Rodie, Jack, 105

Rose, Bob, 171

Rossman, Irene, 75, 81, 98

Rowntree, Ross, 101

Roy, Len, 96

Rupertsland (Manitoba constituency), 21, 92

Russell, Frances, 136, 154

Russell, Grant, 174-175

S

Saskatchewan, 14, 46, 56, 191, 195

Sauvé, Jeanne, 56, 64

Sawka, Aurore, 114

Sawka, Ed, 114

Sayers, Anthony, 4, 6, 131, 201

Scarrow, Howard, 4

Schamber, George, 28, 30, 44-45, 67-68, 79, 82, 86, 103-104, 106-107, 112, 118-120, 167-168

Schreyer, Ed, 3, 17, 20, 28-31, 34, 36-37, 40, 45, 75, 90, 102, 127, 147, 158-159, 163

Schreyer, Lloyd, 102

Schroeder, Vic, 45, 84, 135

Scott, Don, 92, 155

Scotton, Cliff, 102

Scotton, Joyce, 145

Selkirk (Manitoba constituency), 74, 128, 153, 166, 170

Shafransky, Harry, 30-31, 39

Sharp, Mitchell, 83

Sherman, Bud, 49-50

Sinclair, Verna, 109, 114, 208

Small, Catherine, 104

Small, Larry, 103-104

Smallwood, Joey, 83

Smith, Harvey, 146, 155

Socialist Party (Manitoba), 13

Société Franco-Manitobaine, 51, 54

Springfield (Manitoba constituency), 130

St. Boniface, 9, 20-23, 28, 34, 42, 89, 148-149

St. Clements (Manitoba constituency), 21

St. George Stubbs, Lewis, 14

St. Johns (Manitoba constituency), 189

St. Mary's Road, 19, 23-24, 28, 33, 42, 171

St. Matthews (Manitoba constituency), 39

Ste. Rose (Manitoba constituency), 29, 32, 114

St. Vital (Manitoba constituency), 1, 2, 3, 9, 10, 18-25, 27-31, 34-44, 46, 60-63, 128-135, 138-139, 141, 143-145, 147, 153, 156-157, 161-162, 166-173, 197, 199-202, 209-210; and 1986 NDP nomination contest, 67-121

St. Vital Lance, 32

Stanfield, Robert, 95, 107

Starr, Michael, 95

Stevens, Sinclair, 83, 109

Stimpson, Michael, 75, 78, 85, 99, 105, 123, 131

Stinson, Lloyd, 15

Storie, Jerry, 168

Street, David, 69, 75, 78-79, 94, 99, 114, 117, 120-121, 123

Swain, Altje, 90

T

Teillet, Roger-Joseph, 9

Thibault, Nels, 41

Thompson, E.P., 205

Trigwell, Colin, 79-80, 85, 93, 98-99, 105, 110, 113-114, 201-202

Trudeau, Pierre, 52, 177, 195

Trudel, Elaine, 81

Turner, John, 164, 189, 204

Turtle Mountain (Manitoba constituency), 70